THE MIDDLE

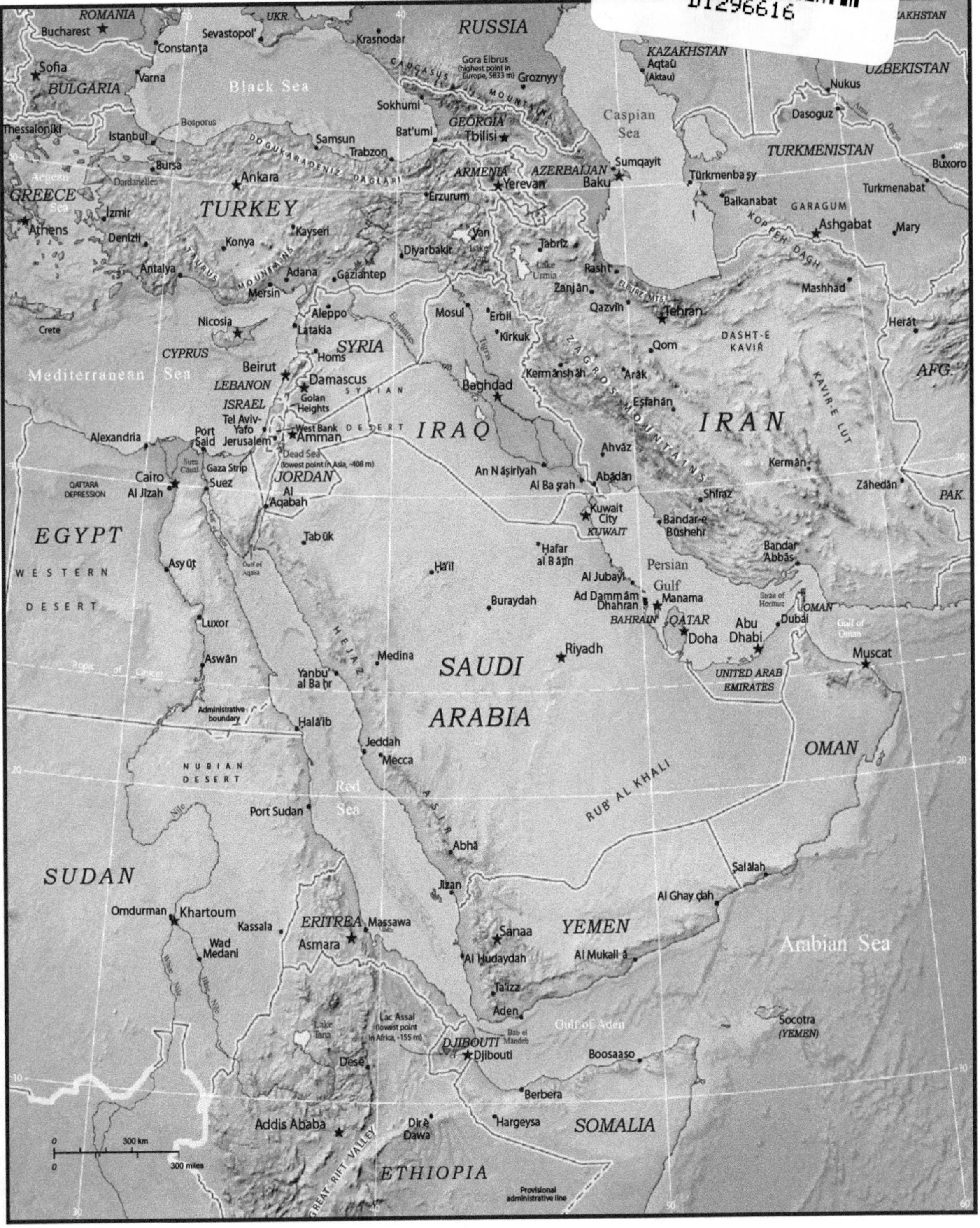

ROMANIA
Bucharest
UKR.
Sevastopol'
Constanța
RUSSIA
Krasnodar
KAZAKHSTAN
Aqtaū (Aktau)
UZBEKISTAN
Sofia
BULGARIA
Varna
Black Sea
Gora Elbrus (highest point in Europe, 5633 m)
CAUCASUS MOUNTAINS
Groznyy
Nukus
Dasoguz
Caspian Sea
Sokhumi
Bosporus
Thessaloniki
Istanbul
Samsun
Trabzon
Bat'umi
GEORGIA
Tbilisi
TURKMENISTAN
Bursa
DOGU KARADENIZ DAGLARI
ARMENIA
AZERBAIJAN
Sumqayit
Aegean Sea
Dardanelles
Ankara
Yerevan
Baku
Türkmenbaşy
Buxoro
Turkmenabat
GREECE
Erzurum
Balkanabat
GARAGUM
İzmir
TURKEY
KOPPEH DAGH
Ashgabat
Mary
Athens
Denizli
Konya
Kayseri
Van
Tabriz
Diyarbakır
Lake Urmia
TAURUS MOUNTAINS
Antalya
Adana
Gaziantep
Rasht
ELBURZ MTS.
Mashhad
Mersin
Zanjān
Qazvin
Aleppo
Mosul
Erbil
Tehran
Herāt
Crete
Nicosia
Latakia
Kirkuk
DASHT-E KAVIR
CYPRUS
SYRIA
Qom
Homs
Euphrates
Tigris
Mediterranean Sea
Beirut
Kermānshāh
Arāk
AFG.
LEBANON
Damascus
ZAGROS MOUNTAINS
KAVIR-E LUT
Golan Heights
SYRIAN
Baghdad
ISRAEL
Eşfahān
Tel Aviv-Yafo
DESERT
IRAN
Alexandria
Port Said
West Bank
Amman
IRAQ
Jerusalem
Dead Sea (lowest point in Asia, -408 m)
Ahvāz
Suez Canal
Gaza Strip
Kermān
JORDAN
An Nāşiriyah
Abādān
QATTARA DEPRESSION
Cairo
Al Jīzah
Suez
Al Başrah
Zāhedān
PAK.
Al 'Aqabah
Shīrāz
Kuwait City
KUWAIT
Bandar-e Būshehr
EGYPT
Tabūk
Hafar al Bāţin
Bandar 'Abbās
WESTERN DESERT
Asyūţ
Gulf of Aqaba
Ḥā'il
Persian Gulf
Al Jubayl
Ad Dammām
Dhahran
Manama
BAHRAIN
Buraydah
Strait of Hormuz
OMAN
Luxor
HEJAZ
QATAR
Doha
Abu Dhabi
Dubai
Gulf of Oman
Riyadh
Muscat
Aswān
Tropic of Cancer
Medina
SAUDI ARABIA
Yanbu' al Baḩr
UNITED ARAB EMIRATES
Administrative boundary
Halā'ib
Jeddah
Mecca
OMAN
NUBIAN DESERT
Red Sea
RUB' AL KHALI
Port Sudan
Nile
ASIR
Abhā
Şalālah
SUDAN
Jīzān
Al Ghayḑah
Omdurman
Khartoum
Kassala
ERITREA
Massawa
Sanaa
YEMEN
Arabian Sea
Asmara
Wad Medani
Al Hudaydah
Al Mukallā
White Nile
Blue Nile
Ta'izz
Aden
Lake Tana
Lac Assal (lowest point in Africa, -155 m)
Bab el Mandeb
Gulf of Aden
Socotra (YEMEN)
DJIBOUTI
Djibouti
Boosaaso
Desē
Berbera
Addis Ababa
Dirē Dawa
Hargeysa
SOMALIA
300 km
300 miles
GREAT RIFT VALLEY
ETHIOPIA
Provisional administrative line

GULF WAR JOURNAL

BOOK ONE - DESERT STORM

CALIBER
COMICS

GULF WAR JOURNAL

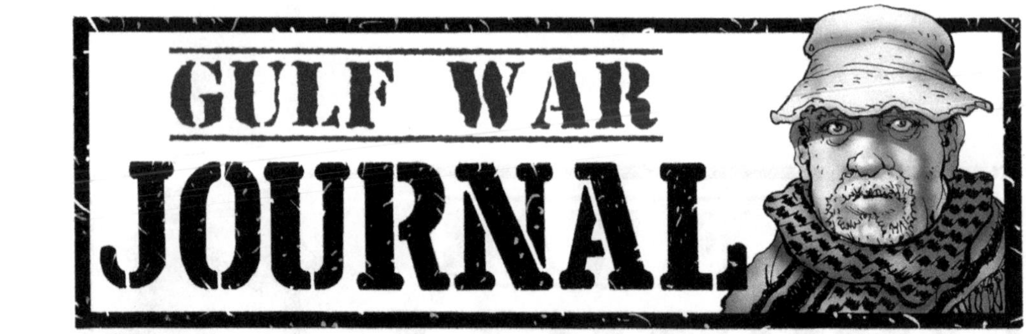

BOOK ONE - DESERT STORM

WRITTEN AND PENCILLED BY

DON LOMAX

INKED BY

ROSE LOMAX

LETTERED BY

CLEM ROBINS
MARK MOORE

This book collects the DESERT STORM JOURNAL issues 1-4
Originally published by Apple Comics

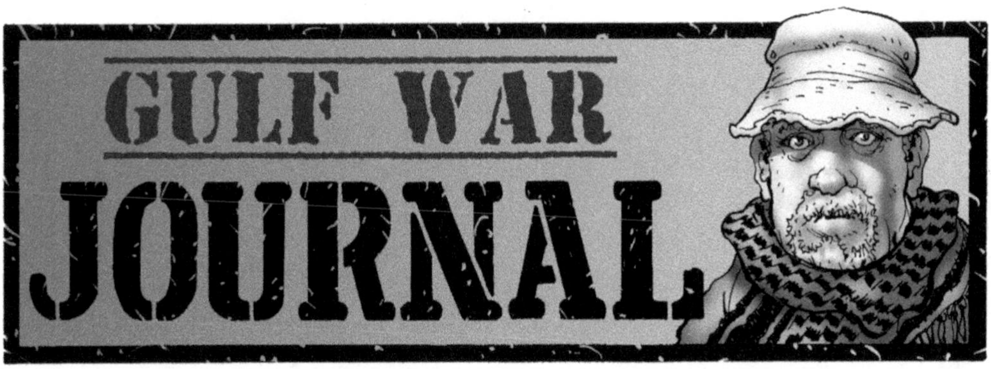
GULF WAR
JOURNAL

A SHORT HISTORY OF GULF WAR JOURNAL
by its creator, Don Lomax

The first Gulf War, for the most part, began on August 2, 1990 with Saddam Hussein's invasion of Kuwait proclaiming the oil rich country a province of Iraq. On August 7, 1990 Operation Desert Shield was initiated by orders from President George H W Bush and the first United States forces arrived in Saudi Arabia to help reclaim sovereignty for the beleaguered Kuwait.

At that time, I was producing my signature feature for Apple Comics, VIETNAM JOURNAL and found myself caught up in the war, like everyone else. My publisher and I began brainstorming one day that, knowing the main character of that series Scott Neithammer (the troops call him 'Journal') like we did, we knew he would have, reluctantly, ended up in that war zone. Even with his advanced age, war correspondents are a breed removed from the average individual. They are drawn to war like a moth to a flame. Then, something happened that I believe is unique in comics. I began writing DESERT STORM JOURNAL in real time. We didn't know, of course, at that time that there would be additional wars to follow in the region which would bring historians to rename the conflict as Gulf War 1. Produced in real time we were not sure what direction the war was going to take. It may have continued for years or fizzled out leaving us with egg on our collective faces. Kudos must be expressed to Mike Catron, the Apple Press publisher, for his faith in the project and adventuresome spirit.

As it was, issue #1 of the comic was published in September 1991 and continued for nine issues. Caliber Comics has now collected all nine issues into a two book graphic novel set under the title GULF WAR JOURNAL.

Desert Storm Begins

Wednesday, January 16, 1991

The Announcement

The White House, 7:06 P.M. EST —

"The liberation of Kuwait has begun. In conjunction with the forces of our coalition partners, the United States has moved under the code name Operation Desert Storm to enforce the mandates of the United Nations Security Council.

"As of 7 o'clock P.M., Operation Desert Storm forces were engaging targets in Iraq and Kuwait."

— Statement by President George Bush, as read by spokesman Marlin Fitzwater

The Speech

The following is the text of President Bush's speech to the nation the night of January 16, 1991, as transcribed by the White House.

The Oval Office, 9:01 P.M. EST —

The President: Just two hours ago, allied air forces began an attack on military targets in Iraq and Kuwait. These attacks continue as I speak. Ground forces are not engaged.

This conflict started August 2nd when the dictator of Iraq invaded a small and helpless neighbor. Kuwait — a member of the Arab League and a member of the United Nations — was crushed; its people brutalized. Five months ago, Saddam Hussein started this cruel war against Kuwait. Tonight, the battle has been joined.

This military action, taken in accord with United Nations resolutions — and with the consent of the United States Congress — follows months of constant and virtually endless diplomatic activity on the part of the United Nations, the United States and many, many other countries. Arab leaders sought what became known as an Arab solution — only to conclude that Saddam Hussein was unwilling to leave Kuwait. Others traveled to Baghdad in a variety of efforts to restore peace and justice. Our Secretary of State, James Baker, held an historic meeting in Geneva — only to be totally rebuffed. This past weekend, in a last ditch effort, the Secretary General of the United Nations went to the Middle East, with peace in his heart — his second such mission. And he came back from Baghdad with no progress at all in getting Saddam Hussein to withdraw from Kuwait.

Now the 28 countries with forces in the Gulf area, have exhausted all reasonable efforts to reach a peaceful resolution, have no choice but to drive Saddam from Kuwait by force. We will not fail.

As I report to you, air attacks are underway against military targets in Iraq. We are determined to knock out Saddam Hussein's nuclear bomb potential. We will also destroy his chemical weapons facilities. Much of Saddam's artillery and tanks will be destroyed. Our operations are designed to best protect the lives of all the coalition forces by targeting Saddam's vast military arsenal. Initial reports from General Schwarzkopf are that our operations are proceedir according to plan.

Our objectives are clear. Saddam Hussein's forces will leave Kuwait. The legitimate government of Kuwait will be restored to its rightful place and Kuwait will once again be free. Iraq will eventually comply with all relevant United Nations resolutions. And then, when peace is restored, it is our hope that Iraq will live as a peaceful and cooperative member of the family of nations, thus, enhancing the security and stability of the Gulf.

Some may ask, why act now? Why not wait? The answer is clear: The world could wait no longer. Sanctions, though having some effect, showed no signs of accomplishing their objective. Sanctions were tried for well over five months, and we and our allies concluded that sanctions alone would not force Saddam from Kuwait.

While the world waited, Saddam Hussein systematically raped, pillaged and plundered a tiny nation, no threat to his own. He subjected the people of Kuwait to unspeakable atrocities — and among those maimed and murdered, innocent children.

While the world waited, Saddam sought to add to the chemical weapons arsenal he now possesses an infinitely more dangerous weapon of mass destruction — a nuclear weapon.

And while the world waited, while the world talked peace and withdrawal, Saddam Hussein dug in and moved massive forces into Kuwait.

While the world waited, while Saddam stalled, more damage was being done to the fragile economies of the Third World, the emerging democracies of Eastern Europe, to the entire world including to our own economy.

The United States, together with the United Nations, exhausted every means at our disposal to bring this crisis to a peaceful end. However, Saddam clearly felt that by stalling and threatening and defying the United Nations he could weaken the forces arrayed against him.

While the world waited, Saddam Hussein met every overture of peace with open contempt. While the world prayed for peace, Saddam prepared for war.

I had hoped that when the United States Congress, in historic debate, took its resolute action, Saddam would realize he could not prevail and would move out of Kuwait in accord with the United Nations resolutions. He did not do that. Instead, he remained intransigent, certain that time was on his side.

Saddam was warned over and over again to comply with the will of the United Nations. Leave Kuwait or be driven out. Saddam has arrogantly rejected all warnings. Instead he tried to make this a dispute between Iraq and the United States of America.

Well, he failed. Tonight, 28 nations — countries from five continents: Europe and Asia, Africa and the Arab League — have forces in the Gulf area standing shoulder to shoulder against Saddam Hussein. These countries had hoped the use of force could be avoided. Regrettably, we now believe that only force will make him leave.

Prior to ordering our forces into battle, I instructed our military commanders to take every necessary step to prevail as quickly as possible and with the greatest degree of protection possible for American and allied servicemen and women. I've told the American people before that this will not be another Vietnam. And I repeat this here tonight. Our troops will have the best possible support in the entire world, and they will not be asked to fight with one hand tied behind their back.

I'm hopeful that this fighting will not go on for long, and that casualties will be held to an absolute minimum.

This is an historic moment. We have, in this past year made great progress in ending the long era of conflict and Cold War. We have before us the opportunity to forge, for ourselves and for future generations, a new world order — a world where the rule of law, not the law of the jungle, governs the conduct of nations.

When we are successful, and we will be, we have a real chance at this new world order — an order in which a credible United Nations can use its peacekeeping role to fulfill the promise and vision of the U.N.'s founders.

We have no argument with the people of Iraq — indeed, for the innocents caught in this conflict, I pray for their safety.

Our goal is not the conquest of Iraq — it is the liberation of Kuwait. It is my hope that somehow the Iraqi people can, even now, convince their dictator that he must lay down his arms, leave Kuwait, and let Iraq itself rejoin the family of peace-loving nations.

Thomas Paine wrote many years ago: "These are the times that try men's souls." Those well-known words are so very true today. But even as planes of

the multinational forces attack Iraq, I prefer to think of peace, not war. I am convinced not only that we will prevail, but that out of the horror of combat will come the recognition that no nation can stand against a world united. No nation will be permitted to brutally assault its neighbor.

No president can easily commit our sons and daughters to war. They are the nation's finest. Ours is an all volunteer force — magnificently trained, highly motivated. The troops know why they're there. And listen to what they say, for they've said it better than any president or prime minister ever could.

Listen to "Hollywood" Huddleston, Marine Lance Corporal. He says, "Let's free these people so we can go home and be free again." He's right. The terrible crimes and tortures committed by Saddam's henchmen against the innocent people of Kuwait are an affront to mankind and a challenge to the freedom of all.

Listen to one of our great officers out there, Marine Lieutenant General Walter Boomer. He said, "There are things worth fighting for. A world in which brutality and lawlessness are allowed to go unchecked isn't the kind of world we're going to want to live in."

Listen to Master Sergeant J.P. Kendall of the 82nd Airborne: "We're here for more than just the price of a gallon of gas. What we're doing is going to chart the future of the world for the next hundred years. It's better to deal with this guy now than five years from now."

And finally, we should all sit up and listen to Jackie Jones, an Army lieutenant, when she says, "If we let him get away with this, who knows what's going to be next?"

I have called upon "Hollywood" and Walter and J.P. and Jackie and all their courageous comrades in arms to do what must be done. Tonight, America and the world are deeply grateful to them and to their families. And let me say to everyone listening or watching tonight: when the troops we've sent in finish their work, I am determined to bring them home as soon as possible.

Tonight, as our forces fight, they and their families are in our prayers. May God bless each and every one of them, and the coalition forces at our side in the Gulf — and may He continue to bless our nation, the United States of America.
— *9:15 P.M. EST*

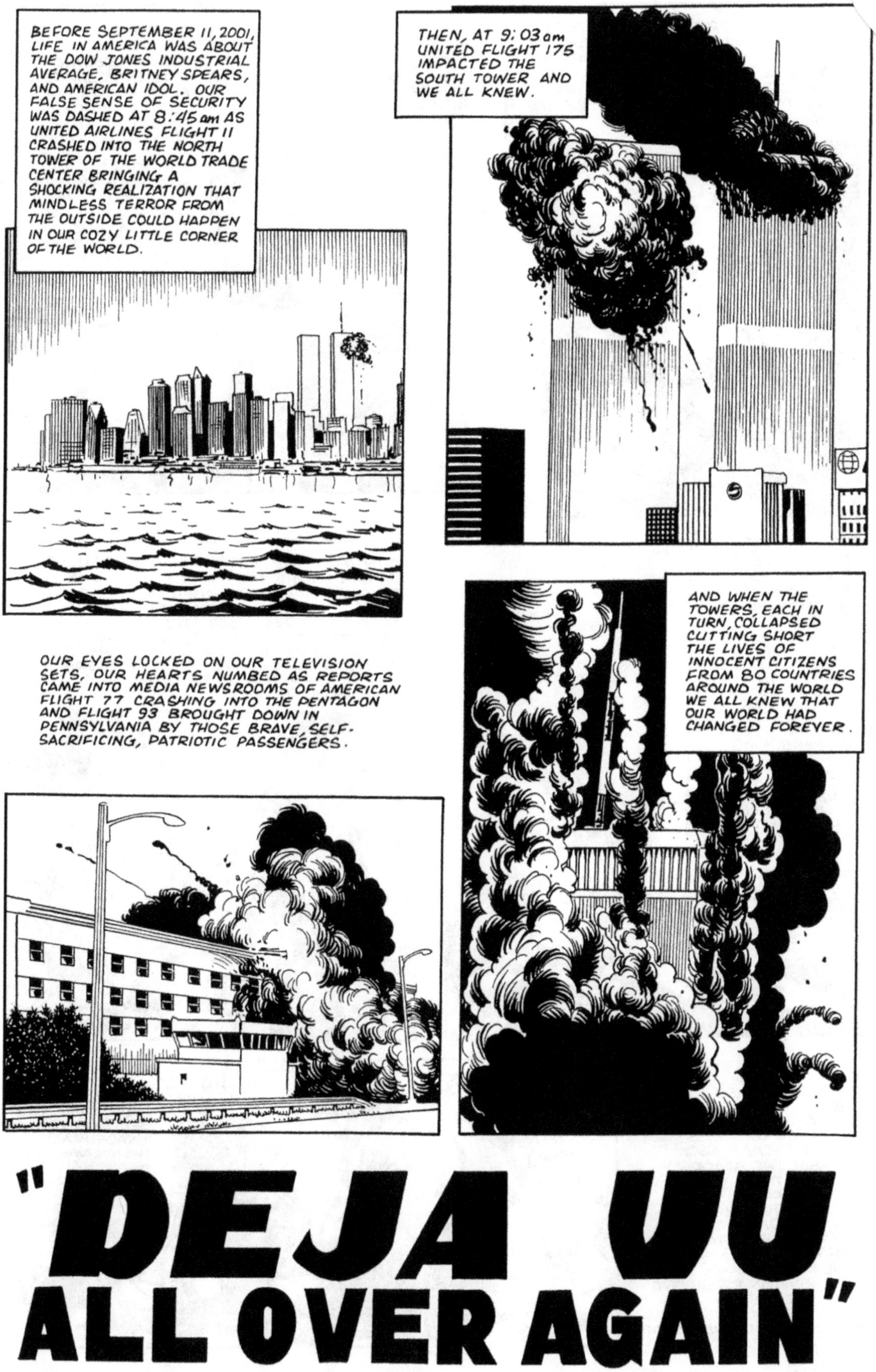
BEFORE SEPTEMBER 11, 2001, LIFE IN AMERICA WAS ABOUT THE DOW JONES INDUSTRIAL AVERAGE, BRITNEY SPEARS, AND AMERICAN IDOL. OUR FALSE SENSE OF SECURITY WAS DASHED AT 8:45 am AS UNITED AIRLINES FLIGHT 11 CRASHED INTO THE NORTH TOWER OF THE WORLD TRADE CENTER BRINGING A SHOCKING REALIZATION THAT MINDLESS TERROR FROM THE OUTSIDE COULD HAPPEN IN OUR COZY LITTLE CORNER OF THE WORLD.
THEN, AT 9:03 am UNITED FLIGHT 175 IMPACTED THE SOUTH TOWER AND WE ALL KNEW.
OUR EYES LOCKED ON OUR TELEVISION SETS, OUR HEARTS NUMBED AS REPORTS CAME INTO MEDIA NEWSROOMS OF AMERICAN FLIGHT 77 CRASHING INTO THE PENTAGON AND FLIGHT 93 BROUGHT DOWN IN PENNSYLVANIA BY THOSE BRAVE, SELF-SACRIFICING, PATRIOTIC PASSENGERS.
AND WHEN THE TOWERS, EACH IN TURN, COLLAPSED CUTTING SHORT THE LIVES OF INNOCENT CITIZENS FROM 80 COUNTRIES AROUND THE WORLD WE ALL KNEW THAT OUR WORLD HAD CHANGED FOREVER.
"DEJA VU ALL OVER AGAIN"

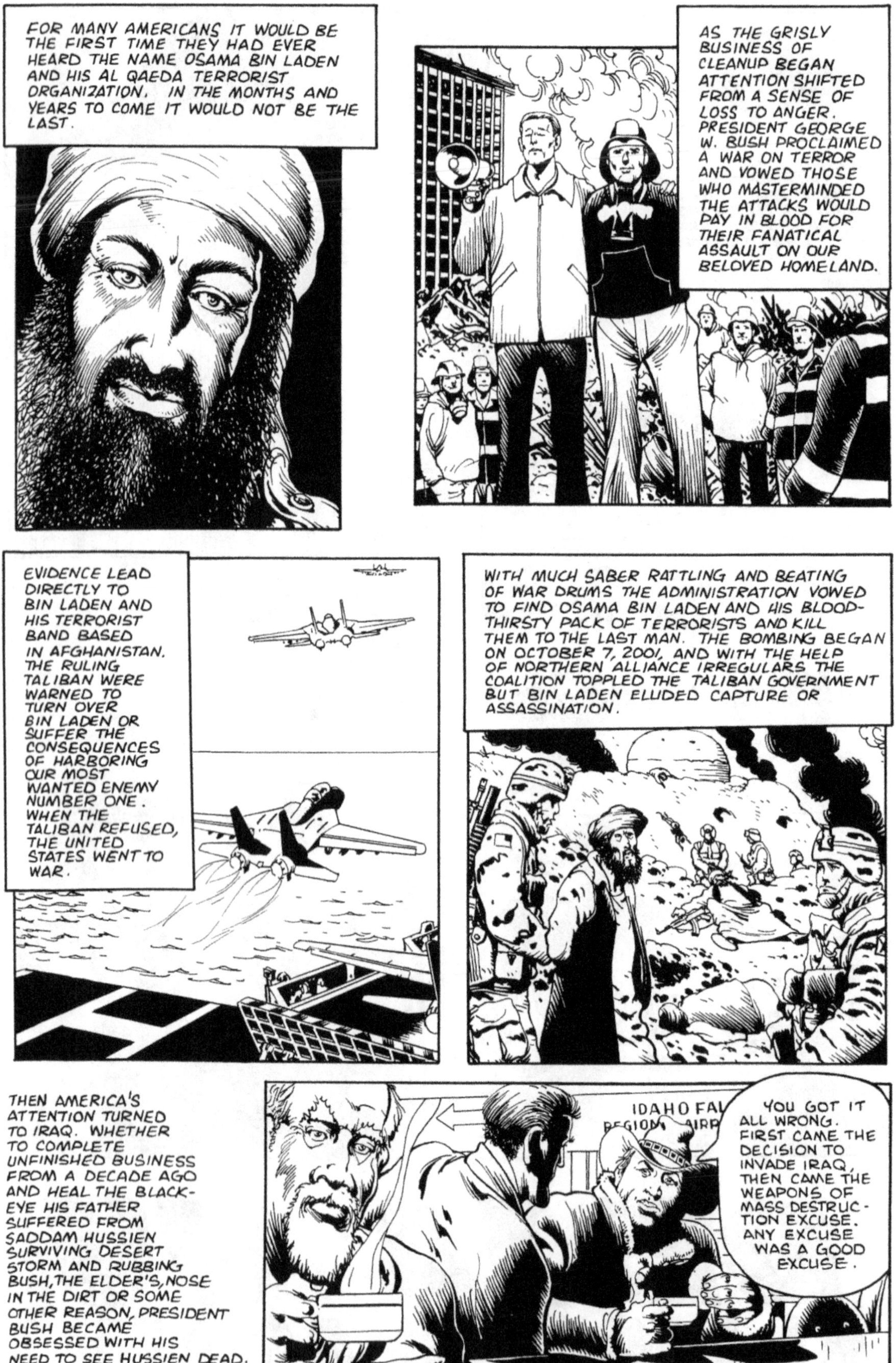
FOR MANY AMERICANS IT WOULD BE THE FIRST TIME THEY HAD EVER HEARD THE NAME OSAMA BIN LADEN AND HIS AL QAEDA TERRORIST ORGANIZATION. IN THE MONTHS AND YEARS TO COME IT WOULD NOT BE THE LAST.
AS THE GRISLY BUSINESS OF CLEANUP BEGAN ATTENTION SHIFTED FROM A SENSE OF LOSS TO ANGER. PRESIDENT GEORGE W. BUSH PROCLAIMED A WAR ON TERROR AND VOWED THOSE WHO MASTERMINDED THE ATTACKS WOULD PAY IN BLOOD FOR THEIR FANATICAL ASSAULT ON OUR BELOVED HOMELAND.
EVIDENCE LEAD DIRECTLY TO BIN LADEN AND HIS TERRORIST BAND BASED IN AFGHANISTAN. THE RULING TALIBAN WERE WARNED TO TURN OVER BIN LADEN OR SUFFER THE CONSEQUENCES OF HARBORING OUR MOST WANTED ENEMY NUMBER ONE. WHEN THE TALIBAN REFUSED, THE UNITED STATES WENT TO WAR.
WITH MUCH SABER RATTLING AND BEATING OF WAR DRUMS THE ADMINISTRATION VOWED TO FIND OSAMA BIN LADEN AND HIS BLOOD-THIRSTY PACK OF TERRORISTS AND KILL THEM TO THE LAST MAN. THE BOMBING BEGAN ON OCTOBER 7, 2001, AND WITH THE HELP OF NORTHERN ALLIANCE IRREGULARS THE COALITION TOPPLED THE TALIBAN GOVERNMENT BUT BIN LADEN ELUDED CAPTURE OR ASSASSINATION.
THEN AMERICA'S ATTENTION TURNED TO IRAQ. WHETHER TO COMPLETE UNFINISHED BUSINESS FROM A DECADE AGO AND HEAL THE BLACK-EYE HIS FATHER SUFFERED FROM SADDAM HUSSIEN SURVIVING DESERT STORM AND RUBBING BUSH, THE ELDER'S, NOSE IN THE DIRT OR SOME OTHER REASON, PRESIDENT BUSH BECAME OBSESSED WITH HIS NEED TO SEE HUSSIEN DEAD.
IDAHO FAL
YOU GOT IT ALL WRONG. FIRST CAME THE DECISION TO INVADE IRAQ, THEN CAME THE WEAPONS OF MASS DESTRUCTION EXCUSE. ANY EXCUSE WAS A GOOD EXCUSE.

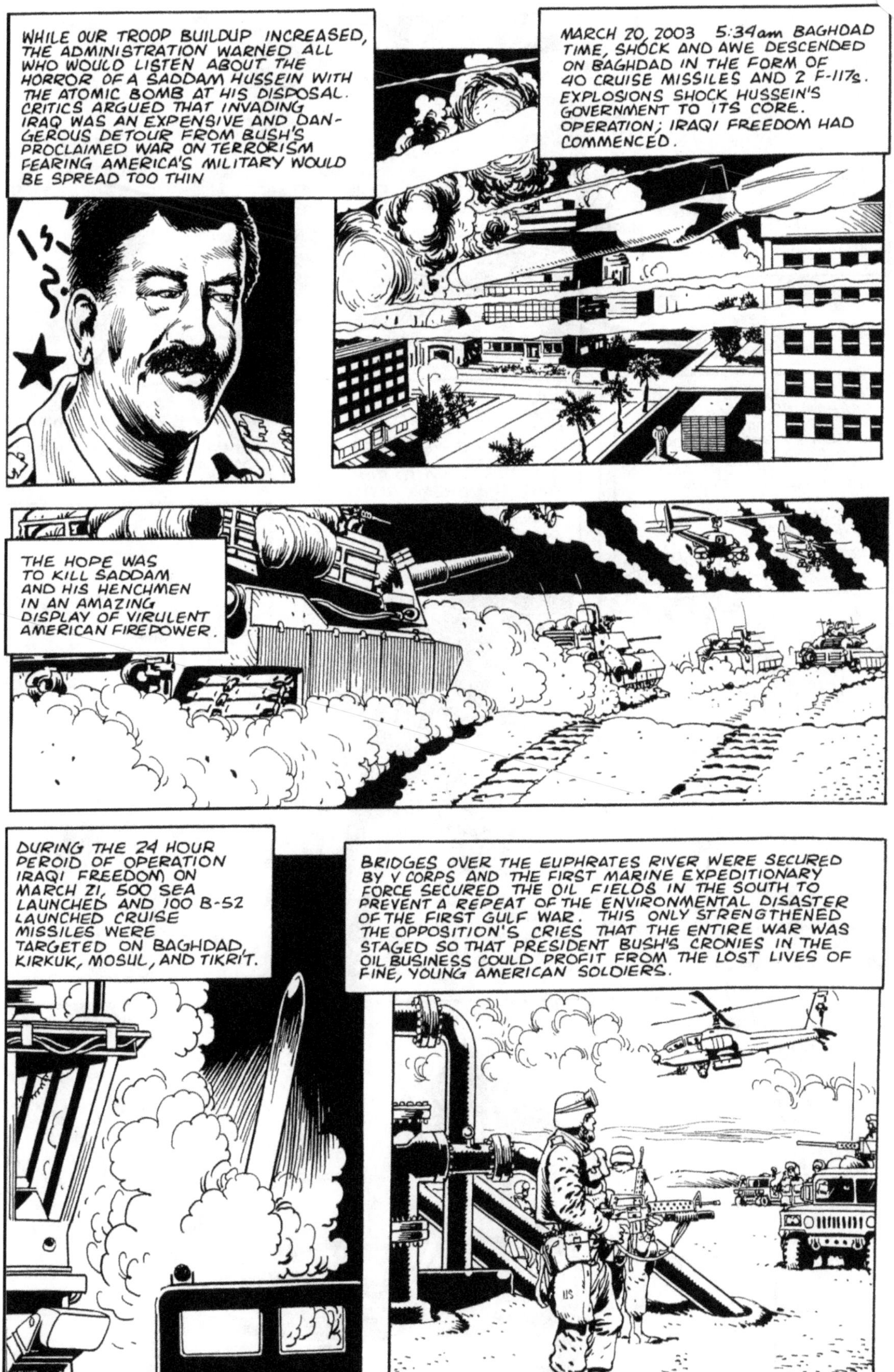
WHILE OUR TROOP BUILDUP INCREASED, THE ADMINISTRATION WARNED ALL WHO WOULD LISTEN ABOUT THE HORROR OF A SADDAM HUSSEIN WITH THE ATOMIC BOMB AT HIS DISPOSAL. CRITICS ARGUED THAT INVADING IRAQ WAS AN EXPENSIVE AND DANGEROUS DETOUR FROM BUSH'S PROCLAIMED WAR ON TERRORISM FEARING AMERICA'S MILITARY WOULD BE SPREAD TOO THIN
MARCH 20, 2003 5:34am BAGHDAD TIME, SHOCK AND AWE DESCENDED ON BAGHDAD IN THE FORM OF 40 CRUISE MISSILES AND 2 F-117s. EXPLOSIONS SHOCK HUSSEIN'S GOVERNMENT TO ITS CORE. OPERATION; IRAQI FREEDOM HAD COMMENCED.
THE HOPE WAS TO KILL SADDAM AND HIS HENCHMEN IN AN AMAZING DISPLAY OF VIRULENT AMERICAN FIREPOWER.
DURING THE 24 HOUR PEROID OF OPERATION IRAQI FREEDOM ON MARCH 21, 500 SEA LAUNCHED AND 100 B-52 LAUNCHED CRUISE MISSILES WERE TARGETED ON BAGHDAD, KIRKUK, MOSUL, AND TIKRIT.
BRIDGES OVER THE EUPHRATES RIVER WERE SECURED BY V CORPS AND THE FIRST MARINE EXPEDITIONARY FORCE SECURED THE OIL FIELDS IN THE SOUTH TO PREVENT A REPEAT OF THE ENVIRONMENTAL DISASTER OF THE FIRST GULF WAR. THIS ONLY STRENGTHENED THE OPPOSITION'S CRIES THAT THE ENTIRE WAR WAS STAGED SO THAT PRESIDENT BUSH'S CRONIES IN THE OIL BUSINESS COULD PROFIT FROM THE LOST LIVES OF FINE, YOUNG AMERICAN SOLDIERS.

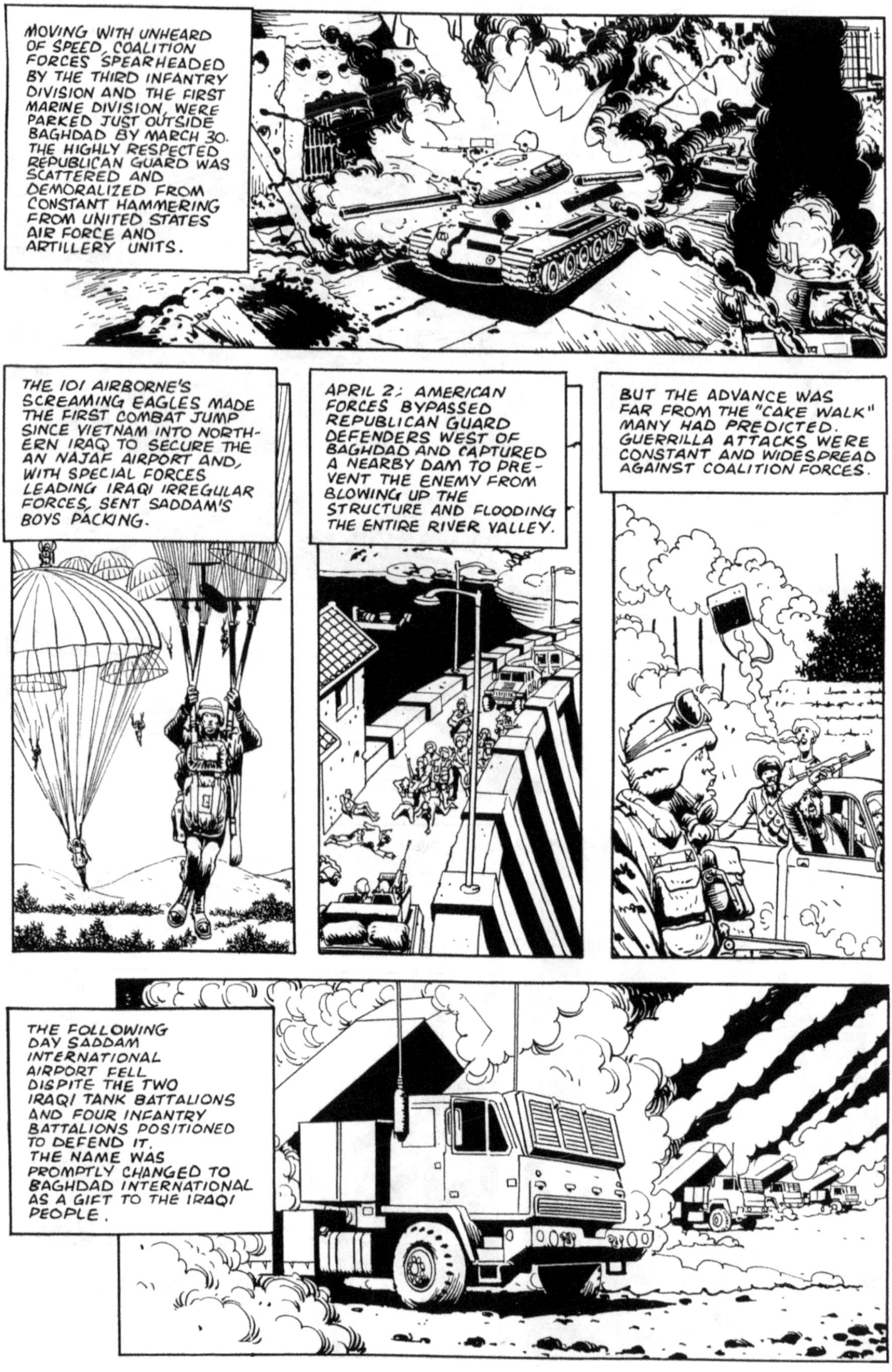
MOVING WITH UNHEARD OF SPEED, COALITION FORCES SPEARHEADED BY THE THIRD INFANTRY DIVISION AND THE FIRST MARINE DIVISION, WERE PARKED JUST OUTSIDE BAGHDAD BY MARCH 30. THE HIGHLY RESPECTED REPUBLICAN GUARD WAS SCATTERED AND DEMORALIZED FROM CONSTANT HAMMERING FROM UNITED STATES AIR FORCE AND ARTILLERY UNITS.
THE 101 AIRBORNE'S SCREAMING EAGLES MADE THE FIRST COMBAT JUMP SINCE VIETNAM INTO NORTHERN IRAQ TO SECURE THE AN NAJAF AIRPORT AND, WITH SPECIAL FORCES LEADING IRAQI IRREGULAR FORCES, SENT SADDAM'S BOYS PACKING.
APRIL 2; AMERICAN FORCES BYPASSED REPUBLICAN GUARD DEFENDERS WEST OF BAGHDAD AND CAPTURED A NEARBY DAM TO PREVENT THE ENEMY FROM BLOWING UP THE STRUCTURE AND FLOODING THE ENTIRE RIVER VALLEY.
BUT THE ADVANCE WAS FAR FROM THE "CAKE WALK" MANY HAD PREDICTED. GUERRILLA ATTACKS WERE CONSTANT AND WIDESPREAD AGAINST COALITION FORCES.
THE FOLLOWING DAY SADDAM INTERNATIONAL AIRPORT FELL DISPITE THE TWO IRAQI TANK BATTALIONS AND FOUR INFANTRY BATTALIONS POSITIONED TO DEFEND IT. THE NAME WAS PROMPTLY CHANGED TO BAGHDAD INTERNATIONAL AS A GIFT TO THE IRAQI PEOPLE.

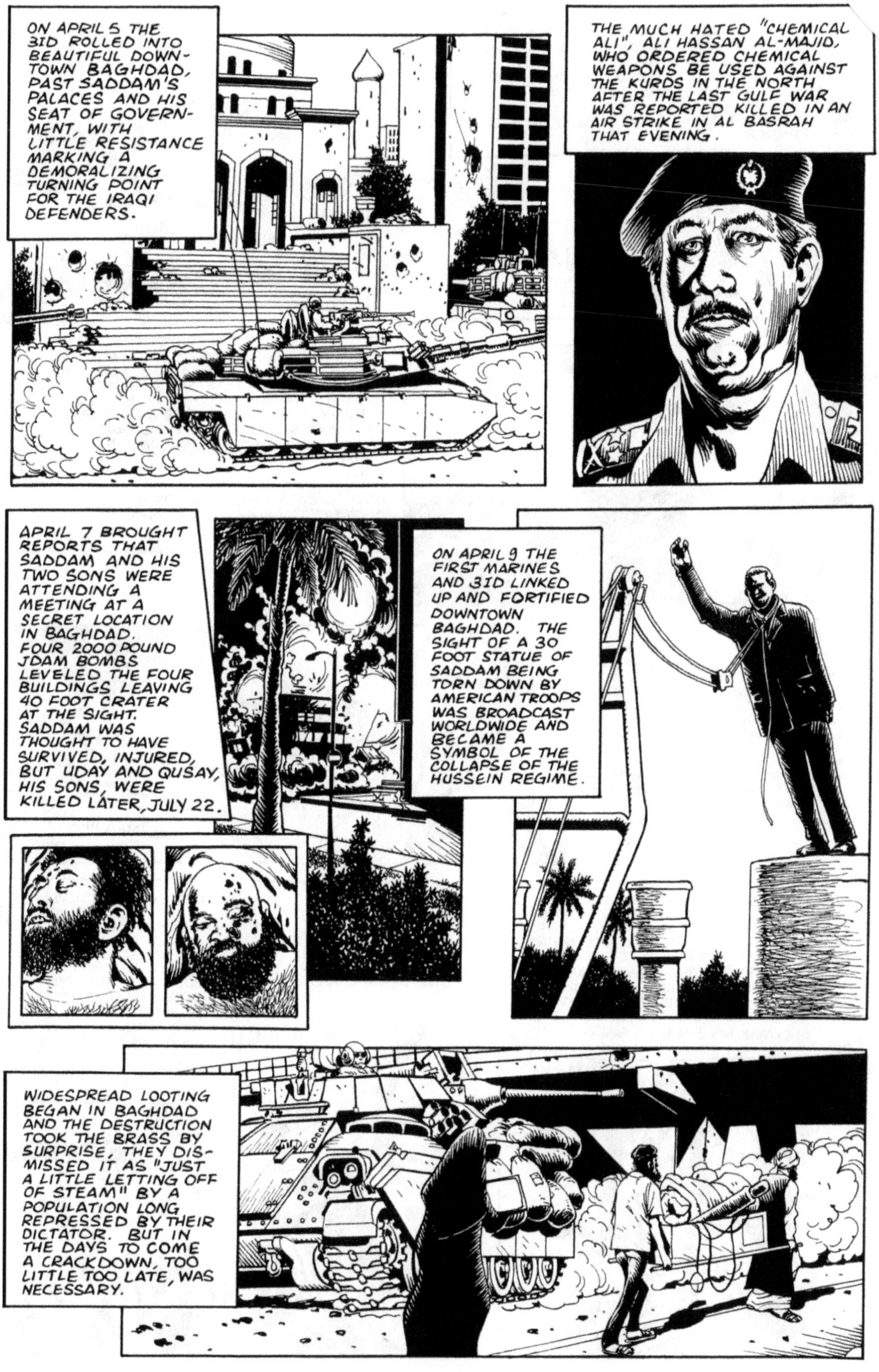
ON APRIL 5 THE 3ID ROLLED INTO BEAUTIFUL DOWN-TOWN BAGHDAD, PAST SADDAM'S PALACES AND HIS SEAT OF GOVERNMENT, WITH LITTLE RESISTANCE MARKING A DEMORALIZING TURNING POINT FOR THE IRAQI DEFENDERS.
THE MUCH HATED "CHEMICAL ALI", ALI HASSAN AL-MAJID, WHO ORDERED CHEMICAL WEAPONS BE USED AGAINST THE KURDS IN THE NORTH AFTER THE LAST GULF WAR WAS REPORTED KILLED IN AN AIR STRIKE IN AL BASRAH THAT EVENING.
APRIL 7 BROUGHT REPORTS THAT SADDAM AND HIS TWO SONS WERE ATTENDING A MEETING AT A SECRET LOCATION IN BAGHDAD. FOUR 2000 POUND JDAM BOMBS LEVELED THE FOUR BUILDINGS LEAVING 40 FOOT CRATER AT THE SIGHT. SADDAM WAS THOUGHT TO HAVE SURVIVED, INJURED, BUT UDAY AND QUSAY, HIS SONS, WERE KILLED LATER, JULY 22.
ON APRIL 9 THE FIRST MARINES AND 3ID LINKED UP AND FORTIFIED DOWNTOWN BAGHDAD. THE SIGHT OF A 30 FOOT STATUE OF SADDAM BEING TORN DOWN BY AMERICAN TROOPS WAS BROADCAST WORLDWIDE AND BECAME A SYMBOL OF THE COLLAPSE OF THE HUSSEIN REGIME.
WIDESPREAD LOOTING BEGAN IN BAGHDAD AND THE DESTRUCTION TOOK THE BRASS BY SURPRISE, THEY DISMISSED IT AS "JUST A LITTLE LETTING OFF OF STEAM" BY A POPULATION LONG REPRESSED BY THEIR DICTATOR. BUT IN THE DAYS TO COME A CRACKDOWN, TOO LITTLE TOO LATE, WAS NECESSARY.

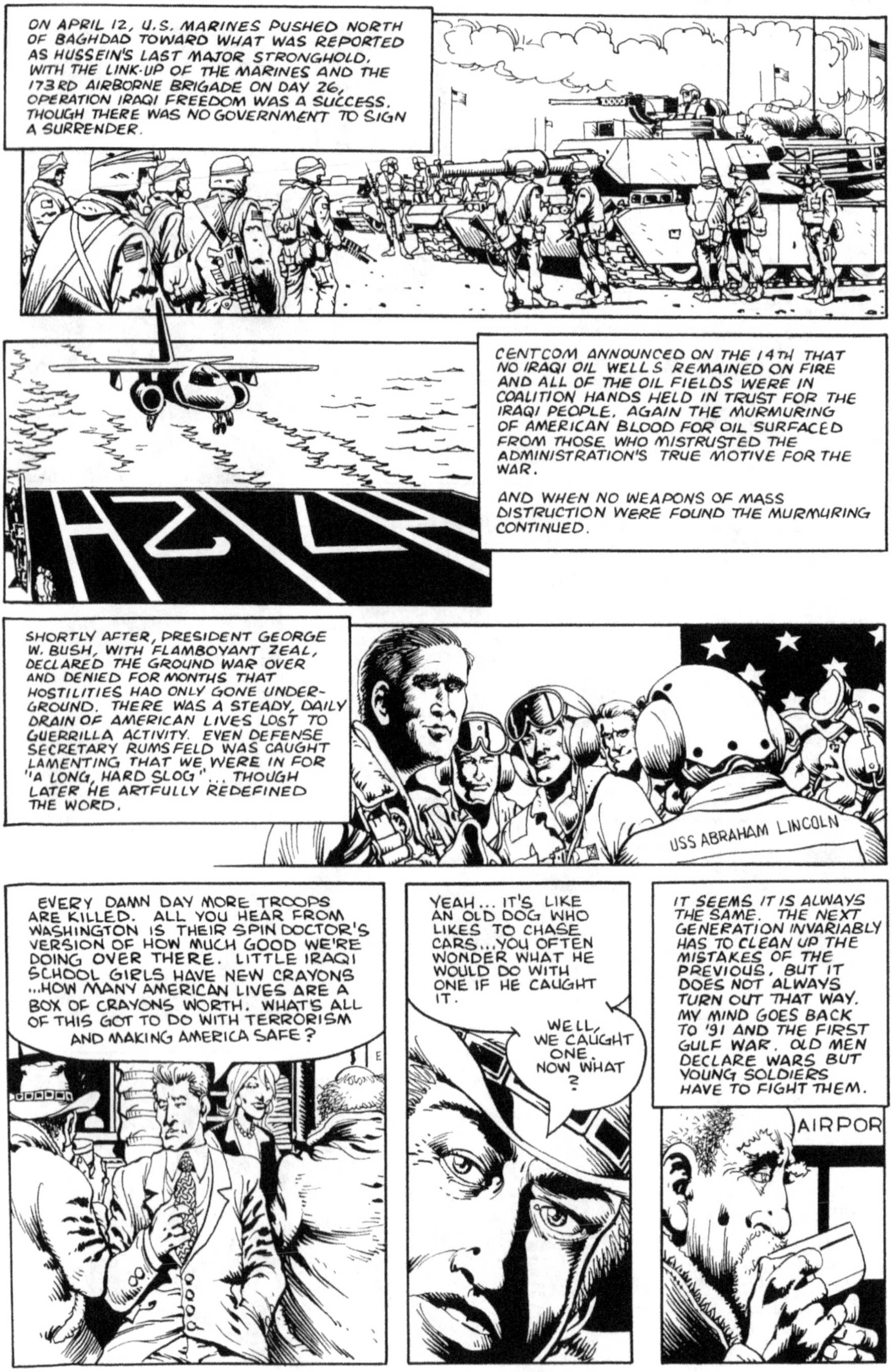
ON APRIL 12, U.S. MARINES PUSHED NORTH OF BAGHDAD TOWARD WHAT WAS REPORTED AS HUSSEIN'S LAST MAJOR STRONGHOLD. WITH THE LINK-UP OF THE MARINES AND THE 173RD AIRBORNE BRIGADE ON DAY 26, OPERATION IRAQI FREEDOM WAS A SUCCESS. THOUGH THERE WAS NO GOVERNMENT TO SIGN A SURRENDER.
CENTCOM ANNOUNCED ON THE 14TH THAT NO IRAQI OIL WELLS REMAINED ON FIRE AND ALL OF THE OIL FIELDS WERE IN COALITION HANDS HELD IN TRUST FOR THE IRAQI PEOPLE. AGAIN THE MURMURING OF AMERICAN BLOOD FOR OIL SURFACED FROM THOSE WHO MISTRUSTED THE ADMINISTRATION'S TRUE MOTIVE FOR THE WAR.
AND WHEN NO WEAPONS OF MASS DISTRUCTION WERE FOUND THE MURMURING CONTINUED.
SHORTLY AFTER, PRESIDENT GEORGE W. BUSH, WITH FLAMBOYANT ZEAL, DECLARED THE GROUND WAR OVER AND DENIED FOR MONTHS THAT HOSTILITIES HAD ONLY GONE UNDER-GROUND. THERE WAS A STEADY, DAILY DRAIN OF AMERICAN LIVES LOST TO GUERRILLA ACTIVITY. EVEN DEFENSE SECRETARY RUMSFELD WAS CAUGHT LAMENTING THAT WE WERE IN FOR "A LONG, HARD SLOG"... THOUGH LATER HE ARTFULLY REDEFINED THE WORD.
USS ABRAHAM LINCOLN
EVERY DAMN DAY MORE TROOPS ARE KILLED. ALL YOU HEAR FROM WASHINGTON IS THEIR SPIN DOCTOR'S VERSION OF HOW MUCH GOOD WE'RE DOING OVER THERE. LITTLE IRAQI SCHOOL GIRLS HAVE NEW CRAYONS ...HOW MANY AMERICAN LIVES ARE A BOX OF CRAYONS WORTH. WHAT'S ALL OF THIS GOT TO DO WITH TERRORISM AND MAKING AMERICA SAFE?
YEAH... IT'S LIKE AN OLD DOG WHO LIKES TO CHASE CARS... YOU OFTEN WONDER WHAT HE WOULD DO WITH ONE IF HE CAUGHT IT.
WELL, WE CAUGHT ONE. NOW WHAT?
IT SEEMS IT IS ALWAYS THE SAME. THE NEXT GENERATION INVARIABLY HAS TO CLEAN UP THE MISTAKES OF THE PREVIOUS, BUT IT DOES NOT ALWAYS TURN OUT THAT WAY. MY MIND GOES BACK TO '91 AND THE FIRST GULF WAR. OLD MEN DECLARE WARS BUT YOUNG SOLDIERS HAVE TO FIGHT THEM.
AIRPOR

GULF WAR JOURNAL

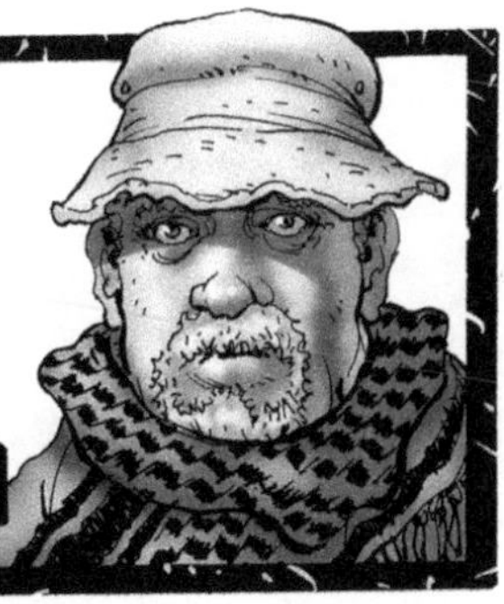

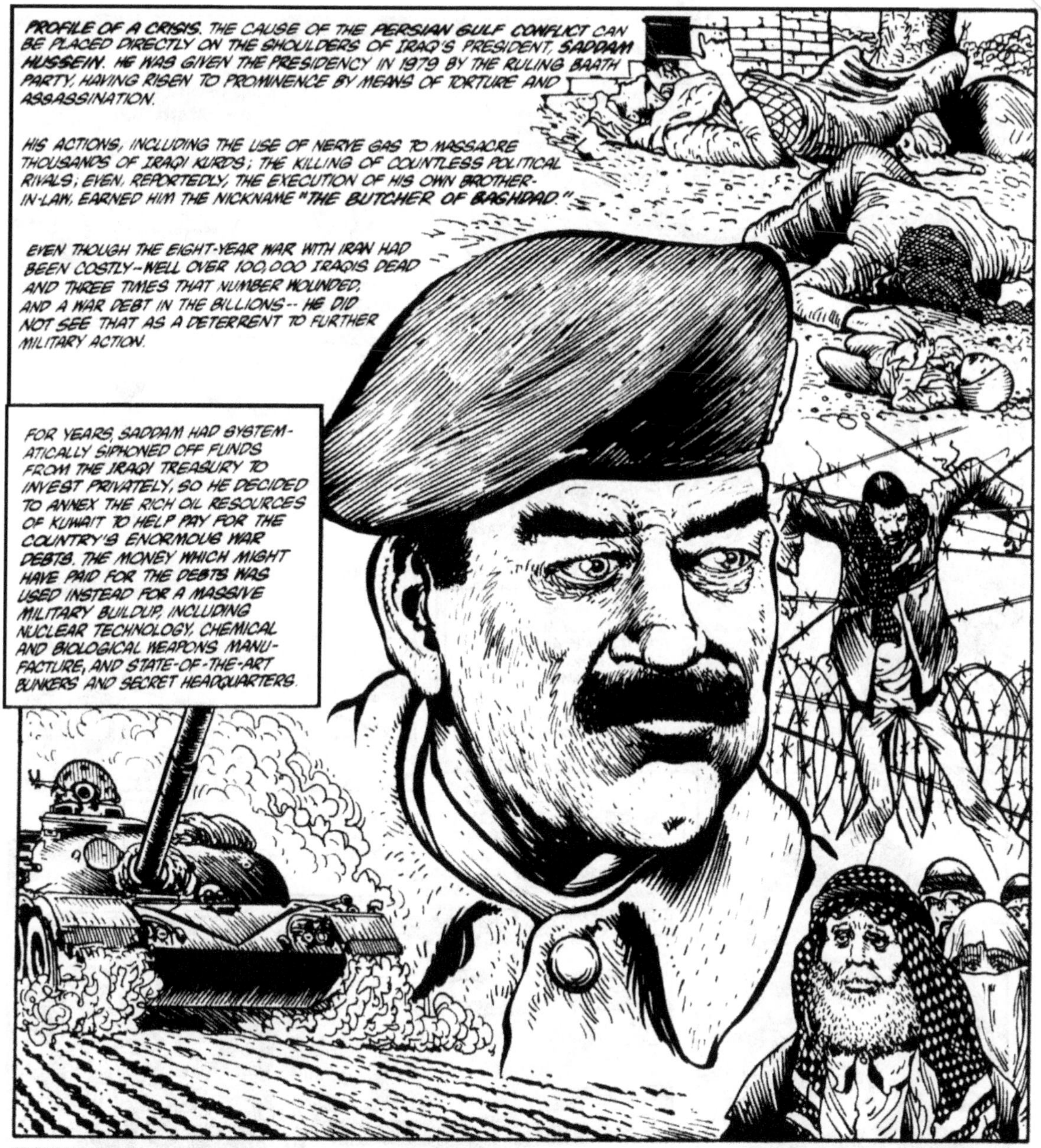
PROFILE OF A CRISIS. THE CAUSE OF THE PERSIAN GULF CONFLICT CAN BE PLACED DIRECTLY ON THE SHOULDERS OF IRAQ'S PRESIDENT, SADDAM HUSSEIN. HE WAS GIVEN THE PRESIDENCY IN 1979 BY THE RULING BAATH PARTY, HAVING RISEN TO PROMINENCE BY MEANS OF TORTURE AND ASSASSINATION.
HIS ACTIONS, INCLUDING THE USE OF NERVE GAS TO MASSACRE THOUSANDS OF IRAQI KURDS; THE KILLING OF COUNTLESS POLITICAL RIVALS; EVEN, REPORTEDLY, THE EXECUTION OF HIS OWN BROTHER-IN-LAW, EARNED HIM THE NICKNAME "THE BUTCHER OF BAGHDAD."
EVEN THOUGH THE EIGHT-YEAR WAR WITH IRAN HAD BEEN COSTLY--WELL OVER 100,000 IRAQIS DEAD AND THREE TIMES THAT NUMBER WOUNDED, AND A WAR DEBT IN THE BILLIONS-- HE DID NOT SEE THAT AS A DETERRENT TO FURTHER MILITARY ACTION.
FOR YEARS, SADDAM HAD SYSTEMATICALLY SIPHONED OFF FUNDS FROM THE IRAQI TREASURY TO INVEST PRIVATELY, SO HE DECIDED TO ANNEX THE RICH OIL RESOURCES OF KUWAIT TO HELP PAY FOR THE COUNTRY'S ENORMOUS WAR DEBTS. THE MONEY WHICH MIGHT HAVE PAID FOR THE DEBTS WAS USED INSTEAD FOR A MASSIVE MILITARY BUILDUP, INCLUDING NUCLEAR TECHNOLOGY, CHEMICAL AND BIOLOGICAL WEAPONS MANUFACTURE, AND STATE-OF-THE-ART BUNKERS AND SECRET HEADQUARTERS.
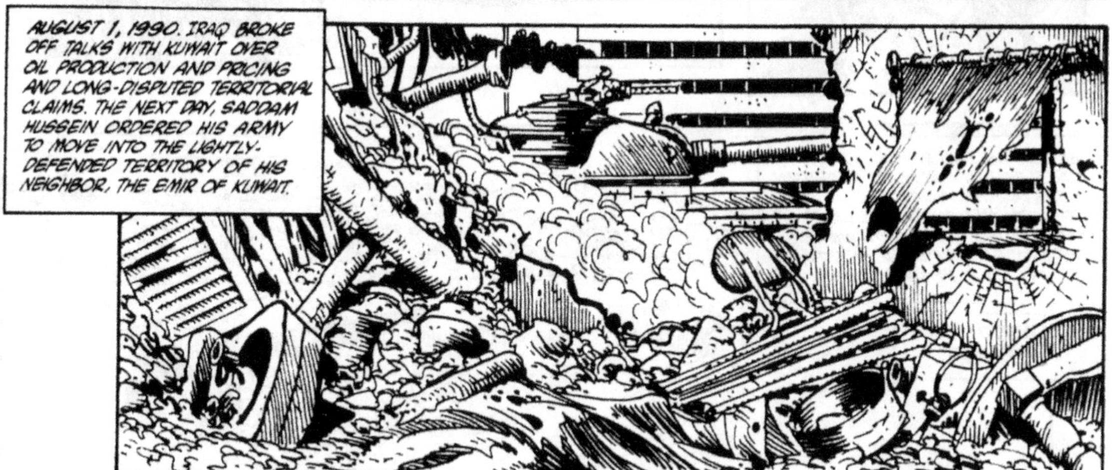
AUGUST 1, 1990. IRAQ BROKE OFF TALKS WITH KUWAIT OVER OIL PRODUCTION AND PRICING AND LONG-DISPUTED TERRITORIAL CLAIMS. THE NEXT DAY, SADDAM HUSSEIN ORDERED HIS ARMY TO MOVE INTO THE LIGHTLY-DEFENDED TERRITORY OF HIS NEIGHBOR, THE EMIR OF KUWAIT.

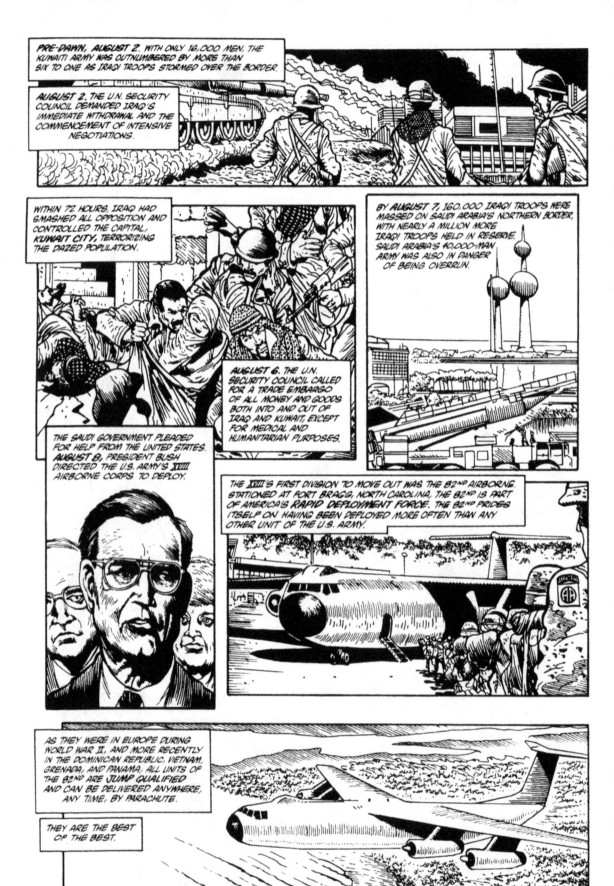

PRE-DAWN, AUGUST 2. WITH ONLY 16,000 MEN, THE KUWAITI ARMY WAS OUTNUMBERED BY MORE THAN SIX TO ONE AS IRAQI TROOPS STORMED OVER THE BORDER.

AUGUST 2. THE U.N. SECURITY COUNCIL DEMANDED IRAQ'S IMMEDIATE WITHDRAWAL AND THE COMMENCEMENT OF INTENSIVE NEGOTIATIONS.

WITHIN 72 HOURS, IRAQ HAD SMASHED ALL OPPOSITION AND CONTROLLED THE CAPITAL, *KUWAIT CITY*, TERRORIZING THE DAZED POPULATION.

BY AUGUST 7, 160,000 IRAQI TROOPS WERE MASSED ON SAUDI ARABIA'S NORTHERN BORDER, WITH NEARLY A MILLION MORE IRAQI TROOPS HELD IN RESERVE. SAUDI ARABIA'S 40,000-MAN ARMY WAS ALSO IN DANGER OF BEING OVERRUN.

AUGUST 6. THE U.N. SECURITY COUNCIL CALLED FOR A TRADE EMBARGO OF ALL MONEY AND GOODS BOTH INTO AND OUT OF IRAQ AND KUWAIT, EXCEPT FOR MEDICAL AND HUMANITARIAN PURPOSES.

THE SAUDI GOVERNMENT PLEADED FOR HELP FROM THE UNITED STATES. AUGUST 8, PRESIDENT BUSH DIRECTED THE U.S. ARMY'S XVIII AIRBORNE CORPS TO DEPLOY.

THE XVIII'S FIRST DIVISION TO MOVE OUT WAS THE 82ND AIRBORNE. STATIONED AT FORT BRAGG, NORTH CAROLINA, THE 82ND IS PART OF AMERICA'S *RAPID DEPLOYMENT FORCE*. THE 82ND PRIDES ITSELF ON HAVING BEEN DEPLOYED MORE OFTEN THAN ANY OTHER UNIT OF THE U.S. ARMY.

AS THEY WERE IN EUROPE DURING WORLD WAR II, AND MORE RECENTLY IN THE DOMINICAN REPUBLIC, VIETNAM, GRENADA, AND PANAMA, ALL UNITS OF THE 82ND ARE *JUMP QUALIFIED* AND CAN BE DELIVERED ANYWHERE, ANY TIME, BY PARACHUTE.

THEY ARE THE BEST OF THE BEST.

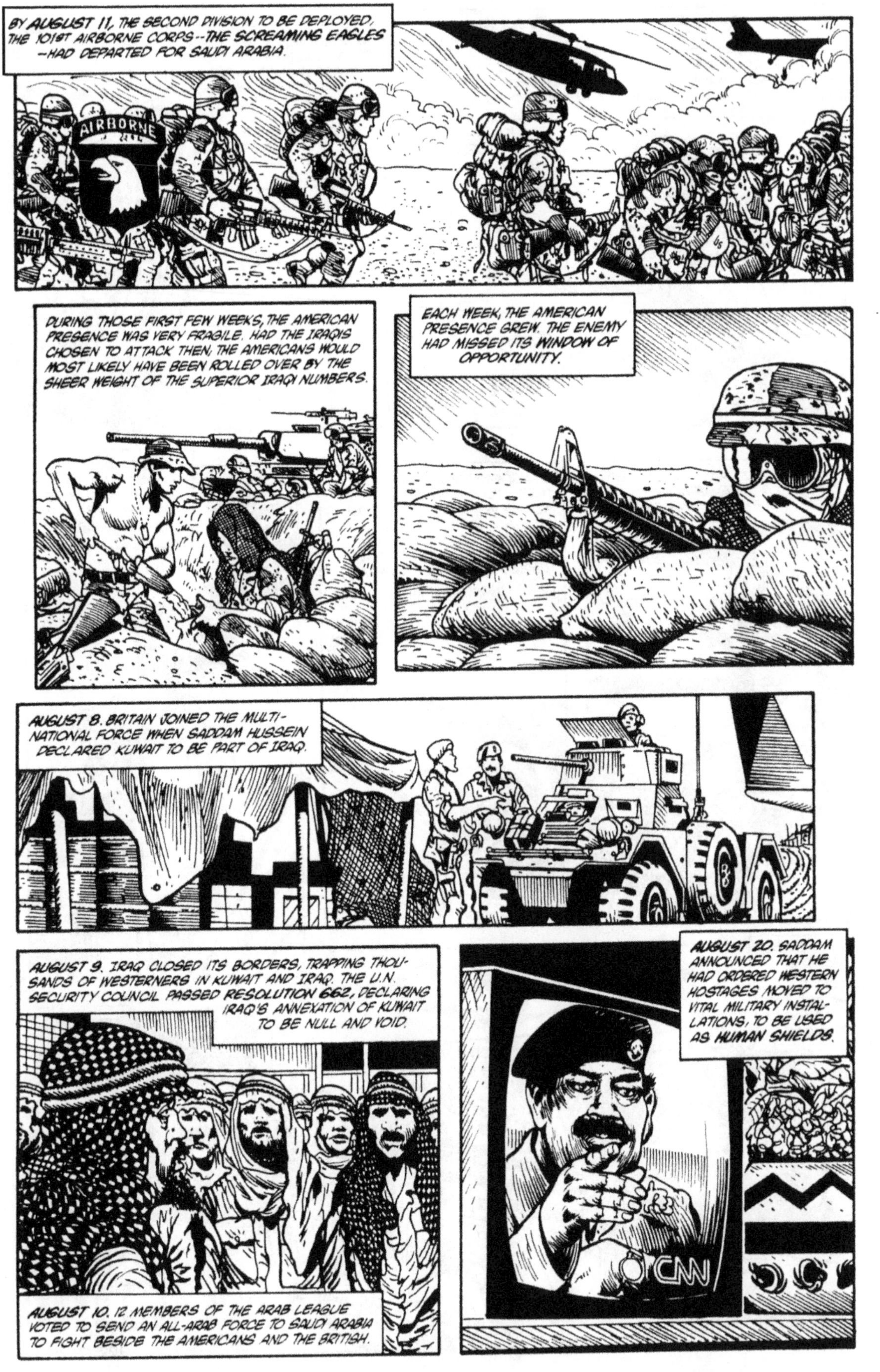
BY AUGUST 11, THE SECOND DIVISION TO BE DEPLOYED, THE 101st AIRBORNE CORPS--THE SCREAMING EAGLES --HAD DEPARTED FOR SAUDI ARABIA.
AIRBORNE
DURING THOSE FIRST FEW WEEKS, THE AMERICAN PRESENCE WAS VERY FRAGILE. HAD THE IRAQIS CHOSEN TO ATTACK THEN, THE AMERICANS WOULD MOST LIKELY HAVE BEEN ROLLED OVER BY THE SHEER WEIGHT OF THE SUPERIOR IRAQI NUMBERS.
EACH WEEK, THE AMERICAN PRESENCE GREW. THE ENEMY HAD MISSED ITS WINDOW OF OPPORTUNITY.
AUGUST 8. BRITAIN JOINED THE MULTI-NATIONAL FORCE WHEN SADDAM HUSSEIN DECLARED KUWAIT TO BE PART OF IRAQ.
AUGUST 9. IRAQ CLOSED ITS BORDERS, TRAPPING THOUSANDS OF WESTERNERS IN KUWAIT AND IRAQ. THE U.N. SECURITY COUNCIL PASSED RESOLUTION 662, DECLARING IRAQ'S ANNEXATION OF KUWAIT TO BE NULL AND VOID.
AUGUST 10. 12 MEMBERS OF THE ARAB LEAGUE VOTED TO SEND AN ALL-ARAB FORCE TO SAUDI ARABIA TO FIGHT BESIDE THE AMERICANS AND THE BRITISH.
AUGUST 20. SADDAM ANNOUNCED THAT HE HAD ORDERED WESTERN HOSTAGES MOVED TO VITAL MILITARY INSTALLATIONS, TO BE USED AS HUMAN SHIELDS.
CNN

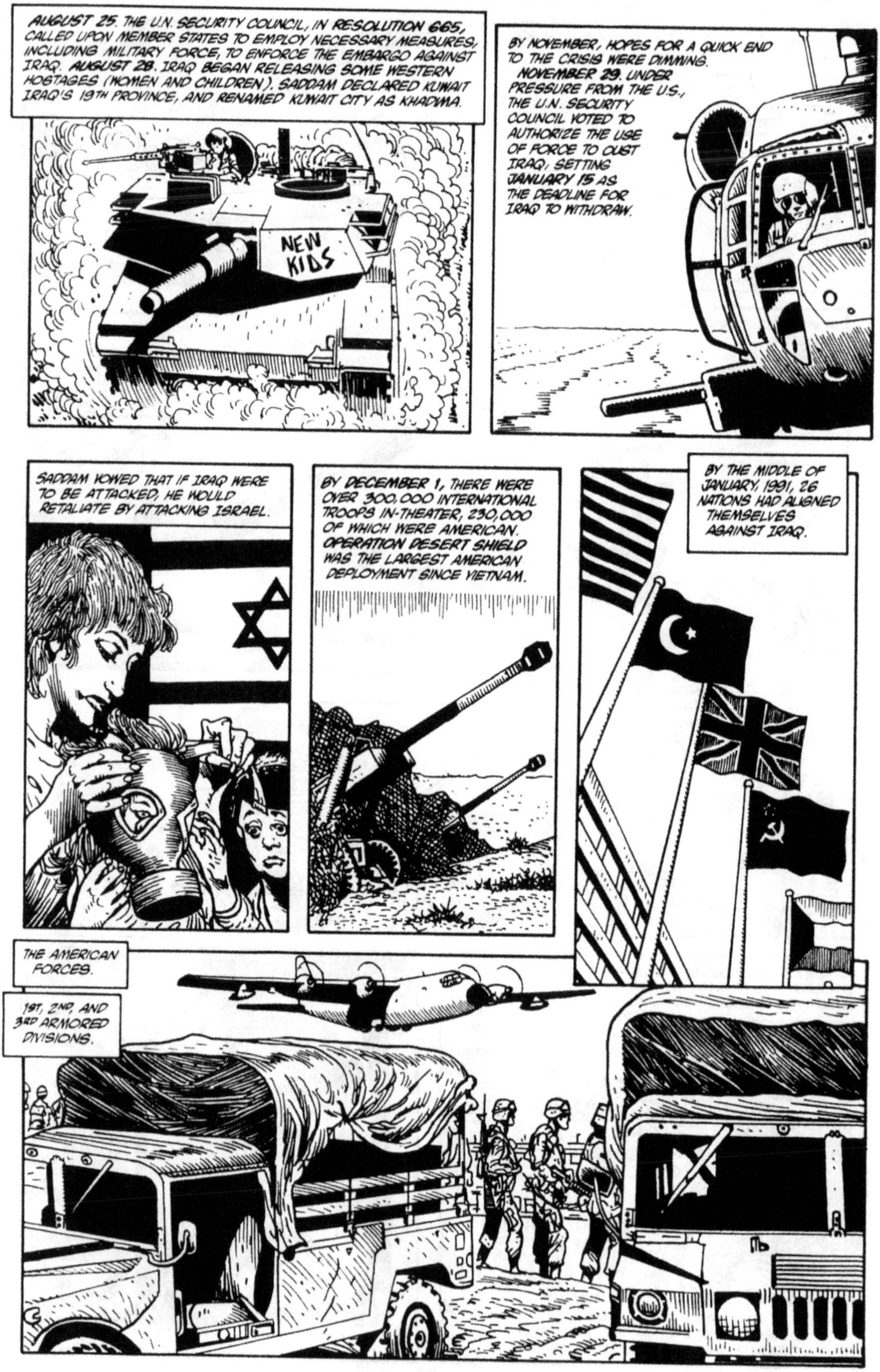

AUGUST 25. THE U.N. SECURITY COUNCIL, IN RESOLUTION 665, CALLED UPON MEMBER STATES TO EMPLOY NECESSARY MEASURES, INCLUDING MILITARY FORCE, TO ENFORCE THE EMBARGO AGAINST IRAQ. AUGUST 28. IRAQ BEGAN RELEASING SOME WESTERN HOSTAGES (WOMEN AND CHILDREN). SADDAM DECLARED KUWAIT IRAQ'S 19TH PROVINCE, AND RENAMED KUWAIT CITY AS KHADIMA.
NEW KIDS
BY NOVEMBER, HOPES FOR A QUICK END TO THE CRISIS WERE DIMMING. NOVEMBER 29. UNDER PRESSURE FROM THE U.S., THE U.N. SECURITY COUNCIL VOTED TO AUTHORIZE THE USE OF FORCE TO OUST IRAQ, SETTING JANUARY 15 AS THE DEADLINE FOR IRAQ TO WITHDRAW.
SADDAM VOWED THAT IF IRAQ WERE TO BE ATTACKED, HE WOULD RETALIATE BY ATTACKING ISRAEL.
BY DECEMBER 1, THERE WERE OVER 300,000 INTERNATIONAL TROOPS IN-THEATER, 230,000 OF WHICH WERE AMERICAN. OPERATION DESERT SHIELD WAS THE LARGEST AMERICAN DEPLOYMENT SINCE VIETNAM.
BY THE MIDDLE OF JANUARY, 1991, 26 NATIONS HAD ALIGNED THEMSELVES AGAINST IRAQ.
THE AMERICAN FORCES.
1ST, 2ND, AND 3RD ARMORED DIVISIONS.

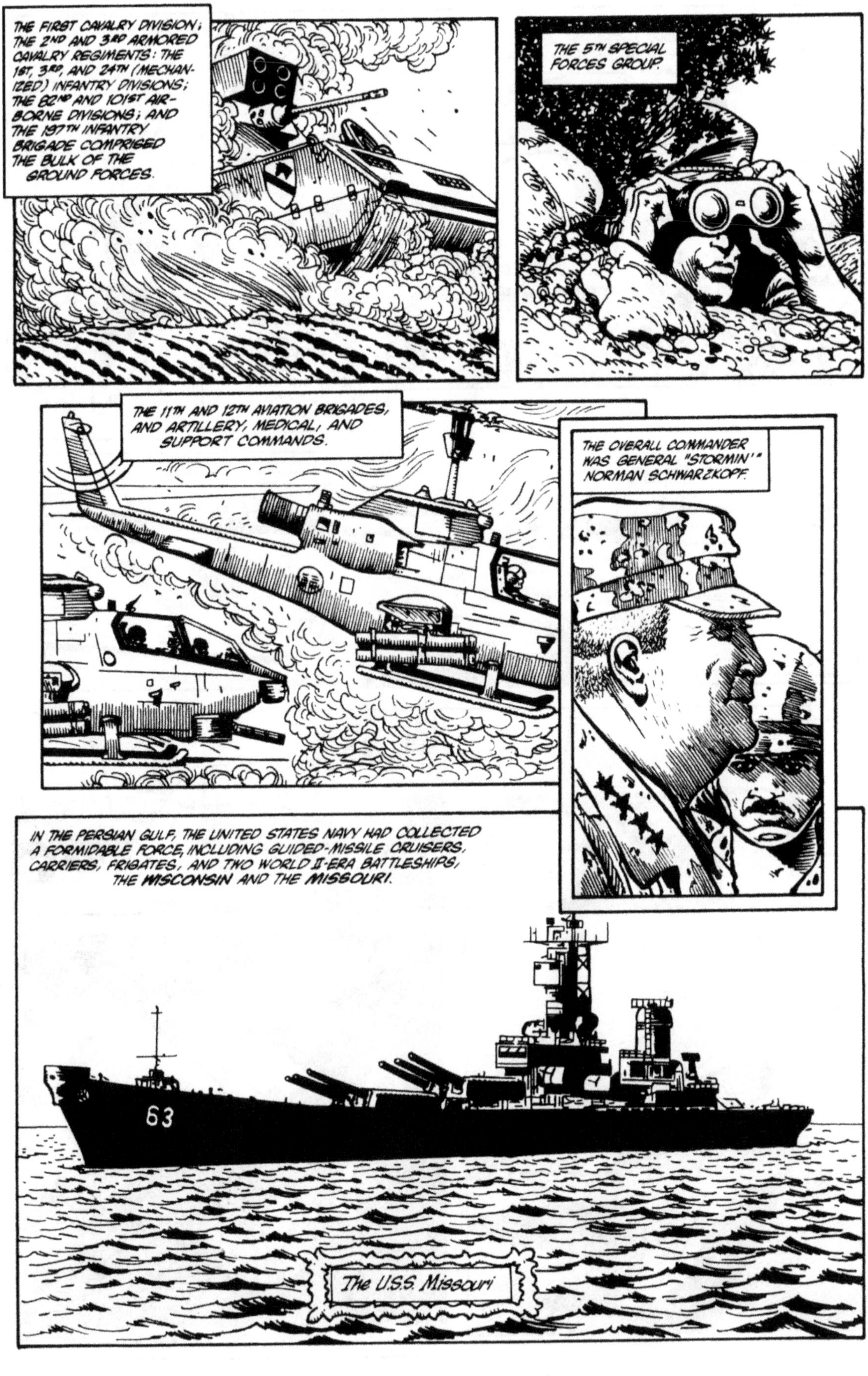
THE FIRST CAVALRY DIVISION; THE 2ND AND 3RD ARMORED CAVALRY REGIMENTS: THE 1ST, 3RD, AND 24TH (MECHANIZED) INFANTRY DIVISIONS; THE 82ND AND 101ST AIRBORNE DIVISIONS; AND THE 197TH INFANTRY BRIGADE COMPRISED THE BULK OF THE GROUND FORCES.
THE 5TH SPECIAL FORCES GROUP.
THE 11TH AND 12TH AVIATION BRIGADES, AND ARTILLERY, MEDICAL, AND SUPPORT COMMANDS.
THE OVERALL COMMANDER WAS GENERAL "STORMIN'" NORMAN SCHWARZKOPF.
IN THE PERSIAN GULF, THE UNITED STATES NAVY HAD COLLECTED A FORMIDABLE FORCE, INCLUDING GUIDED-MISSILE CRUISERS, CARRIERS, FRIGATES, AND TWO WORLD II-ERA BATTLESHIPS, THE WISCONSIN AND THE MISSOURI.
63
The U.S.S. Missouri

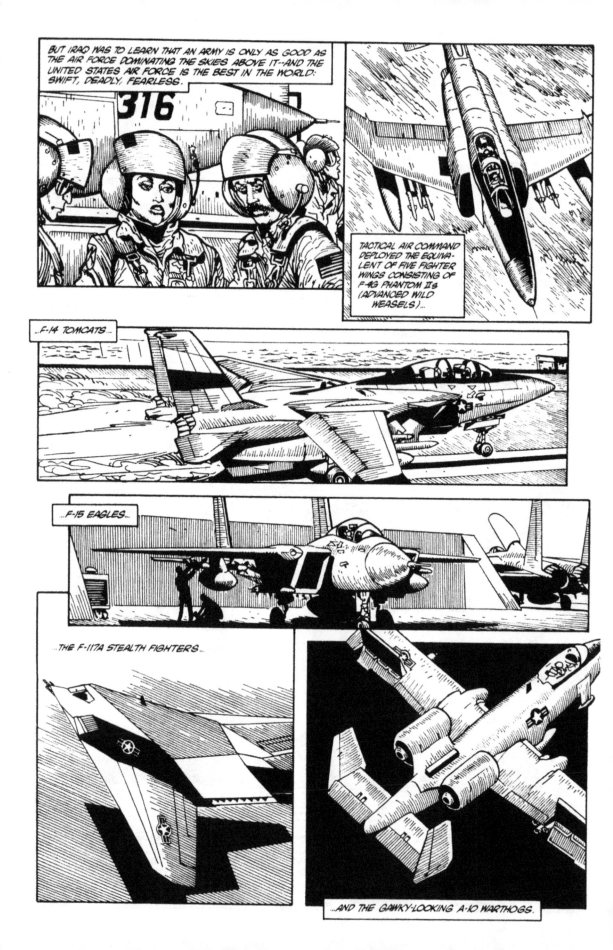

BUT IRAQ WAS TO LEARN THAT AN ARMY IS ONLY AS GOOD AS THE AIR FORCE DOMINATING THE SKIES ABOVE IT--AND THE UNITED STATES AIR FORCE IS THE BEST IN THE WORLD: SWIFT, DEADLY, FEARLESS.

TACTICAL AIR COMMAND DEPLOYED THE EQUIVALENT OF FIVE FIGHTER WINGS CONSISTING OF F-4G PHANTOM IIs (ADVANCED WILD WEASELS)...

...F-14 TOMCATS...

...F-15 EAGLES...

...THE F-117A STEALTH FIGHTERS...

...AND THE GAWKY-LOOKING A-10 WARTHOGS.

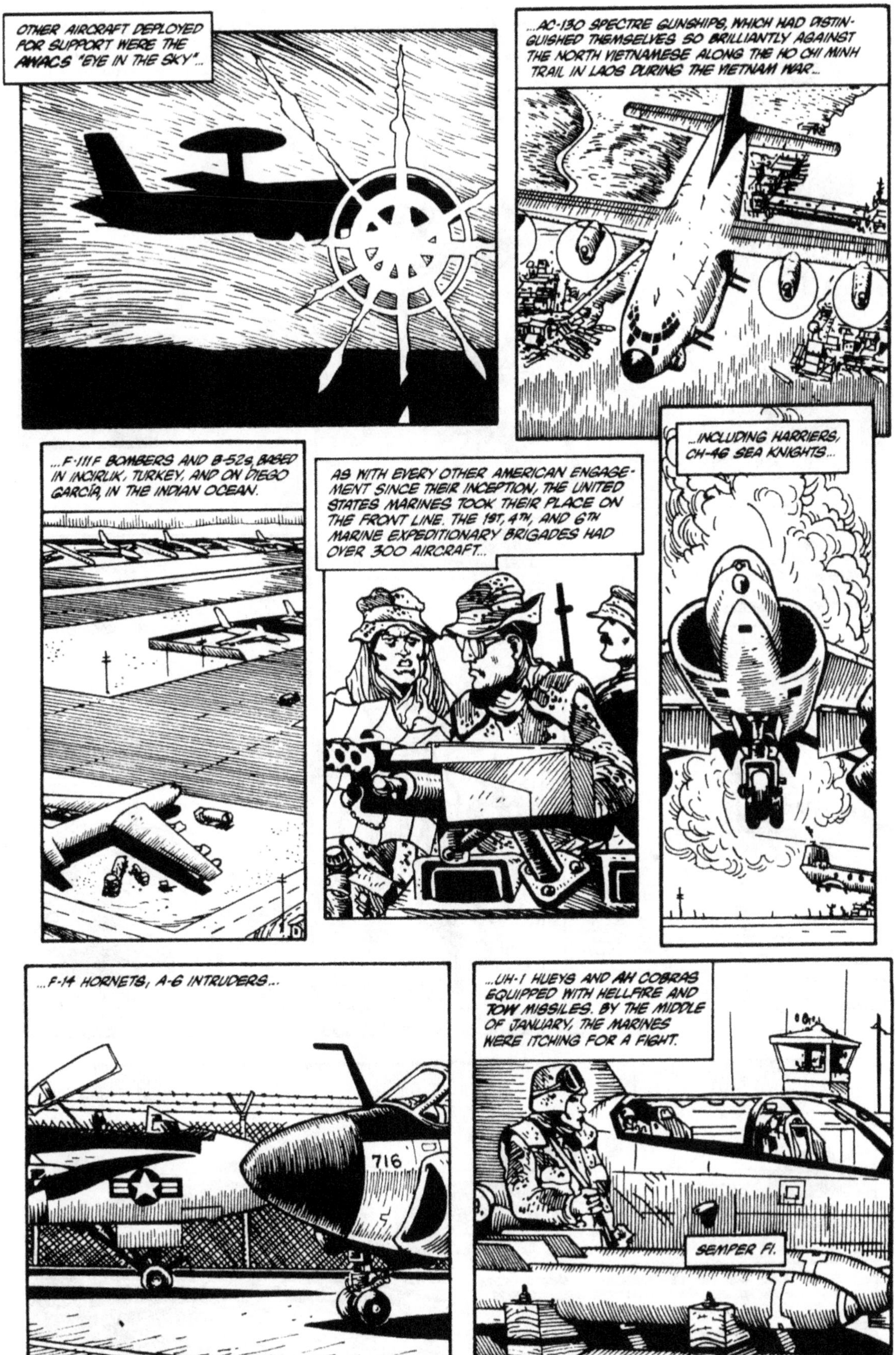
OTHER AIRCRAFT DEPLOYED FOR SUPPORT WERE THE AWACS "EYE IN THE SKY"...
...AC-130 SPECTRE GUNSHIPS, WHICH HAD DISTINGUISHED THEMSELVES SO BRILLIANTLY AGAINST THE NORTH VIETNAMESE ALONG THE HO CHI MINH TRAIL IN LAOS DURING THE VIETNAM WAR...
...F-111F BOMBERS AND B-52s, BASED IN INCIRLIK, TURKEY, AND ON DIEGO GARCIA, IN THE INDIAN OCEAN.
AS WITH EVERY OTHER AMERICAN ENGAGEMENT SINCE THEIR INCEPTION, THE UNITED STATES MARINES TOOK THEIR PLACE ON THE FRONT LINE. THE 1ST, 4TH, AND 6TH MARINE EXPEDITIONARY BRIGADES HAD OVER 300 AIRCRAFT...
...INCLUDING HARRIERS, CH-46 SEA KNIGHTS...
...F-14 HORNETS, A-6 INTRUDERS...
716
...UH-1 HUEYS AND AH COBRAS EQUIPPED WITH HELLFIRE AND TOW MISSILES. BY THE MIDDLE OF JANUARY, THE MARINES WERE ITCHING FOR A FIGHT.
SEMPER FI.

THE IRAQI FORCES.
BAGHDAD CLAIMED TO HAVE OVER A MILLION TROOPS UNDER ARMS, WITH OVER 850,000 ADDITIONAL MEN IN THE POPULAR MILITIA.

THE REPUBLICAN GUARD WAS AN ELITE CORPS OF TWO ARMORED DIVISIONS AND THREE INFANTRY DIVISIONS ALONG WITH A SPECIAL FORCES DIVISION. THEY WERE SADDAM HUSSEIN'S PRIDE AND JOY. BY EARLY 1991, BAGHDAD HAD ADDED ANOTHER 130,000 TROOPS TO BRING THE REPUBLICAN GUARD'S STRENGTH TO 11 DIVISIONS.

IRAQ'S AIR FORCE CONSISTED OF TWO BOMBER SQUADRONS, 13 FIGHTER SQUADRONS, AND 16 INTERCEPTOR SQUADRONS MADE UP PRIMARILY OF RUSSIAN MIGs AND FRENCH MIRAGES.

WITH VIRTUALLY NO COASTLINE UNTIL IT INVADED KUWAIT, IRAQ'S NAVY HAD CONSISTED OF FOUR GUIDED MISSILE FRIGATES AND A COUPLE OF DOZEN PATROL BOATS, SOME ALSO CARRYING MISSILES.

SADDAM'S FORCES WERE SAID TO BE BATTLE-HARDENED VETERANS, WELL-ARMED AND OUTFITTED, WITH THE POTENTIAL TO FARE WELL AGAINST THE COALITION.

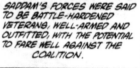

IRAQ ALSO HELD A PAIR OF DEADLY, DIRTY WILD CARDS. THE FIRST WAS THE ABILITY TO LAUNCH THEIR OWN MODIFIED SOVIET SCUD MISSILES AGAINST SAUDI ARABIA AND THE CIVILIAN POPULATION OF ISRAEL.

THE SECOND WAS THE POSSESSION OF BIOLOGICAL AND CHEMICAL WEAPONS--AND THE WILLINGNESS TO USE THEM AGAINST THE ALLIED FORCES.

"read my lips: no more Vietnams!"

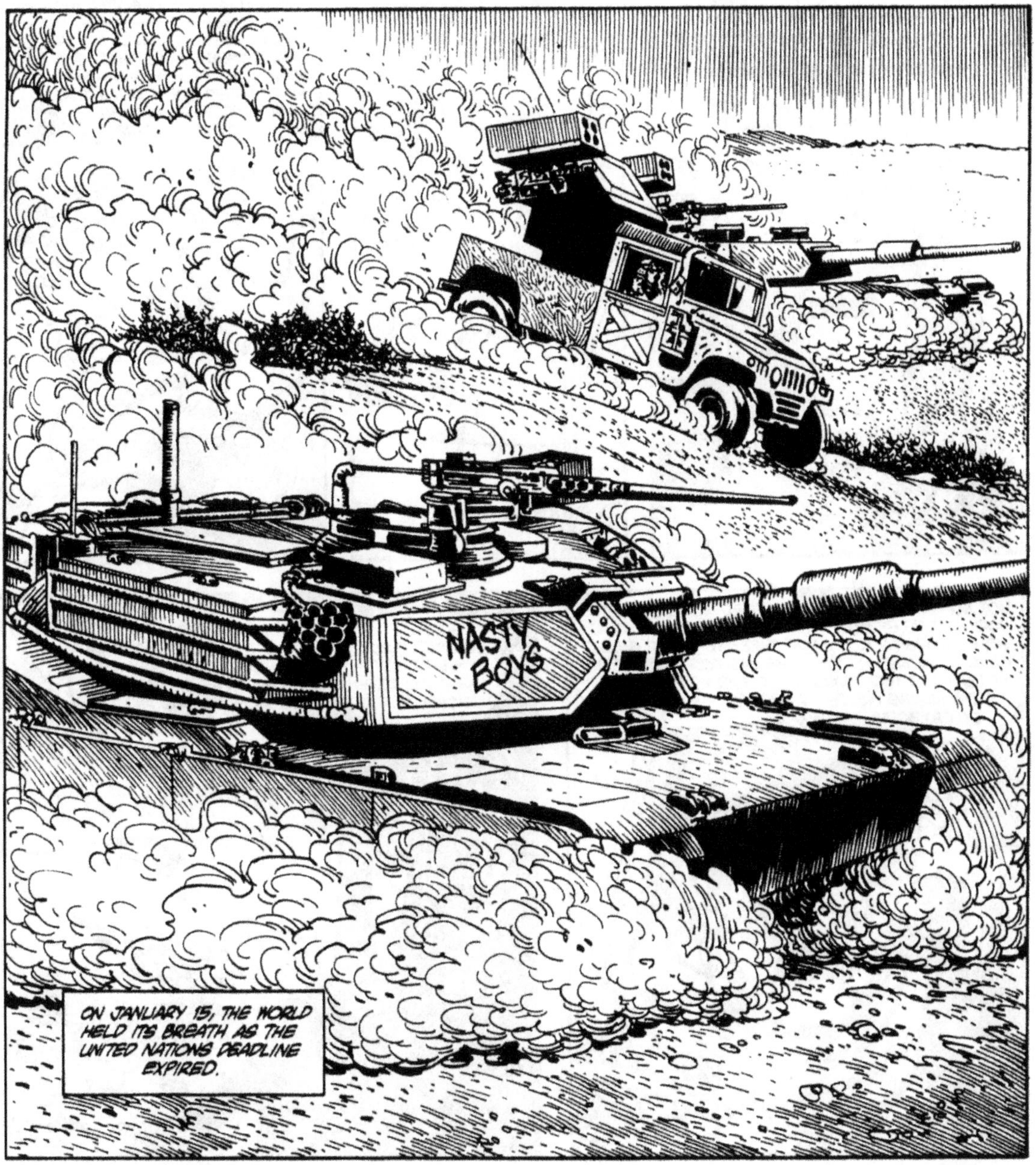
NASTY BOYS
ON JANUARY 15, THE WORLD HELD ITS BREATH AS THE UNITED NATIONS DEADLINE EXPIRED.

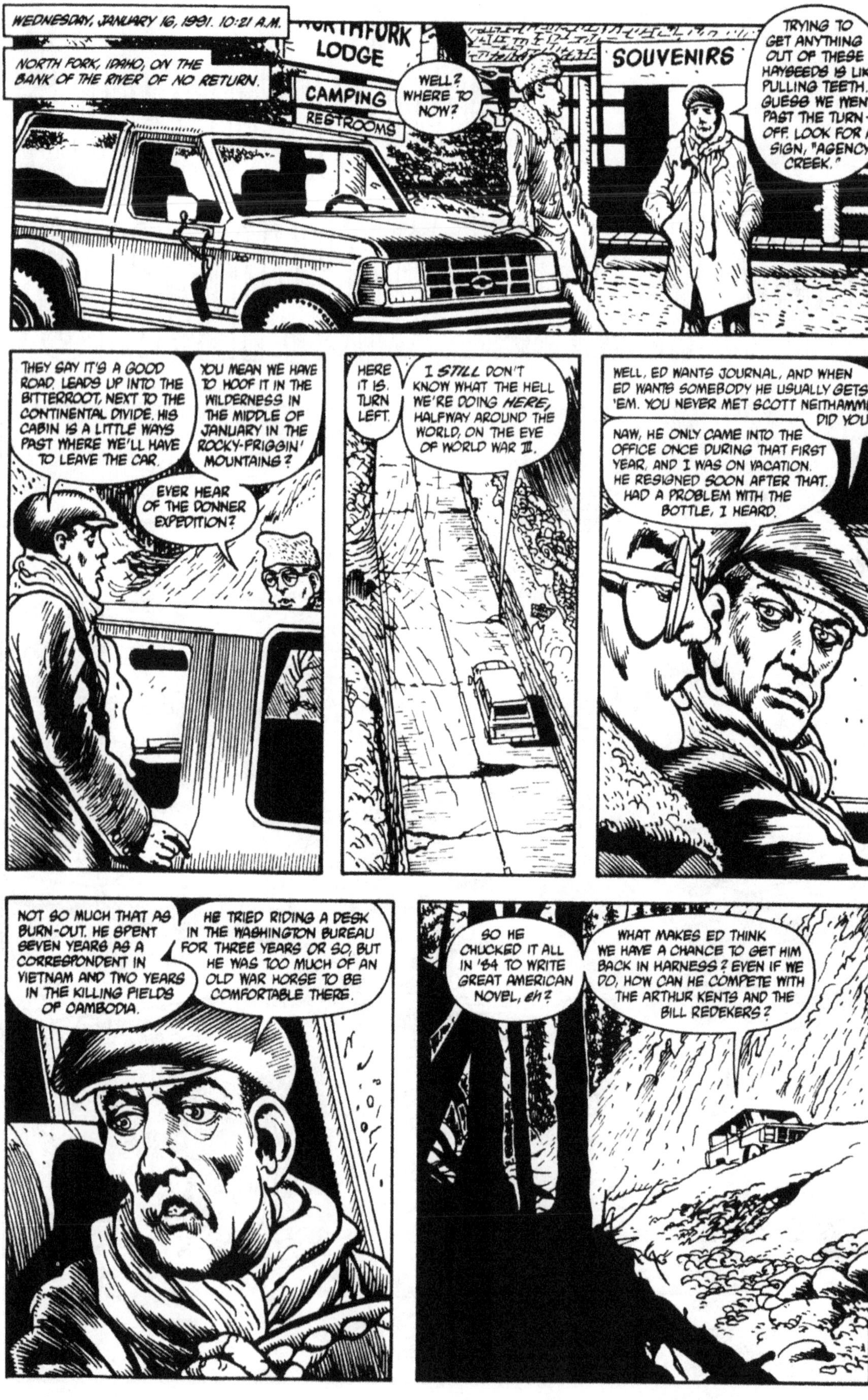
WEDNESDAY, JANUARY 16, 1991. 10:21 A.M.
NORTH FORK, IDAHO, ON THE BANK OF THE RIVER OF NO RETURN.
LODGE
CAMPING
RESTROOMS
SOUVENIRS
WELL? WHERE TO NOW?
TRYING TO GET ANYTHING OUT OF THESE HAYSEEDS IS LIKE PULLING TEETH. I GUESS WE WENT PAST THE TURN-OFF. LOOK FOR A SIGN, "AGENCY CREEK."
THEY SAY IT'S A GOOD ROAD. LEADS UP INTO THE BITTERROOT, NEXT TO THE CONTINENTAL DIVIDE. HIS CABIN IS A LITTLE WAYS PAST WHERE WE'LL HAVE TO LEAVE THE CAR.
YOU MEAN WE HAVE TO HOOF IT IN THE WILDERNESS IN THE MIDDLE OF JANUARY IN THE ROCKY-FRIGGIN' MOUNTAINS?
EVER HEAR OF THE DONNER EXPEDITION?
HERE IT IS. TURN LEFT.
I STILL DON'T KNOW WHAT THE HELL WE'RE DOING HERE, HALFWAY AROUND THE WORLD, ON THE EVE OF WORLD WAR III.
WELL, ED WANTS JOURNAL, AND WHEN ED WANTS SOMEBODY HE USUALLY GETS 'EM. YOU NEVER MET SCOTT NEITHAMMER, DID YOU?
NAW, HE ONLY CAME INTO THE OFFICE ONCE DURING THAT FIRST YEAR, AND I WAS ON VACATION. HE RESIGNED SOON AFTER THAT. HAD A PROBLEM WITH THE BOTTLE, I HEARD.
NOT SO MUCH THAT AS BURN-OUT. HE SPENT SEVEN YEARS AS A CORRESPONDENT IN VIETNAM AND TWO YEARS IN THE KILLING FIELDS OF CAMBODIA.
HE TRIED RIDING A DESK IN THE WASHINGTON BUREAU FOR THREE YEARS OR SO, BUT HE WAS TOO MUCH OF AN OLD WAR HORSE TO BE COMFORTABLE THERE.
SO HE CHUCKED IT ALL IN '84 TO WRITE GREAT AMERICAN NOVEL, eh?
WHAT MAKES ED THINK WE HAVE A CHANCE TO GET HIM BACK IN HARNESS? EVEN IF WE DO, HOW CAN HE COMPETE WITH THE ARTHUR KENTS AND THE BILL REDEKERS?

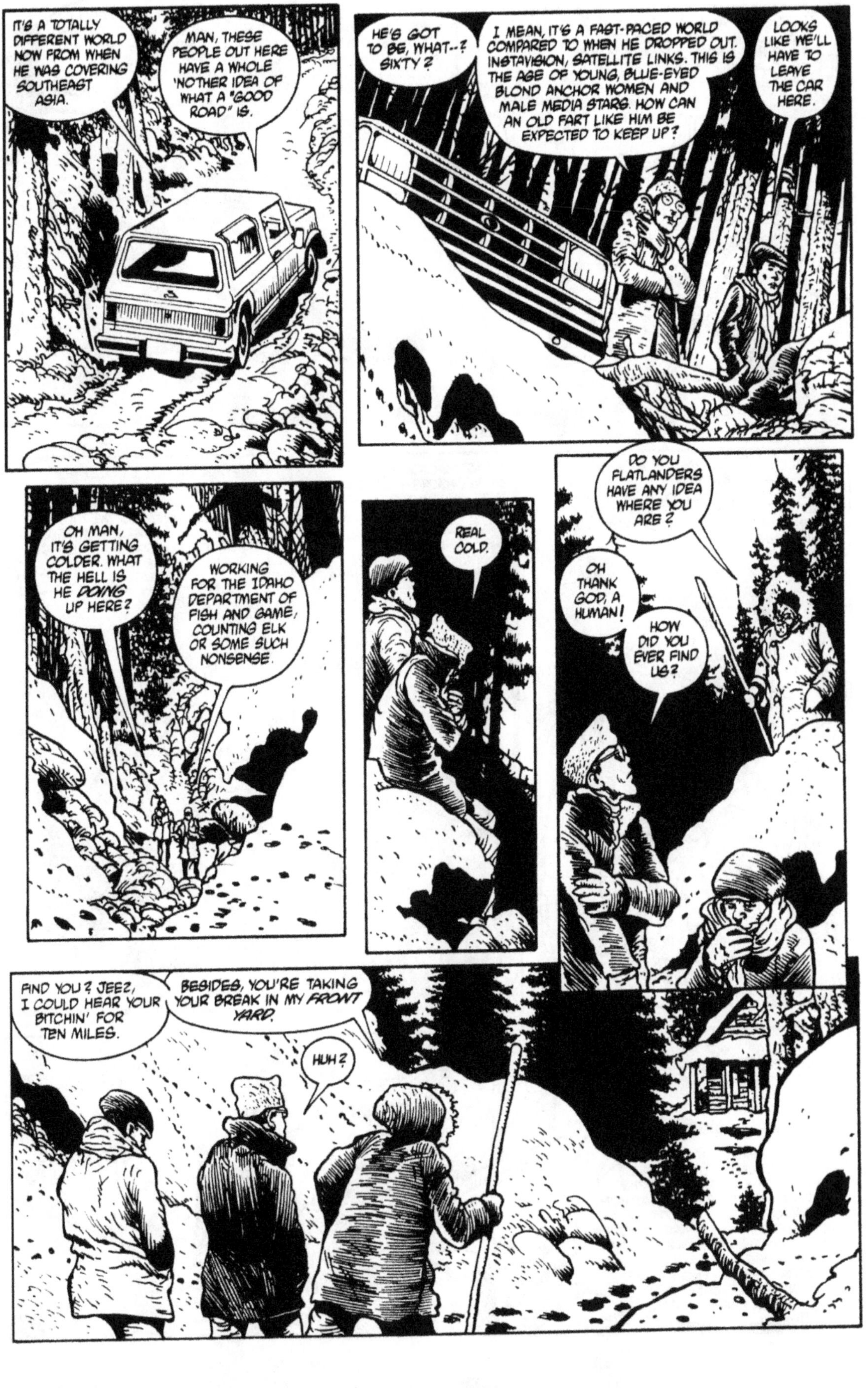
IT'S A TOTALLY DIFFERENT WORLD NOW FROM WHEN HE WAS COVERING SOUTHEAST ASIA.
MAN, THESE PEOPLE OUT HERE HAVE A WHOLE 'NOTHER IDEA OF WHAT A "GOOD ROAD" IS.
HE'S GOT TO BE, WHAT--? SIXTY?
I MEAN, IT'S A FAST-PACED WORLD COMPARED TO WHEN HE DROPPED OUT. INSTAVISION, SATELLITE LINKS. THIS IS THE AGE OF YOUNG, BLUE-EYED BLOND ANCHOR WOMEN AND MALE MEDIA STARS. HOW CAN AN OLD FART LIKE HIM BE EXPECTED TO KEEP UP?
LOOKS LIKE WE'LL HAVE TO LEAVE THE CAR HERE.
OH MAN, IT'S GETTING COLDER. WHAT THE HELL IS HE DOING UP HERE?
WORKING FOR THE IDAHO DEPARTMENT OF FISH AND GAME, COUNTING ELK OR SOME SUCH NONSENSE.
REAL COLD.
DO YOU FLATLANDERS HAVE ANY IDEA WHERE YOU ARE?
OH THANK GOD, A HUMAN!
HOW DID YOU EVER FIND US?
FIND YOU? JEEZ, I COULD HEAR YOUR BITCHIN' FOR TEN MILES.
BESIDES, YOU'RE TAKING YOUR BREAK IN MY FRONT YARD.
HUH?

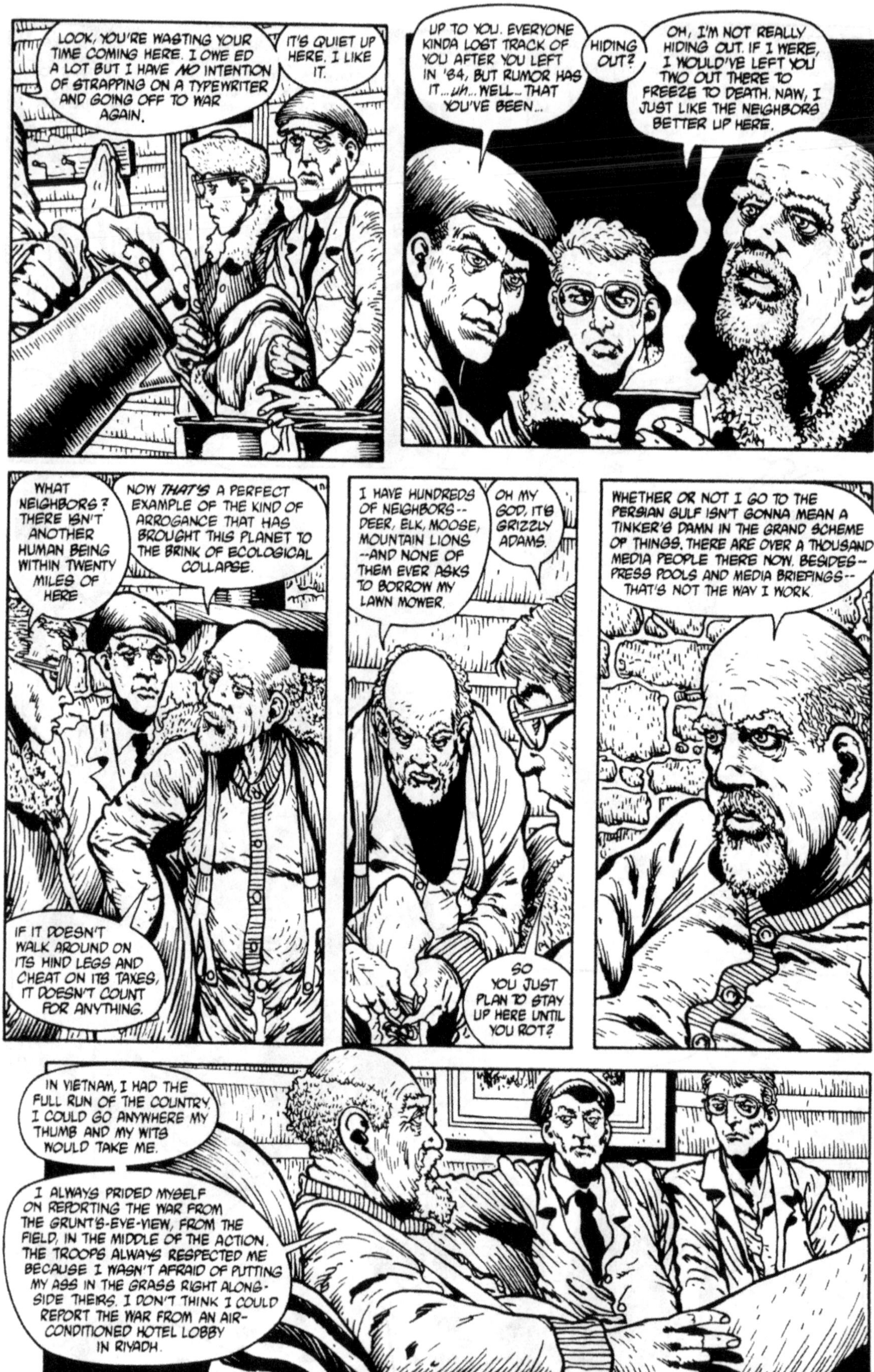
LOOK, YOU'RE WASTING YOUR TIME COMING HERE. I OWE ED A LOT BUT I HAVE NO INTENTION OF STRAPPING ON A TYPEWRITER AND GOING OFF TO WAR AGAIN.
IT'S QUIET UP HERE. I LIKE IT.
UP TO YOU. EVERYONE KINDA LOST TRACK OF YOU AFTER YOU LEFT IN '84, BUT RUMOR HAS IT... UH... WELL... THAT YOU'VE BEEN...
HIDING OUT?
OH, I'M NOT REALLY HIDING OUT. IF I WERE, I WOULD'VE LEFT YOU TWO OUT THERE TO FREEZE TO DEATH. NAW, I JUST LIKE THE NEIGHBORS BETTER UP HERE.
WHAT NEIGHBORS? THERE ISN'T ANOTHER HUMAN BEING WITHIN TWENTY MILES OF HERE.
NOW THAT'S A PERFECT EXAMPLE OF THE KIND OF ARROGANCE THAT HAS BROUGHT THIS PLANET TO THE BRINK OF ECOLOGICAL COLLAPSE.
IF IT DOESN'T WALK AROUND ON ITS HIND LEGS AND CHEAT ON ITS TAXES, IT DOESN'T COUNT FOR ANYTHING.
I HAVE HUNDREDS OF NEIGHBORS-- DEER, ELK, MOOSE, MOUNTAIN LIONS --AND NONE OF THEM EVER ASKS TO BORROW MY LAWN MOWER.
OH MY GOD, IT'S GRIZZLY ADAMS.
SO YOU JUST PLAN TO STAY UP HERE UNTIL YOU ROT?
WHETHER OR NOT I GO TO THE PERSIAN GULF ISN'T GONNA MEAN A TINKER'S DAMN IN THE GRAND SCHEME OF THINGS. THERE ARE OVER A THOUSAND MEDIA PEOPLE THERE NOW. BESIDES-- PRESS POOLS AND MEDIA BRIEFINGS-- THAT'S NOT THE WAY I WORK.
IN VIETNAM, I HAD THE FULL RUN OF THE COUNTRY. I COULD GO ANYWHERE MY THUMB AND MY WITS WOULD TAKE ME.
I ALWAYS PRIDED MYSELF ON REPORTING THE WAR FROM THE GRUNT'S-EYE-VIEW, FROM THE FIELD, IN THE MIDDLE OF THE ACTION. THE TROOPS ALWAYS RESPECTED ME BECAUSE I WASN'T AFRAID OF PUTTING MY ASS IN THE GRASS RIGHT ALONG-SIDE THEIRS. I DON'T THINK I COULD REPORT THE WAR FROM AN AIR-CONDITIONED HOTEL LOBBY IN RIYADH.

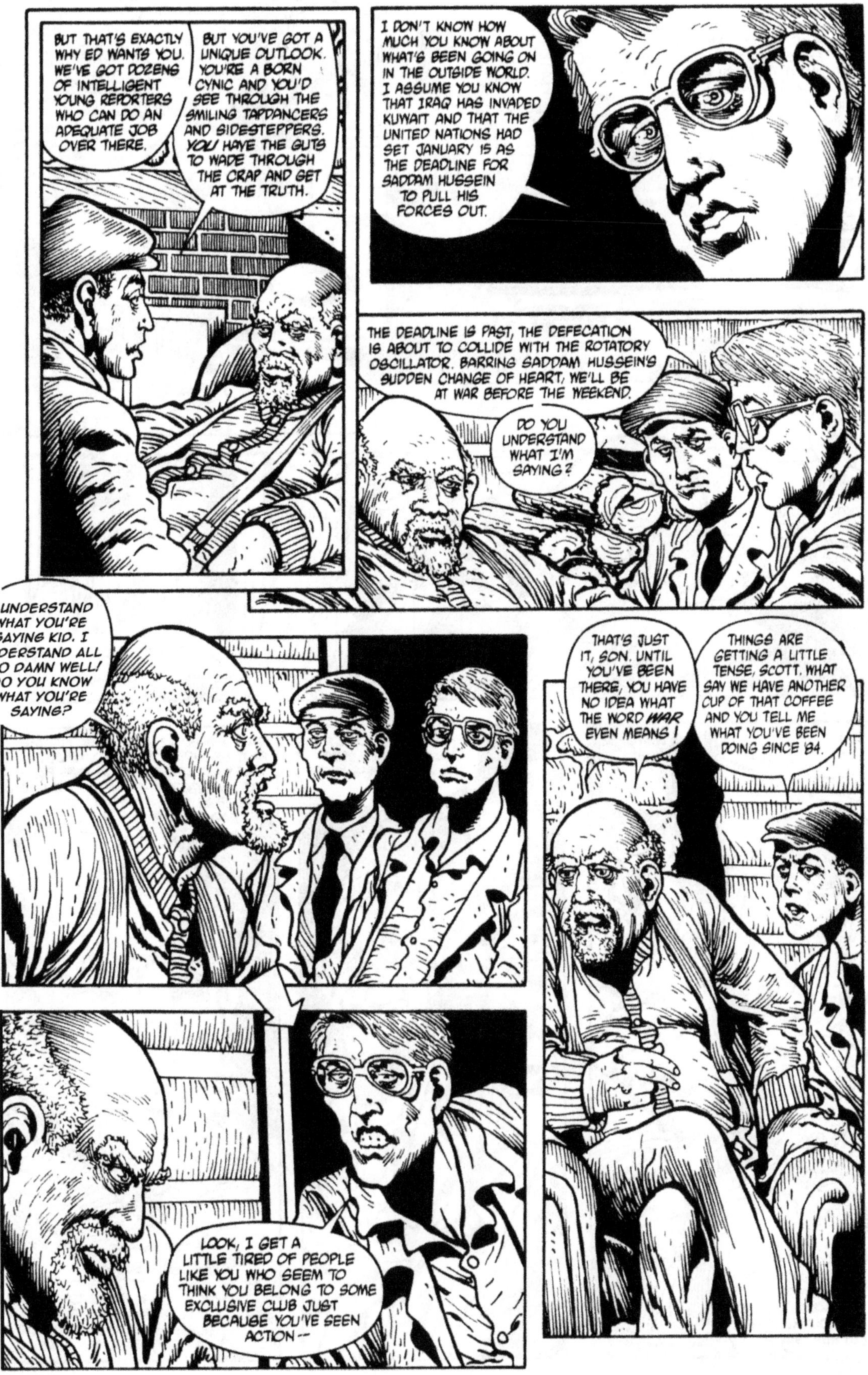
BUT THAT'S EXACTLY WHY ED WANTS YOU. WE'VE GOT DOZENS OF INTELLIGENT YOUNG REPORTERS WHO CAN DO AN ADEQUATE JOB OVER THERE.
BUT YOU'VE GOT A UNIQUE OUTLOOK. YOU'RE A BORN CYNIC AND YOU'D SEE THROUGH THE SMILING TAPDANCERS AND SIDESTEPPERS. YOU HAVE THE GUTS TO WADE THROUGH THE CRAP AND GET AT THE TRUTH.
I DON'T KNOW HOW MUCH YOU KNOW ABOUT WHAT'S BEEN GOING ON IN THE OUTSIDE WORLD. I ASSUME YOU KNOW THAT IRAQ HAS INVADED KUWAIT AND THAT THE UNITED NATIONS HAD SET JANUARY 15 AS THE DEADLINE FOR SADDAM HUSSEIN TO PULL HIS FORCES OUT.
THE DEADLINE IS PAST, THE DEFECATION IS ABOUT TO COLLIDE WITH THE ROTATORY OSCILLATOR. BARRING SADDAM HUSSEIN'S SUDDEN CHANGE OF HEART, WE'LL BE AT WAR BEFORE THE WEEKEND.
DO YOU UNDERSTAND WHAT I'M SAYING?
I UNDERSTAND WHAT YOU'RE SAYING KID. I UNDERSTAND ALL TOO DAMN WELL! DO YOU KNOW WHAT YOU'RE SAYING?
LOOK, I GET A LITTLE TIRED OF PEOPLE LIKE YOU WHO SEEM TO THINK YOU BELONG TO SOME EXCLUSIVE CLUB JUST BECAUSE YOU'VE SEEN ACTION--
THAT'S JUST IT, SON. UNTIL YOU'VE BEEN THERE, YOU HAVE NO IDEA WHAT THE WORD WAR EVEN MEANS!
THINGS ARE GETTING A LITTLE TENSE, SCOTT. WHAT SAY WE HAVE ANOTHER CUP OF THAT COFFEE AND YOU TELL ME WHAT YOU'VE BEEN DOING SINCE '84.

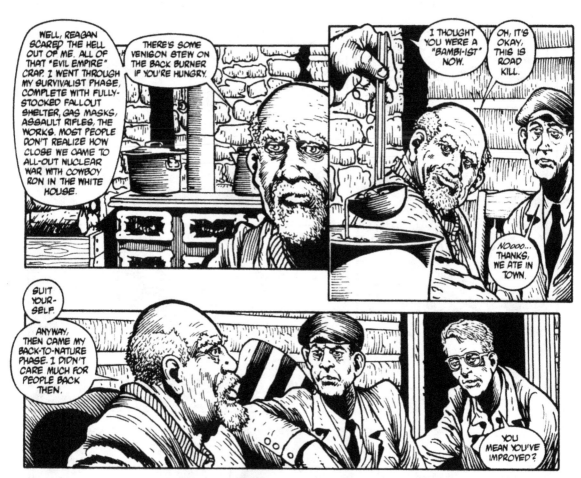

WELL, REAGAN SCARED THE HELL OUT OF ME. ALL OF THAT "EVIL EMPIRE" CRAP. I WENT THROUGH MY SURVIVALIST PHASE, COMPLETE WITH FULLY-STOCKED FALLOUT SHELTER, GAS MASKS, ASSAULT RIFLES, THE WORKS. MOST PEOPLE DON'T REALIZE HOW CLOSE WE CAME TO ALL-OUT NUCLEAR WAR WITH COWBOY RON IN THE WHITE HOUSE.

THERE'S SOME VENISON STEW ON THE BACK BURNER IF YOU'RE HUNGRY.

I THOUGHT YOU WERE A "BAMBI-IST" NOW.

OH, IT'S OKAY, THIS IS ROAD KILL.

NOOOO... THANKS, WE ATE IN TOWN.

SUIT YOUR-SELF.

ANYWAY, THEN CAME MY BACK-TO-NATURE PHASE. I DIDN'T CARE MUCH FOR PEOPLE BACK THEN.

YOU MEAN YOU'VE IMPROVED?

GIVE IT A REST, TED.

YOU KNOW, YOU CAN DROP THIS GOOD COP, BAD COP ROUTINE. IT WENT OUT WITH "STARSKY AND HUTCH."

ED *SAID* YOU WOULDN'T FALL FOR IT, BUT WHAT THE HELL? IT WAS WORTH A TRY.

SO YOU TOOK THIS JOB?

YEAH. I TRIED TO START OVER, PUT THE PAST BEHIND ME, BUT I FOUND OUT THAT WHAT I WAS RUNNING AWAY FROM WAS *INSIDE* ME--I CARRY IT WITH ME WHEREVER I GO. I'M TRYING TO LEARN TO LIVE WITH IT.

I HAD PLANS TO MOVE TO ALASKA, BUT I GUESS WHAT I'M LOOKING FOR DOESN'T EXIST ANY MORE.

I HEAR THAT THE CALIFORNIA SPOILERS ARE MOVING UP THE COAST. IN TWENTY YEARS, ALASKA'LL BE JUST LIKE L.A. WHAT A SHAME.

IT'S CALLED PROGRESS, MAN. NOTHING STAYS THE SAME FOREVER.

WELL, LIKE WE SAID BEFORE, WE REALIZE YOU'RE PRETTY WELL OUT OF IT UP HERE, SO WE'D LIKE TO BRING YOU UP TO DATE ON CURRENT EVENTS.

WELL, LIKE I SAID BEFORE, THERE'S NO PLACE TO HIDE. WHAT SAY WE SEE WHAT'S BEEN HAPPENING IN THE WORLD?

WHA--? YOU'VE GOT TV CLEAR UP HERE?

SO MUCH FOR OUR "MORE INFORMED THAN THOU" ATTITUDE.

CNN?

YEAH, I GOT A DISH ON TOP OF THE HILL BEHIND THE CABIN.

...ON THE LINE IN BAGHDAD ARE BERNARD SHAW, JOHN HOLLIMAN, AND PETER ARNETT...

DID YOU EVER MEET ARNETT WHEN YOU WERE IN VIETNAM?

MANY TIMES. I REMEMBER ONE PARTICULAR EVENING IN A "BOOM-BOOM ROOM" IN AN KHE, DISNEYLAND EAST. PETER ARNETT, GEORGE ESPER, TIM PAGE, AND MYSELF WERE DOWNING SHOOTERS AND TRADING LIES WHEN...

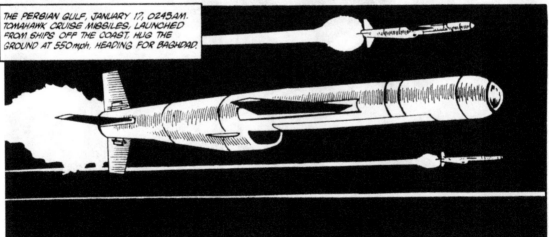

THE PERSIAN GULF, JANUARY 17, 0245 A.M. TOMAHAWK CRUISE MISSILES, LAUNCHED FROM SHIPS OFF THE COAST, HUG THE GROUND AT 550 mph, HEADING FOR BAGHDAD.

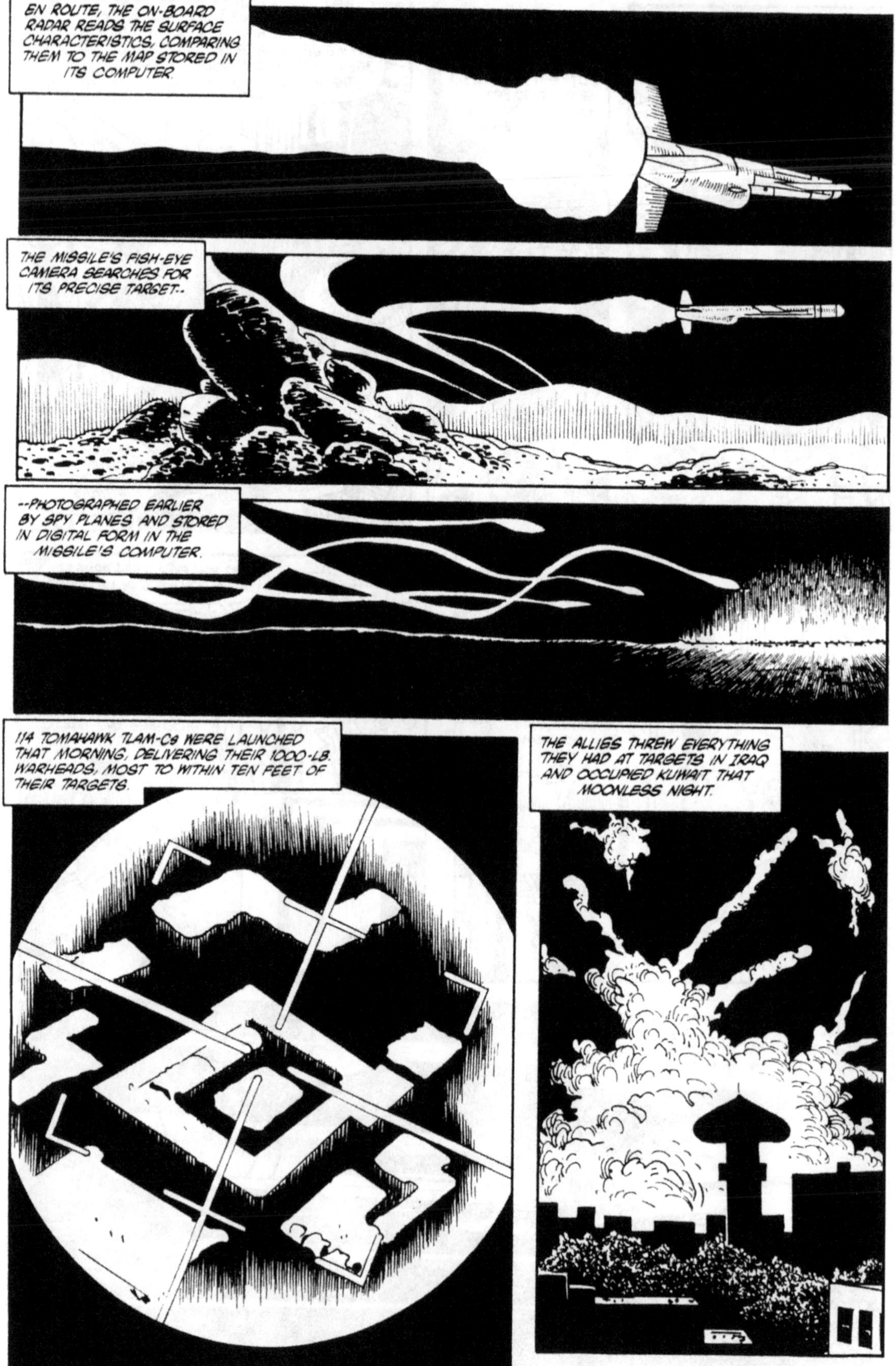
EN ROUTE, THE ON-BOARD RADAR READS THE SURFACE CHARACTERISTICS, COMPARING THEM TO THE MAP STORED IN ITS COMPUTER.
THE MISSILE'S FISH-EYE CAMERA SEARCHES FOR ITS PRECISE TARGET--
--PHOTOGRAPHED EARLIER BY SPY PLANES AND STORED IN DIGITAL FORM IN THE MISSILE'S COMPUTER.
114 TOMAHAWK TLAM-Cs WERE LAUNCHED THAT MORNING, DELIVERING THEIR 1000-LB. WARHEADS, MOST TO WITHIN TEN FEET OF THEIR TARGETS.
THE ALLIES THREW EVERYTHING THEY HAD AT TARGETS IN IRAQ AND OCCUPIED KUWAIT THAT MOONLESS NIGHT.

IRAQI ANTI-AIRCRAFT FIRE LIT UP BAGHDAD, FIRING BLINDLY, FRANTICALLY, AT BOMBERS WHICH WERE NOT THERE.

THE MISSION OF THE FIRST MANNED WAVE WAS TO "SWEEP" THE SKY OVER BAGHDAD OF ANY IRAQI RESISTANCE IN PREPARATION FOR THE HEAVY BOMBERS TO FOLLOW.

TOMAHAWK TARGETS INCLUDED SCUD MISSILE BASES, COMMAND FACILITIES, COMMUNICATIONS, AIRFIELDS, CHEMICAL AND NUCLEAR WEAPONS FACTORIES, AND THE REPUBLICAN GUARD.

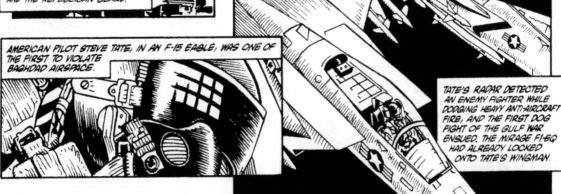

AMERICAN PILOT STEVE TATE, IN AN F-15 EAGLE, WAS ONE OF THE FIRST TO VIOLATE BAGHDAD AIRSPACE.

TATE'S RADAR DETECTED AN ENEMY FIGHTER WHILE DODGING HEAVY ANTI-AIRCRAFT FIRE, AND THE FIRST DOG FIGHT OF THE GULF WAR ENSUED. THE MIRAGE F1-EQ HAD ALREADY LOCKED ONTO TATE'S WINGMAN.

TATE PYLONED TIGHTLY, LOCKED HIM UP, AND FIRED A SPARROW RADAR-GUIDED MISSILE UP HIS TAILPIPE.

THE MIRAGE BURST INTO FLAMES AND TRAILED FIRE DOWN TO THE GROUND, A SAMPLE OF WHAT WAS TO FOLLOW.

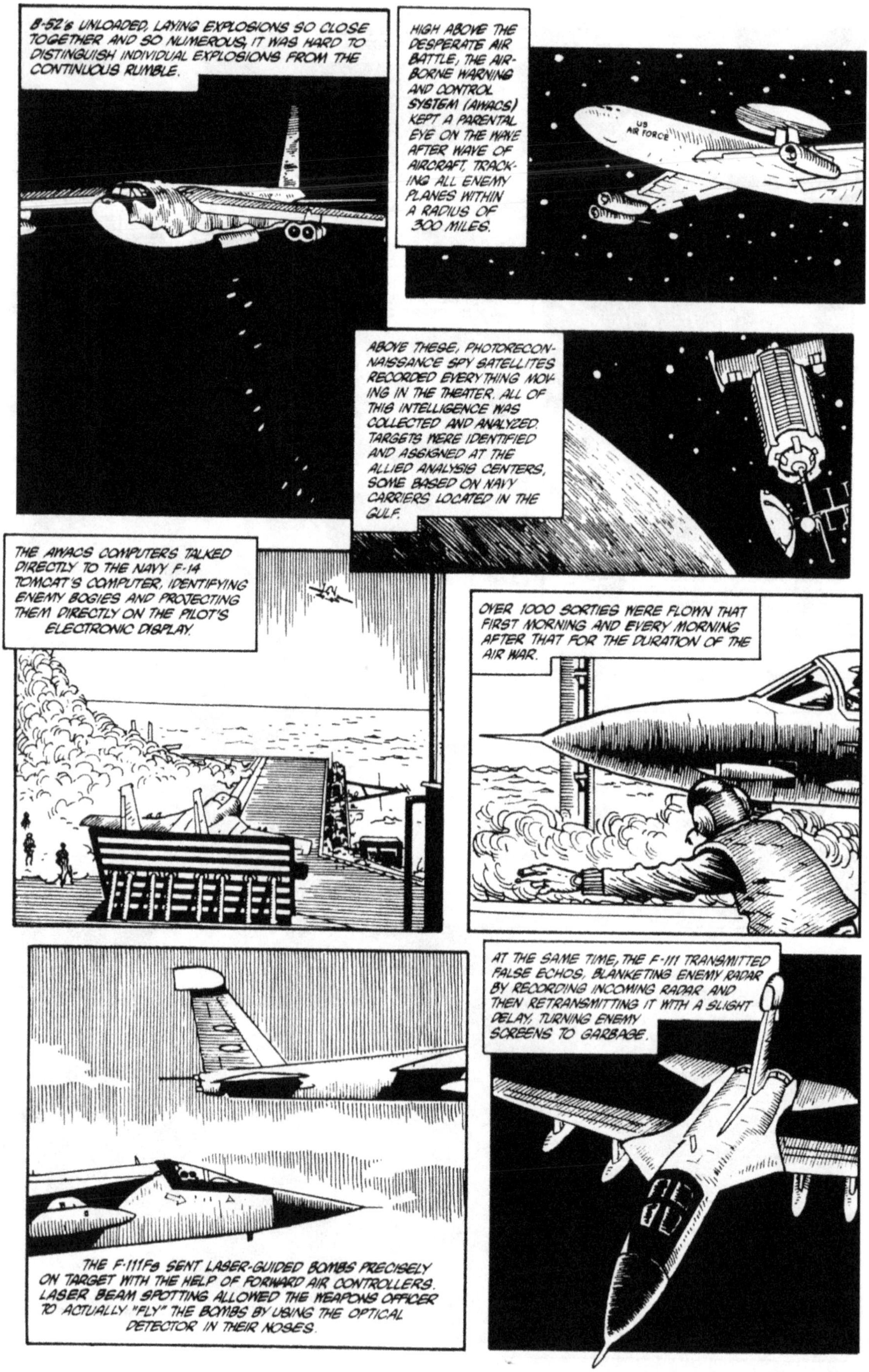
B-52's UNLOADED, LAYING EXPLOSIONS SO CLOSE TOGETHER AND SO NUMEROUS, IT WAS HARD TO DISTINGUISH INDIVIDUAL EXPLOSIONS FROM THE CONTINUOUS RUMBLE.
HIGH ABOVE THE DESPERATE AIR BATTLE, THE AIR-BORNE WARNING AND CONTROL SYSTEM (AWACS) KEPT A PARENTAL EYE ON THE WAVE AFTER WAVE OF AIRCRAFT, TRACKING ALL ENEMY PLANES WITHIN A RADIUS OF 300 MILES.
US AIR FORCE
ABOVE THESE, PHOTORECONNAISSANCE SPY SATELLITES RECORDED EVERYTHING MOVING IN THE THEATER. ALL OF THIS INTELLIGENCE WAS COLLECTED AND ANALYZED. TARGETS WERE IDENTIFIED AND ASSIGNED AT THE ALLIED ANALYSIS CENTERS, SOME BASED ON NAVY CARRIERS LOCATED IN THE GULF.
THE AWACS COMPUTERS TALKED DIRECTLY TO THE NAVY F-14 TOMCAT'S COMPUTER, IDENTIFYING ENEMY BOGIES AND PROJECTING THEM DIRECTLY ON THE PILOT'S ELECTRONIC DISPLAY.
OVER 1000 SORTIES WERE FLOWN THAT FIRST MORNING AND EVERY MORNING AFTER THAT FOR THE DURATION OF THE AIR WAR.
THE F-111Fs SENT LASER-GUIDED BOMBS PRECISELY ON TARGET WITH THE HELP OF FORWARD AIR CONTROLLERS. LASER BEAM SPOTTING ALLOWED THE WEAPONS OFFICER TO ACTUALLY "FLY" THE BOMBS BY USING THE OPTICAL DETECTOR IN THEIR NOSES.
AT THE SAME TIME, THE F-111 TRANSMITTED FALSE ECHOS, BLANKETING ENEMY RADAR BY RECORDING INCOMING RADAR AND THEN RETRANSMITTING IT WITH A SLIGHT DELAY, TURNING ENEMY SCREENS TO GARBAGE.

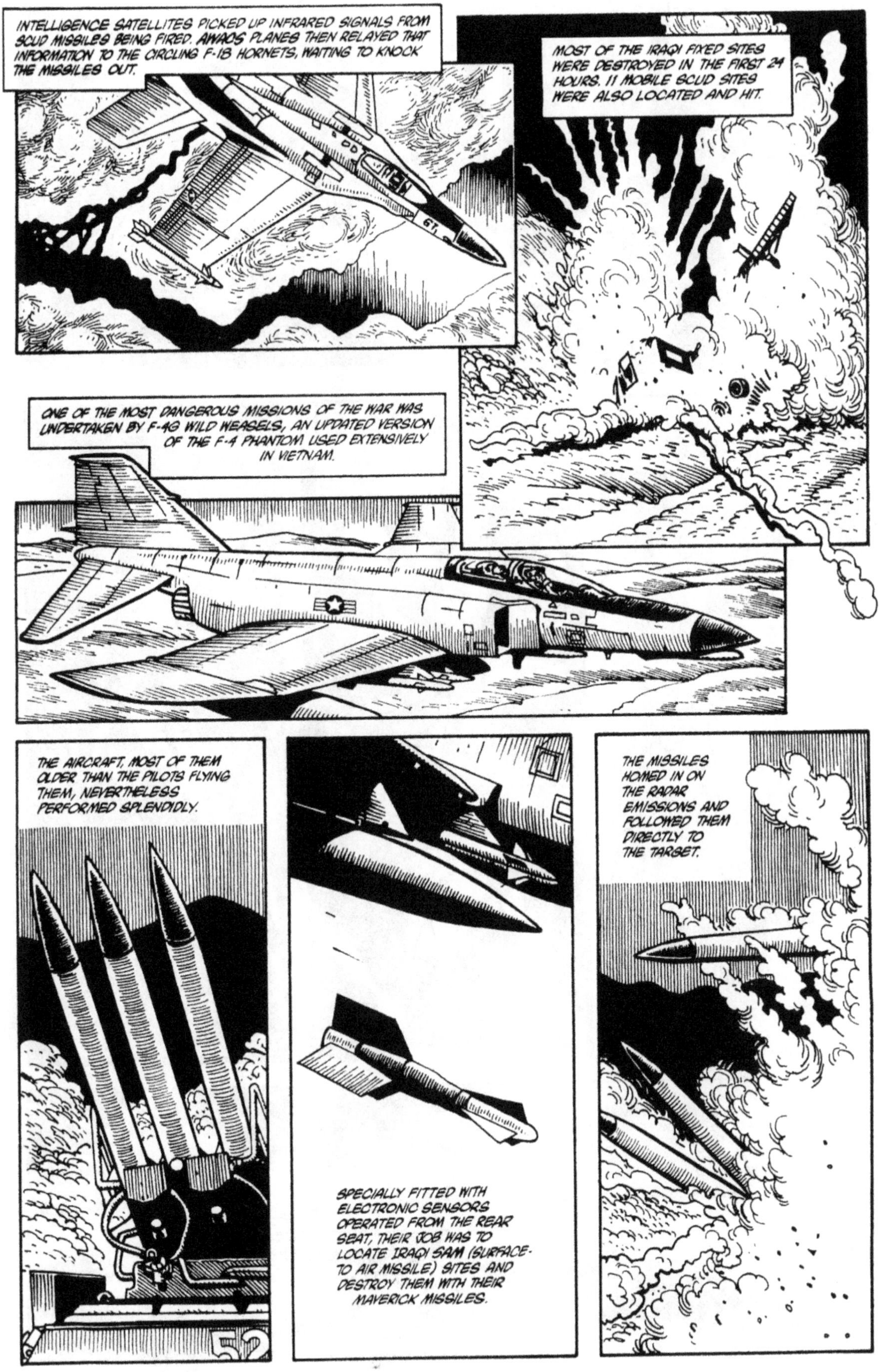
INTELLIGENCE SATELLITES PICKED UP INFRARED SIGNALS FROM SCUD MISSILES BEING FIRED. AWACS PLANES THEN RELAYED THAT INFORMATION TO THE CIRCLING F-18 HORNETS, WAITING TO KNOCK THE MISSILES OUT.
MOST OF THE IRAQI FIXED SITES WERE DESTROYED IN THE FIRST 24 HOURS. 11 MOBILE SCUD SITES WERE ALSO LOCATED AND HIT.
ONE OF THE MOST DANGEROUS MISSIONS OF THE WAR WAS UNDERTAKEN BY F-4G WILD WEASELS, AN UPDATED VERSION OF THE F-4 PHANTOM USED EXTENSIVELY IN VIETNAM.
THE AIRCRAFT, MOST OF THEM OLDER THAN THE PILOTS FLYING THEM, NEVERTHELESS PERFORMED SPLENDIDLY.
SPECIALLY FITTED WITH ELECTRONIC SENSORS OPERATED FROM THE REAR SEAT, THEIR JOB WAS TO LOCATE IRAQI SAM (SURFACE-TO AIR MISSILE) SITES AND DESTROY THEM WITH THEIR MAVERICK MISSILES.
THE MISSILES HOMED IN ON THE RADAR EMISSIONS AND FOLLOWED THEM DIRECTLY TO THE TARGET.
52

THOUGH MANY SAMs WERE FIRED, THE WILD WEASELS VIRTUALLY ELIMINATED THAT THREAT DURING THE FIRST FEW HOURS.

IRAQI ELECTRONIC JAMMING OF THE F-4s ALLOWED SOME VERY FEW SAMs TO FIND THEIR MARK.

OVER BAGHDAD, ANTI-AIRCRAFT FIRE FILLED THE SKY. THE IRAQI RADAR WAS OVERWHELMED BY THE NUMBER OF ALLIED AIRCRAFT.

THE OLD DAYS OF THE LONG, LOW APPROACHES NEEDED FOR BOMBING RUNS, WHICH HAD LED TO A HEAVY ATTRITION RATE FROM ANTI-AIRCRAFT FIRE DURING WORLD WAR II, WERE OVER.

F-14s, 15s, 16s AND 18s FLEW ABOVE 10,000 FEET, OUT OF RANGE OF THE FLAK. AT THE LAST MINUTE, THEY ROLLED OVER AND DOVE EARTHWARD, LIKE DARTS OUT OF THE NIGHT SKY--

--TO DELIVER THEIR ORDNANCE AND CLIMB BACK TO SAFETY IN ONLY SECONDS. THESE AIRCRAFT ARE SO MANEUVERABLE, THE PILOTS WERE ACTUALLY ABLE TO SEE THE ANTI-AIRCRAFT FIRE COMING AT THEM, AND DODGE IT.

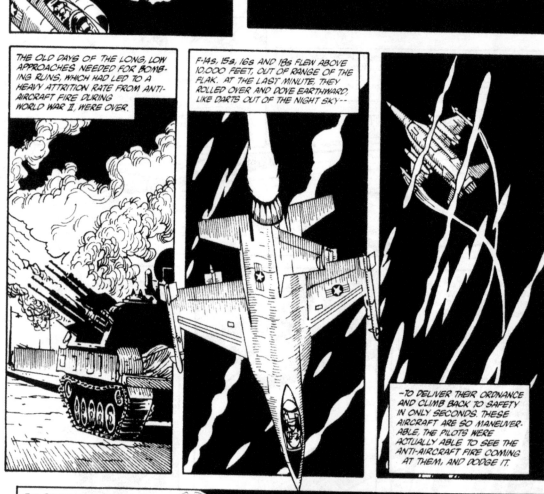

THE BRITISH EMPLOYED THEIR TORNADOS TO DROP JP233 RUNWAY ATTACK MUNITIONS TO CRATER ENEMY AIR FIELDS, AND TO SCATTER THOUSANDS OF HAND-GRENADE-LIKE "BOMBLETS" TO MAKE REPAIRS MORE DIFFICULT.

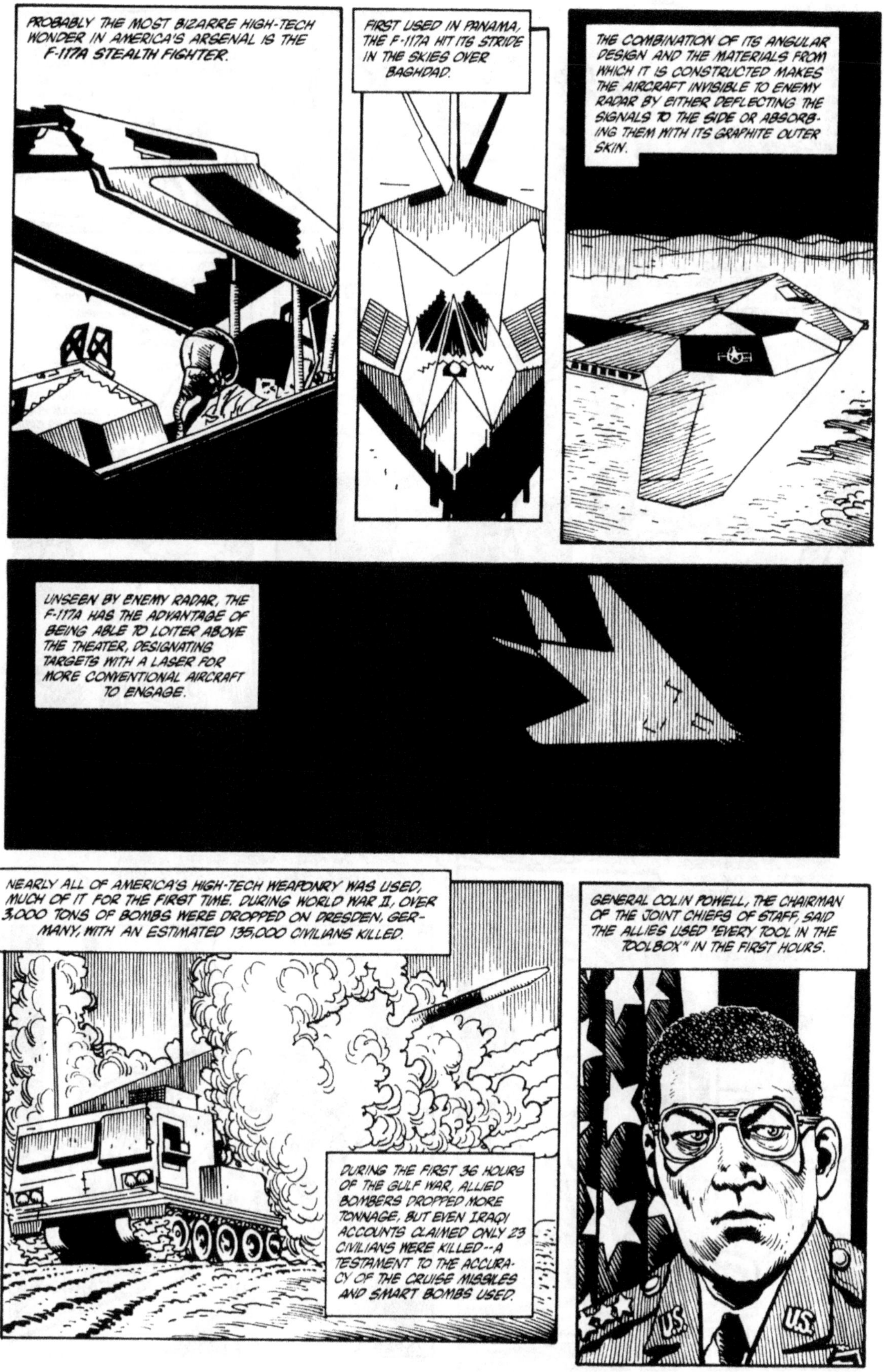
PROBABLY THE MOST BIZARRE HIGH-TECH WONDER IN AMERICA'S ARSENAL IS THE F-117A STEALTH FIGHTER.
FIRST USED IN PANAMA, THE F-117A HIT ITS STRIDE IN THE SKIES OVER BAGHDAD.
THE COMBINATION OF ITS ANGULAR DESIGN AND THE MATERIALS FROM WHICH IT IS CONSTRUCTED MAKES THE AIRCRAFT INVISIBLE TO ENEMY RADAR BY EITHER DEFLECTING THE SIGNALS TO THE SIDE OR ABSORBING THEM WITH ITS GRAPHITE OUTER SKIN.
UNSEEN BY ENEMY RADAR, THE F-117A HAS THE ADVANTAGE OF BEING ABLE TO LOITER ABOVE THE THEATER, DESIGNATING TARGETS WITH A LASER FOR MORE CONVENTIONAL AIRCRAFT TO ENGAGE.
NEARLY ALL OF AMERICA'S HIGH-TECH WEAPONRY WAS USED, MUCH OF IT FOR THE FIRST TIME. DURING WORLD WAR II, OVER 3,000 TONS OF BOMBS WERE DROPPED ON DRESDEN, GERMANY, WITH AN ESTIMATED 135,000 CIVILIANS KILLED.
DURING THE FIRST 36 HOURS OF THE GULF WAR, ALLIED BOMBERS DROPPED MORE TONNAGE, BUT EVEN IRAQI ACCOUNTS CLAIMED ONLY 23 CIVILIANS WERE KILLED--A TESTAMENT TO THE ACCURACY OF THE CRUISE MISSILES AND SMART BOMBS USED.
GENERAL COLIN POWELL, THE CHAIRMAN OF THE JOINT CHIEFS OF STAFF, SAID THE ALLIES USED "EVERY TOOL IN THE TOOLBOX" IN THE FIRST HOURS.
U.S.
U.S.

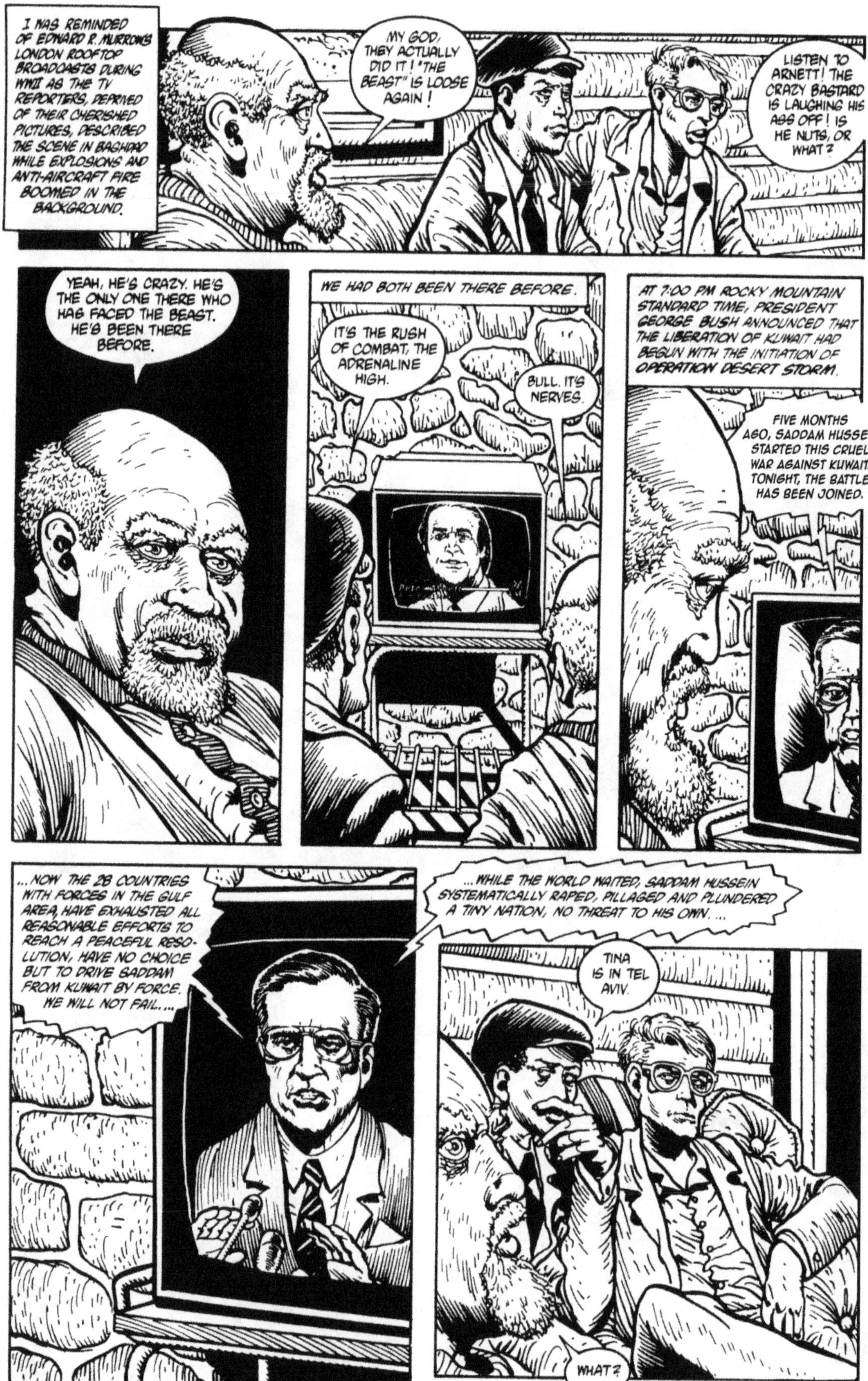
I WAS REMINDED OF EDWARD R. MURROW'S LONDON ROOFTOP BROADCASTS DURING WWII AS THE TV REPORTERS, DEPRIVED OF THEIR CHERISHED PICTURES, DESCRIBED THE SCENE IN BAGHDAD WHILE EXPLOSIONS AND ANTI-AIRCRAFT FIRE BOOMED IN THE BACKGROUND.
MY GOD, THEY ACTUALLY DID IT! "THE BEAST" IS LOOSE AGAIN!
LISTEN TO ARNETT! THE CRAZY BASTARD IS LAUGHING HIS ASS OFF! IS HE NUTS, OR WHAT?
YEAH, HE'S CRAZY. HE'S THE ONLY ONE THERE WHO HAS FACED THE BEAST. HE'S BEEN THERE BEFORE.
WE HAD BOTH BEEN THERE BEFORE.
IT'S THE RUSH OF COMBAT, THE ADRENALINE HIGH.
BULL. IT'S NERVES.
AT 7:00 PM ROCKY MOUNTAIN STANDARD TIME, PRESIDENT GEORGE BUSH ANNOUNCED THAT THE LIBERATION OF KUWAIT HAD BEGUN WITH THE INITIATION OF OPERATION DESERT STORM.
FIVE MONTHS AGO, SADDAM HUSSEIN STARTED THIS CRUEL WAR AGAINST KUWAIT. TONIGHT, THE BATTLE HAS BEEN JOINED.
...NOW THE 28 COUNTRIES WITH FORCES IN THE GULF AREA, HAVE EXHAUSTED ALL REASONABLE EFFORTS TO REACH A PEACEFUL RESOLUTION, HAVE NO CHOICE BUT TO DRIVE SADDAM FROM KUWAIT BY FORCE. WE WILL NOT FAIL....
...WHILE THE WORLD WAITED, SADDAM HUSSEIN SYSTEMATICALLY RAPED, PILLAGED AND PLUNDERED A TINY NATION, NO THREAT TO HIS OWN. ...
TINA IS IN TEL AVIV.
WHAT?

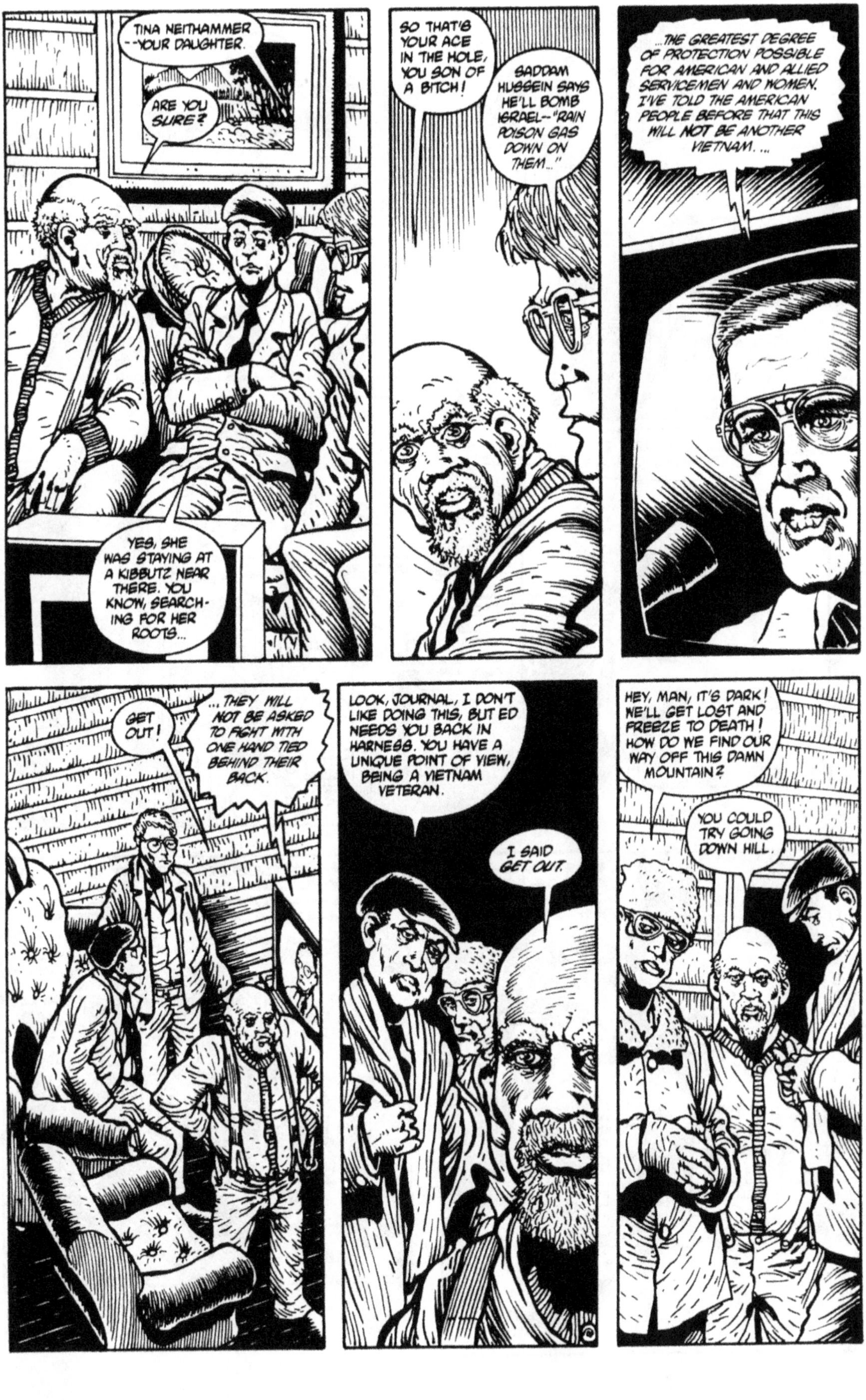
TINA NEITHAMMER --YOUR DAUGHTER.
ARE YOU SURE?
YES, SHE WAS STAYING AT A KIBBUTZ NEAR THERE. YOU KNOW, SEARCHING FOR HER ROOTS...
SO THAT'S YOUR ACE IN THE HOLE, YOU SON OF A BITCH!
SADDAM HUSSEIN SAYS HE'LL BOMB ISRAEL--"RAIN POISON GAS DOWN ON THEM..."
...THE GREATEST DEGREE OF PROTECTION POSSIBLE FOR AMERICAN AND ALLIED SERVICEMEN AND WOMEN. I'VE TOLD THE AMERICAN PEOPLE BEFORE THAT THIS WILL NOT BE ANOTHER VIETNAM. ...
GET OUT!
...THEY WILL NOT BE ASKED TO FIGHT WITH ONE HAND TIED BEHIND THEIR BACK.
LOOK, JOURNAL, I DON'T LIKE DOING THIS, BUT ED NEEDS YOU BACK IN HARNESS. YOU HAVE A UNIQUE POINT OF VIEW, BEING A VIETNAM VETERAN.
I SAID GET OUT.
HEY, MAN, IT'S DARK! WE'LL GET LOST AND FREEZE TO DEATH! HOW DO WE FIND OUR WAY OFF THIS DAMN MOUNTAIN?
YOU COULD TRY GOING DOWN HILL.

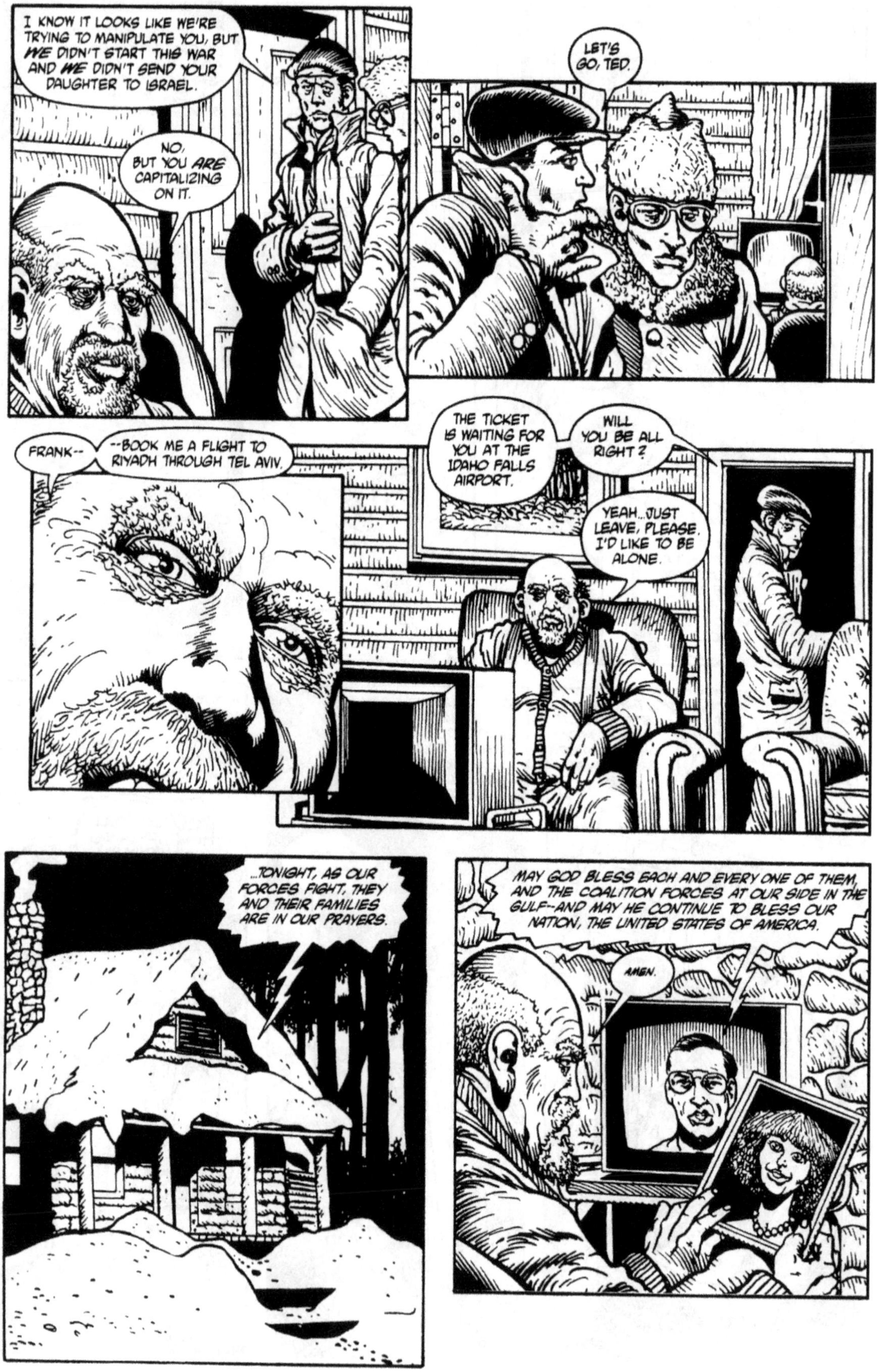

I KNOW IT LOOKS LIKE WE'RE TRYING TO MANIPULATE YOU, BUT WE DIDN'T START THIS WAR AND WE DIDN'T SEND YOUR DAUGHTER TO ISRAEL.
NO, BUT YOU ARE CAPITALIZING ON IT.
LET'S GO, TED.
FRANK--
--BOOK ME A FLIGHT TO RIYADH THROUGH TEL AVIV.
THE TICKET IS WAITING FOR YOU AT THE IDAHO FALLS AIRPORT.
WILL YOU BE ALL RIGHT?
YEAH...JUST LEAVE, PLEASE. I'D LIKE TO BE ALONE.
...TONIGHT, AS OUR FORCES FIGHT, THEY AND THEIR FAMILIES ARE IN OUR PRAYERS.
MAY GOD BLESS EACH AND EVERY ONE OF THEM, AND THE COALITION FORCES AT OUR SIDE IN THE GULF--AND MAY HE CONTINUE TO BLESS OUR NATION, THE UNITED STATES OF AMERICA.
AMEN.

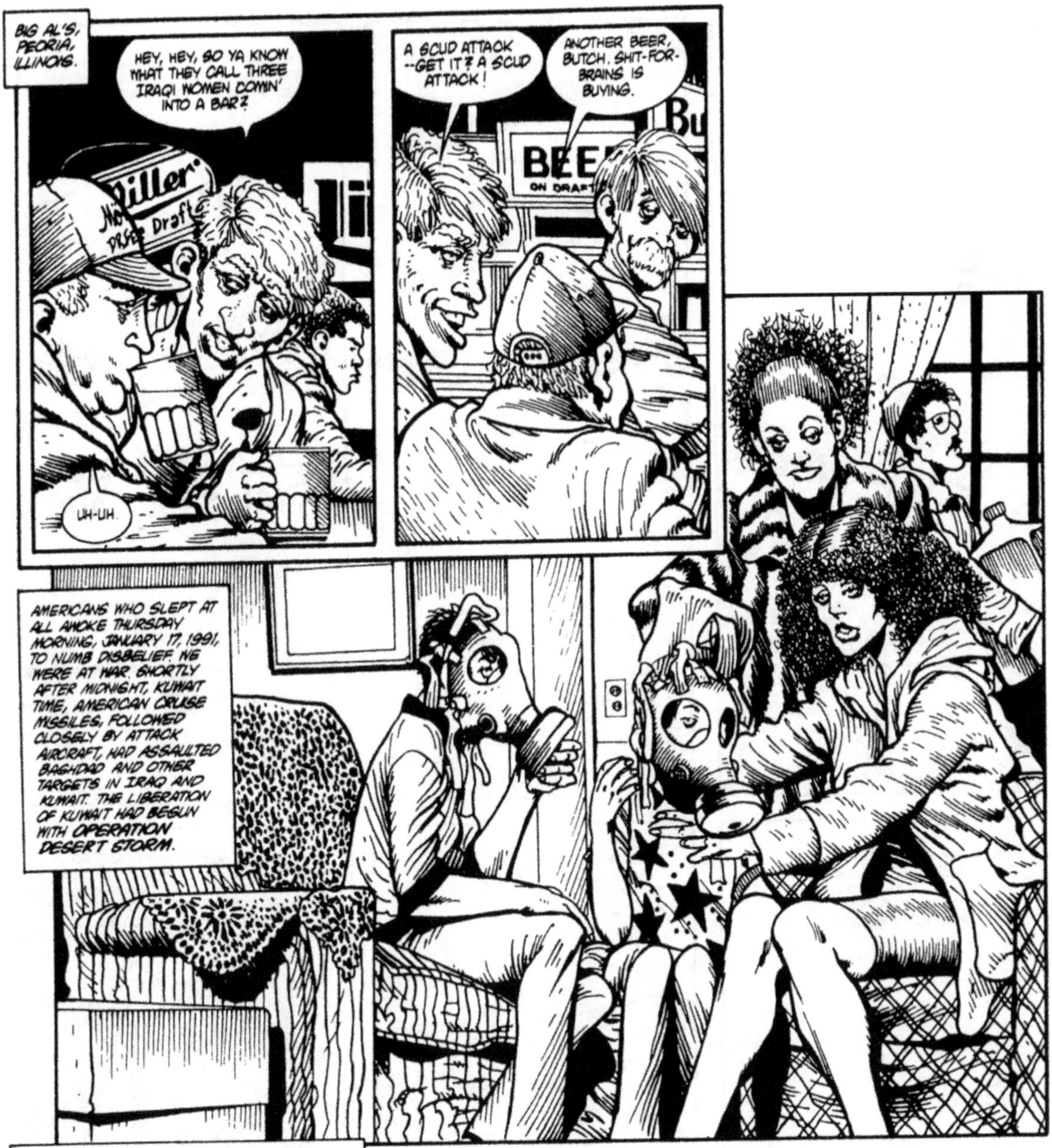
BIG AL'S, PEORIA, ILLINOIS.
HEY, HEY, SO YA KNOW WHAT THEY CALL THREE IRAQI WOMEN COMIN' INTO A BAR?
UH-UH.
A SCUD ATTACK --GET IT? A SCUD ATTACK!
ANOTHER BEER, BUTCH. SHIT-FOR-BRAINS IS BUYING.
BEER ON DRAFT
AMERICANS WHO SLEPT AT ALL AWOKE THURSDAY MORNING, JANUARY 17, 1991, TO NUMB DISBELIEF. WE WERE AT WAR. SHORTLY AFTER MIDNIGHT, KUWAIT TIME, AMERICAN CRUISE MISSILES, FOLLOWED CLOSELY BY ATTACK AIRCRAFT, HAD ASSAULTED BAGHDAD AND OTHER TARGETS IN IRAQ AND KUWAIT. THE LIBERATION OF KUWAIT HAD BEGUN WITH OPERATION DESERT STORM.

ISRAEL'S CIVILIAN POPULATION PREPARED FOR THE WORST. SADDAM HUSSEIN HAD PROMISED THAT IF COALITION FORCES CALLED HIS BLUFF, HE WOULD ATTACK ISRAEL WITH CHEMICAL WEAPONS MOUNTED ON SCUD MISSILES. SO FAR, ISRAEL HAD NO MILITARY INVOLVEMENT IN THE GULF CRISIS.

DEATH RAIN

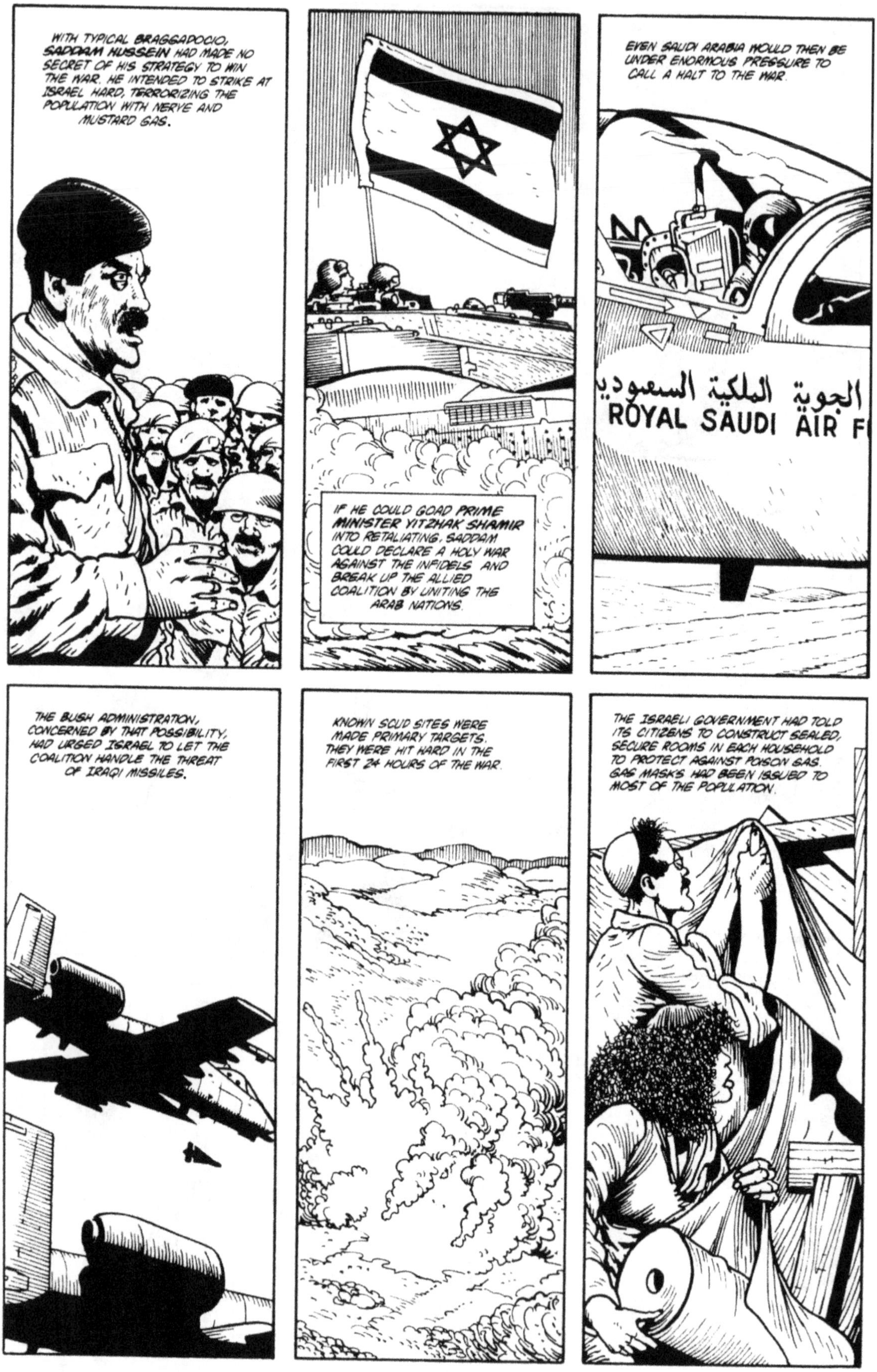

WITH TYPICAL BRAGGADOCIO, SADDAM HUSSEIN HAD MADE NO SECRET OF HIS STRATEGY TO WIN THE WAR. HE INTENDED TO STRIKE AT ISRAEL HARD, TERRORIZING THE POPULATION WITH NERVE AND MUSTARD GAS.
IF HE COULD GOAD PRIME MINISTER YITZHAK SHAMIR INTO RETALIATING, SADDAM COULD DECLARE A HOLY WAR AGAINST THE INFIDELS AND BREAK UP THE ALLIED COALITION BY UNITING THE ARAB NATIONS.
EVEN SAUDI ARABIA WOULD THEN BE UNDER ENORMOUS PRESSURE TO CALL A HALT TO THE WAR.
الجوية الملكية السعودي
ROYAL SAUDI AIR F
THE BUSH ADMINISTRATION, CONCERNED BY THAT POSSIBILITY, HAD URGED ISRAEL TO LET THE COALITION HANDLE THE THREAT OF IRAQI MISSILES.
KNOWN SCUD SITES WERE MADE PRIMARY TARGETS. THEY WERE HIT HARD IN THE FIRST 24 HOURS OF THE WAR.
THE ISRAELI GOVERNMENT HAD TOLD ITS CITIZENS TO CONSTRUCT SEALED, SECURE ROOMS IN EACH HOUSEHOLD TO PROTECT AGAINST POISON GAS. GAS MASKS HAD BEEN ISSUED TO MOST OF THE POPULATION.

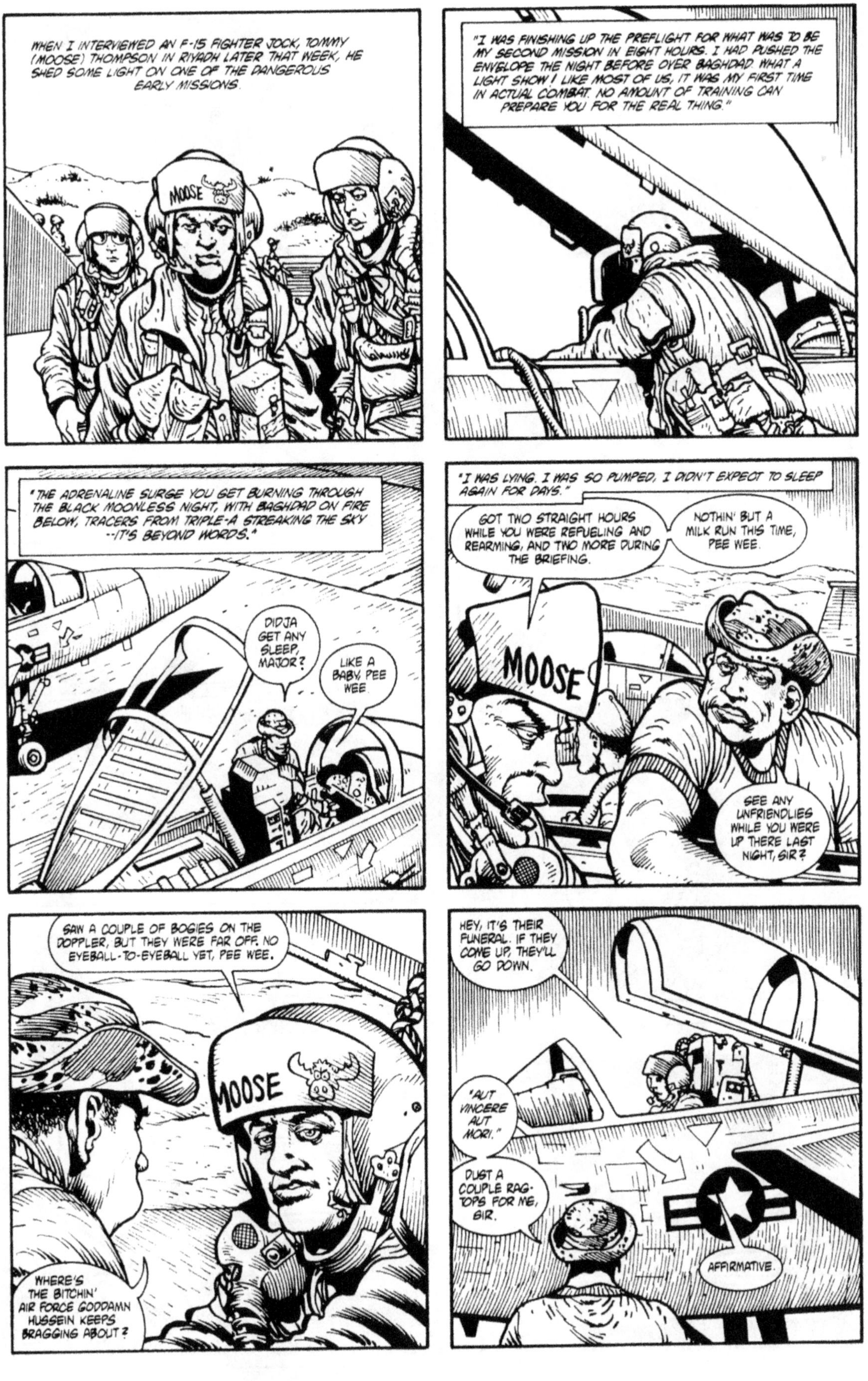
WHEN I INTERVIEWED AN F-15 FIGHTER JOCK, TOMMY (MOOSE) THOMPSON IN RIYADH LATER THAT WEEK, HE SHED SOME LIGHT ON ONE OF THE DANGEROUS EARLY MISSIONS.
MOOSE
"I WAS FINISHING UP THE PREFLIGHT FOR WHAT WAS TO BE MY SECOND MISSION IN EIGHT HOURS. I HAD PUSHED THE ENVELOPE THE NIGHT BEFORE OVER BAGHDAD. WHAT A LIGHT SHOW! LIKE MOST OF US, IT WAS MY FIRST TIME IN ACTUAL COMBAT. NO AMOUNT OF TRAINING CAN PREPARE YOU FOR THE REAL THING."
"THE ADRENALINE SURGE YOU GET BURNING THROUGH THE BLACK MOONLESS NIGHT, WITH BAGHDAD ON FIRE BELOW, TRACERS FROM TRIPLE-A STREAKING THE SKY --IT'S BEYOND WORDS."
DIDJA GET ANY SLEEP, MAJOR?
LIKE A BABY, PEE WEE.
"I WAS LYING. I WAS SO PUMPED, I DIDN'T EXPECT TO SLEEP AGAIN FOR DAYS."
GOT TWO STRAIGHT HOURS WHILE YOU WERE REFUELING AND REARMING, AND TWO MORE DURING THE BRIEFING.
NOTHIN' BUT A MILK RUN THIS TIME, PEE WEE.
MOOSE
SEE ANY UNFRIENDLIES WHILE YOU WERE UP THERE LAST NIGHT, SIR?
SAW A COUPLE OF BOGIES ON THE DOPPLER, BUT THEY WERE FAR OFF. NO EYEBALL-TO-EYEBALL YET, PEE WEE.
MOOSE
WHERE'S THE BITCHIN' AIR FORCE GODDAMN HUSSEIN KEEPS BRAGGING ABOUT?
HEY, IT'S THEIR FUNERAL. IF THEY COME UP, THEY'LL GO DOWN.
"AUT VINCERE AUT MORI."
DUST A COUPLE RAG-TOPS FOR ME, SIR.
AFFIRMATIVE.

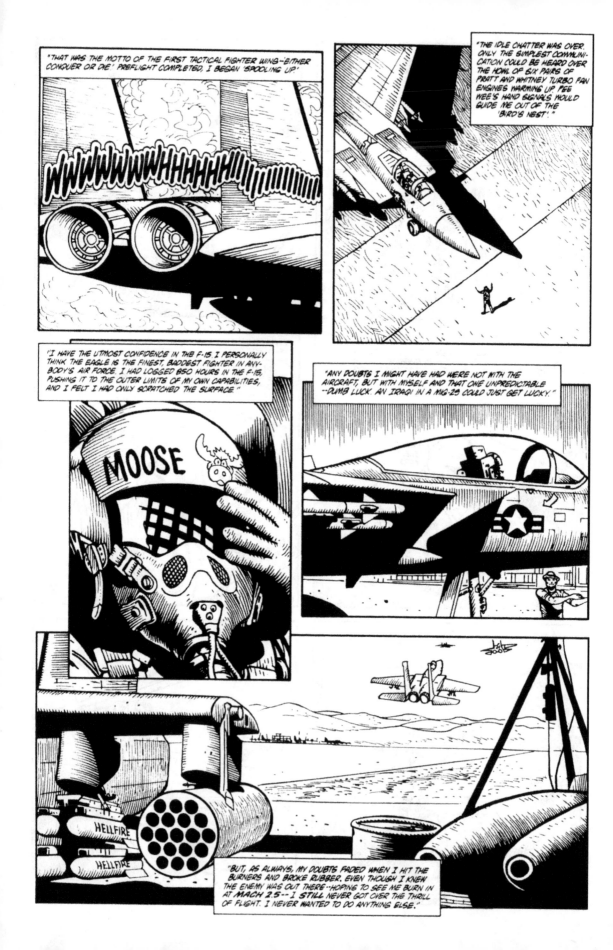

"THAT WAS THE MOTTO OF THE FIRST TACTICAL FIGHTER WING—'EITHER CONQUER OR DIE.' PREFLIGHT COMPLETED, I BEGAN 'SPOOLING UP.'"

WWWWWWWHHHHHH!!

"THE IDLE CHATTER WAS OVER. ONLY THE SIMPLEST COMMUNICATION COULD BE HEARD OVER THE HOWL OF SIX PAIRS OF PRATT AND WHITNEY TURBO FAN ENGINES WARMING UP. PEE WEE'S HAND SIGNALS WOULD GUIDE ME OUT OF THE 'BIRD'S NEST'."

"I HAVE THE UTMOST CONFIDENCE IN THE F-15. I PERSONALLY THINK THE EAGLE IS THE FINEST, BADDEST FIGHTER IN ANYBODY'S AIR FORCE. I HAD LOGGED 850 HOURS IN THE F-15, PUSHING IT TO THE OUTER LIMITS OF MY OWN CAPABILITIES, AND I FELT I HAD ONLY SCRATCHED THE SURFACE."

MOOSE

"ANY DOUBTS I MIGHT HAVE HAD WERE NOT WITH THE AIRCRAFT, BUT WITH MYSELF AND THAT ONE UNPREDICTABLE --DUMB LUCK. AN IRAQI IN A MIG-29 COULD JUST GET LUCKY."

HELLFIRE

HELLFIRE

"BUT, AS ALWAYS, MY DOUBTS FADED WHEN I HIT THE BURNERS AND BROKE RUBBER. EVEN THOUGH I KNEW THE ENEMY WAS OUT THERE--HOPING TO SEE ME BURN IN AT MACH 2.5-- I STILL NEVER GOT OVER THE THRILL OF FLIGHT. I NEVER WANTED TO DO ANYTHING ELSE."

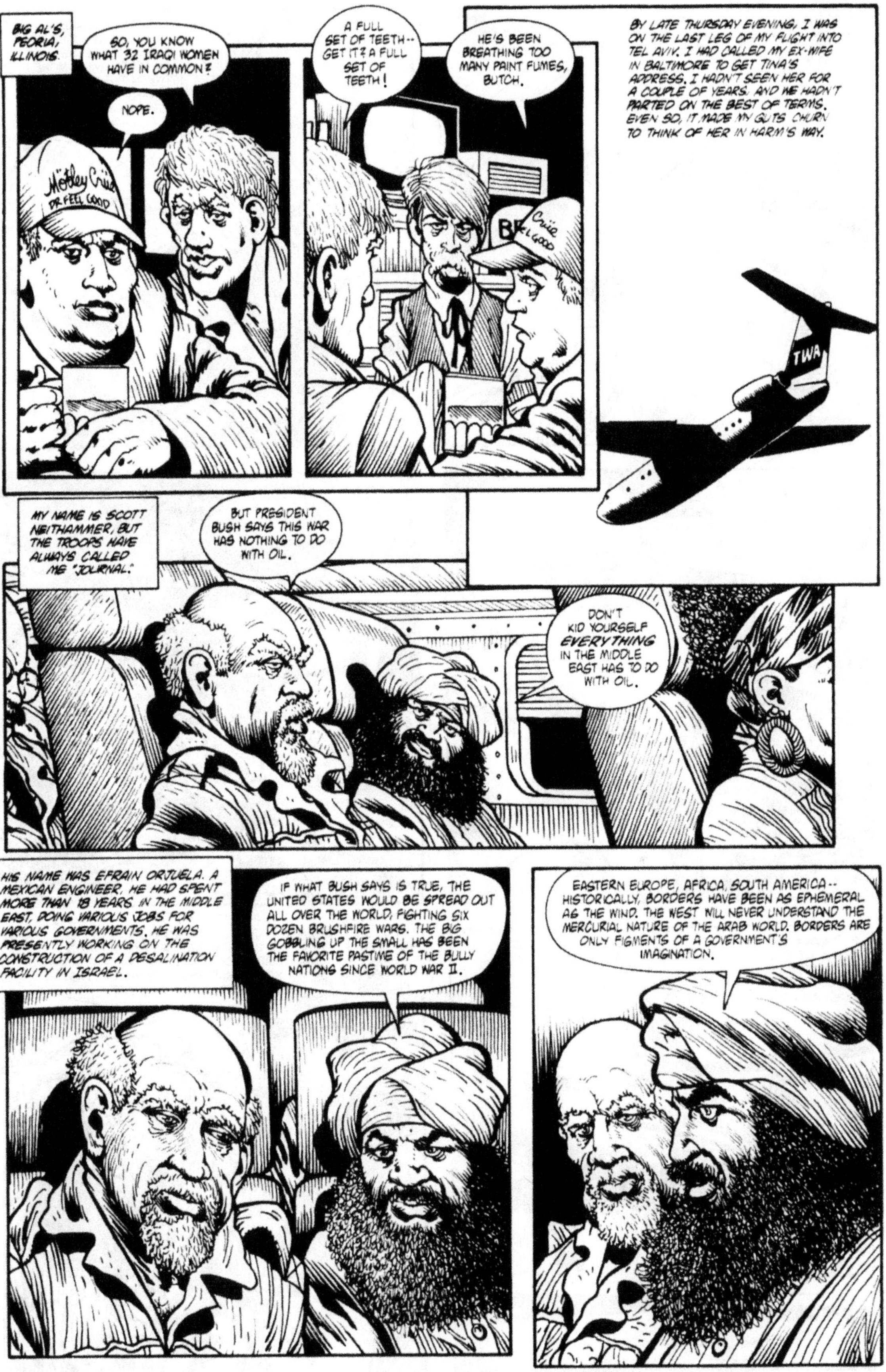
BIG AL'S, PEORIA, ILLINOIS.
SO, YOU KNOW WHAT 32 IRAQI WOMEN HAVE IN COMMON?
NOPE.
A FULL SET OF TEETH-- GET IT? A FULL SET OF TEETH!
HE'S BEEN BREATHING TOO MANY PAINT FUMES, BUTCH.
BY LATE THURSDAY EVENING, I WAS ON THE LAST LEG OF MY FLIGHT INTO TEL AVIV. I HAD CALLED MY EX-WIFE IN BALTIMORE TO GET TINA'S ADDRESS. I HADN'T SEEN HER FOR A COUPLE OF YEARS. AND WE HADN'T PARTED ON THE BEST OF TERMS. EVEN SO, IT MADE MY GUTS CHURN TO THINK OF HER IN HARM'S WAY.
TWA
MY NAME IS SCOTT NEITHAMMER, BUT THE TROOPS HAVE ALWAYS CALLED ME "JOURNAL."
BUT PRESIDENT BUSH SAYS THIS WAR HAS NOTHING TO DO WITH OIL.
DON'T KID YOURSELF. EVERYTHING IN THE MIDDLE EAST HAS TO DO WITH OIL.
HIS NAME WAS EFRAIN ORJUELA. A MEXICAN ENGINEER, HE HAD SPENT MORE THAN 18 YEARS IN THE MIDDLE EAST, DOING VARIOUS JOBS FOR VARIOUS GOVERNMENTS. HE WAS PRESENTLY WORKING ON THE CONSTRUCTION OF A DESALINATION FACILITY IN ISRAEL.
IF WHAT BUSH SAYS IS TRUE, THE UNITED STATES WOULD BE SPREAD OUT ALL OVER THE WORLD, FIGHTING SIX DOZEN BRUSHFIRE WARS. THE BIG GOBBLING UP THE SMALL HAS BEEN THE FAVORITE PASTIME OF THE BULLY NATIONS SINCE WORLD WAR II.
EASTERN EUROPE, AFRICA, SOUTH AMERICA-- HISTORICALLY, BORDERS HAVE BEEN AS EPHEMERAL AS THE WIND. THE WEST WILL NEVER UNDERSTAND THE MERCURIAL NATURE OF THE ARAB WORLD. BORDERS ARE ONLY FIGMENTS OF A GOVERNMENT'S IMAGINATION.

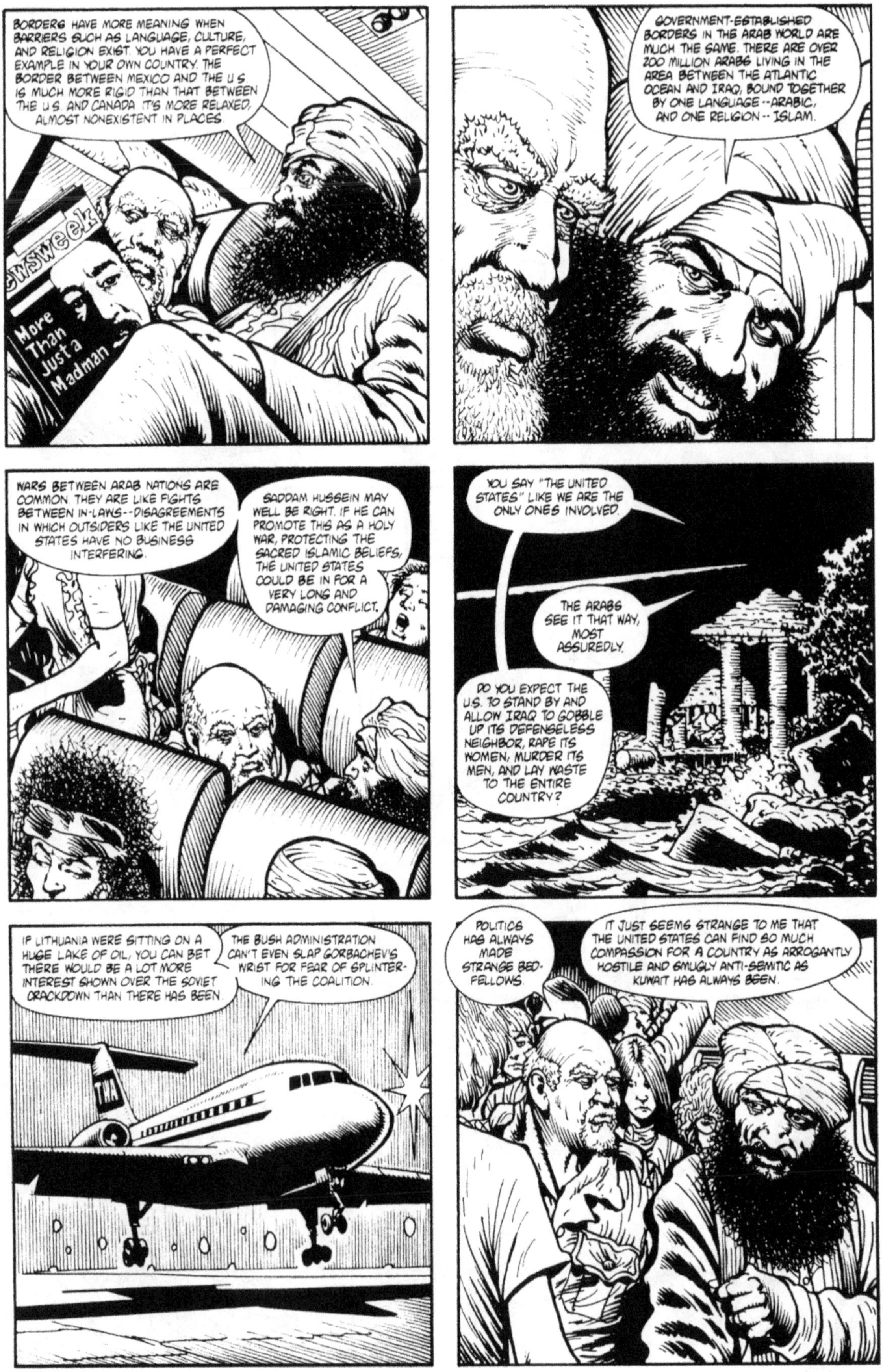
BORDERS HAVE MORE MEANING WHEN BARRIERS SUCH AS LANGUAGE, CULTURE, AND RELIGION EXIST. YOU HAVE A PERFECT EXAMPLE IN YOUR OWN COUNTRY. THE BORDER BETWEEN MEXICO AND THE U.S. IS MUCH MORE RIGID THAN THAT BETWEEN THE U.S. AND CANADA. IT'S MORE RELAXED, ALMOST NONEXISTENT IN PLACES.
More Than Just a Madman
GOVERNMENT-ESTABLISHED BORDERS IN THE ARAB WORLD ARE MUCH THE SAME. THERE ARE OVER 200 MILLION ARABS LIVING IN THE AREA BETWEEN THE ATLANTIC OCEAN AND IRAQ, BOUND TOGETHER BY ONE LANGUAGE--ARABIC, AND ONE RELIGION--ISLAM.
WARS BETWEEN ARAB NATIONS ARE COMMON. THEY ARE LIKE FIGHTS BETWEEN IN-LAWS--DISAGREEMENTS IN WHICH OUTSIDERS LIKE THE UNITED STATES HAVE NO BUSINESS INTERFERING.
SADDAM HUSSEIN MAY WELL BE RIGHT. IF HE CAN PROMOTE THIS AS A HOLY WAR, PROTECTING THE SACRED ISLAMIC BELIEFS, THE UNITED STATES COULD BE IN FOR A VERY LONG AND DAMAGING CONFLICT.
YOU SAY "THE UNITED STATES" LIKE WE ARE THE ONLY ONES INVOLVED.
THE ARABS SEE IT THAT WAY, MOST ASSUREDLY.
DO YOU EXPECT THE U.S. TO STAND BY AND ALLOW IRAQ TO GOBBLE UP ITS DEFENSELESS NEIGHBOR, RAPE ITS WOMEN, MURDER ITS MEN, AND LAY WASTE TO THE ENTIRE COUNTRY?
IF LITHUANIA WERE SITTING ON A HUGE LAKE OF OIL, YOU CAN BET THERE WOULD BE A LOT MORE INTEREST SHOWN OVER THE SOVIET CRACKDOWN THAN THERE HAS BEEN.
THE BUSH ADMINISTRATION CAN'T EVEN SLAP GORBACHEV'S WRIST FOR FEAR OF SPLINTERING THE COALITION.
POLITICS HAS ALWAYS MADE STRANGE BED-FELLOWS.
IT JUST SEEMS STRANGE TO ME THAT THE UNITED STATES CAN FIND SO MUCH COMPASSION FOR A COUNTRY AS ARROGANTLY HOSTILE AND SMUGLY ANTI-SEMITIC AS KUWAIT HAS ALWAYS BEEN.

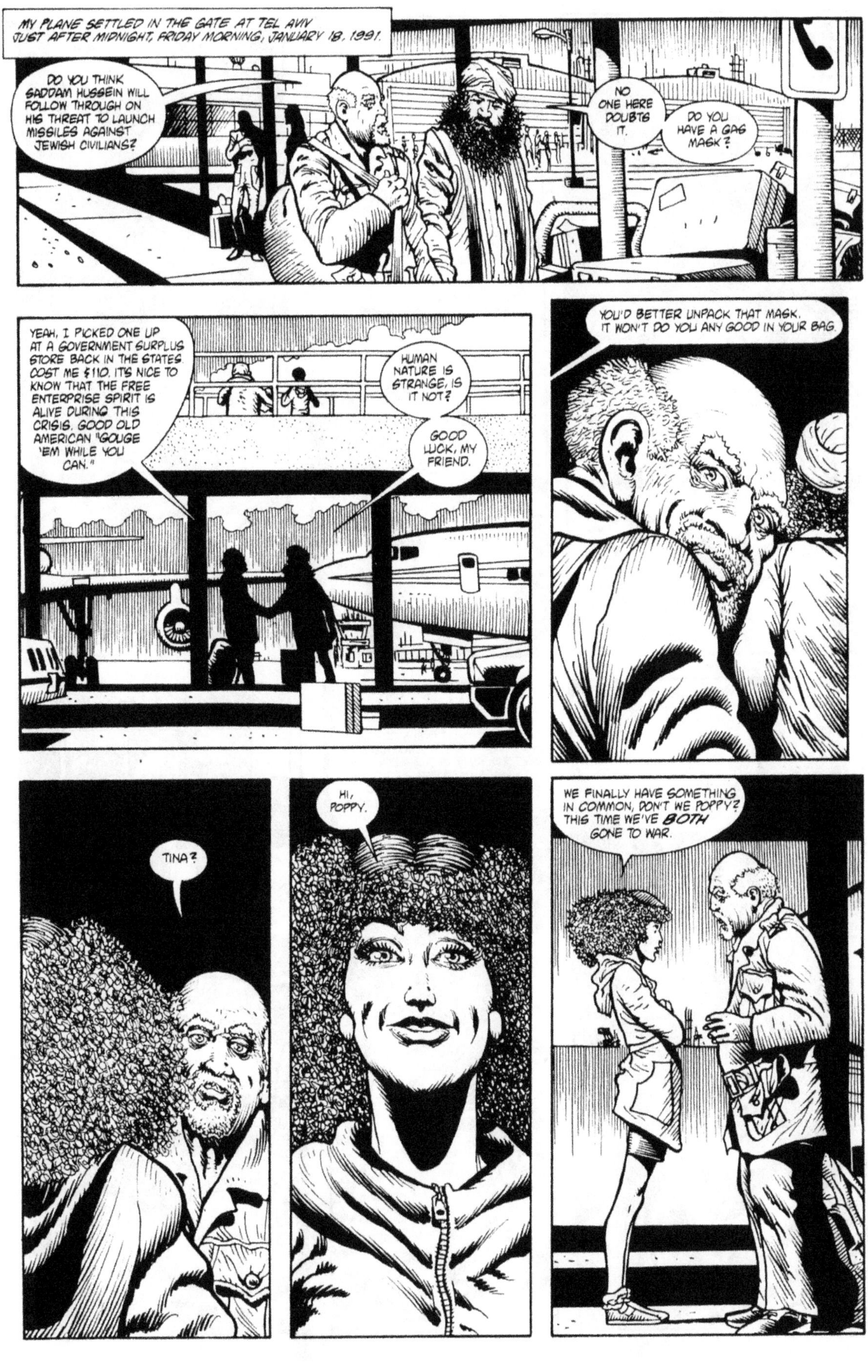
MY PLANE SETTLED IN THE GATE AT TEL AVIV JUST AFTER MIDNIGHT, FRIDAY MORNING, JANUARY 18, 1991.
DO YOU THINK SADDAM HUSSEIN WILL FOLLOW THROUGH ON HIS THREAT TO LAUNCH MISSILES AGAINST JEWISH CIVILIANS?
NO ONE HERE DOUBTS IT.
DO YOU HAVE A GAS MASK?
YEAH, I PICKED ONE UP AT A GOVERNMENT SURPLUS STORE BACK IN THE STATES. COST ME $110. IT'S NICE TO KNOW THAT THE FREE ENTERPRISE SPIRIT IS ALIVE DURING THIS CRISIS. GOOD OLD AMERICAN "GOUGE 'EM WHILE YOU CAN."
HUMAN NATURE IS STRANGE, IS IT NOT?
GOOD LUCK, MY FRIEND.
YOU'D BETTER UNPACK THAT MASK. IT WON'T DO YOU ANY GOOD IN YOUR BAG.
TINA?
HI, POPPY.
WE FINALLY HAVE SOMETHING IN COMMON, DON'T WE POPPY? THIS TIME WE'VE BOTH GONE TO WAR.

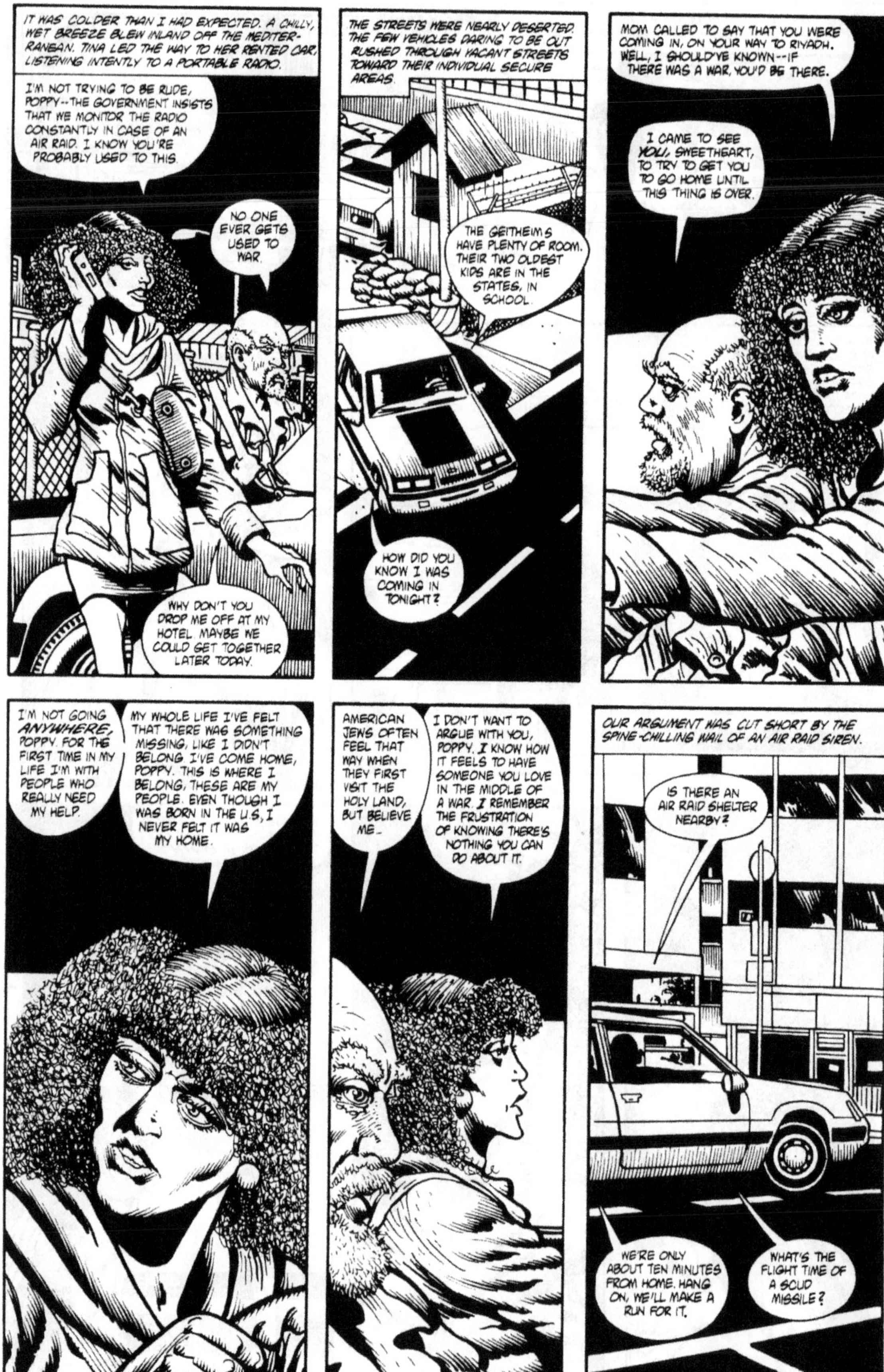
IT WAS COLDER THAN I HAD EXPECTED. A CHILLY, WET BREEZE BLEW INLAND OFF THE MEDITER-RANEAN. TINA LED THE WAY TO HER RENTED CAR, LISTENING INTENTLY TO A PORTABLE RADIO.
I'M NOT TRYING TO BE RUDE, POPPY--THE GOVERNMENT INSISTS THAT WE MONITOR THE RADIO CONSTANTLY IN CASE OF AN AIR RAID. I KNOW YOU'RE PROBABLY USED TO THIS.
NO ONE EVER GETS USED TO WAR.
WHY DON'T YOU DROP ME OFF AT MY HOTEL. MAYBE WE COULD GET TOGETHER LATER TODAY.
THE STREETS WERE NEARLY DESERTED. THE FEW VEHICLES DARING TO BE OUT RUSHED THROUGH VACANT STREETS TOWARD THEIR INDIVIDUAL SECURE AREAS.
THE GEITHEIM'S HAVE PLENTY OF ROOM. THEIR TWO OLDEST KIDS ARE IN THE STATES, IN SCHOOL.
HOW DID YOU KNOW I WAS COMING IN TONIGHT?
MOM CALLED TO SAY THAT YOU WERE COMING IN, ON YOUR WAY TO RIYADH. WELL, I SHOULD'VE KNOWN--IF THERE WAS A WAR, YOU'D BE THERE.
I CAME TO SEE YOU, SWEETHEART, TO TRY TO GET YOU TO GO HOME UNTIL THIS THING IS OVER.
I'M NOT GOING ANYWHERE, POPPY. FOR THE FIRST TIME IN MY LIFE I'M WITH PEOPLE WHO REALLY NEED MY HELP.
MY WHOLE LIFE I'VE FELT THAT THERE WAS SOMETHING MISSING, LIKE I DIDN'T BELONG. I'VE COME HOME, POPPY. THIS IS WHERE I BELONG. THESE ARE MY PEOPLE. EVEN THOUGH I WAS BORN IN THE U.S., I NEVER FELT IT WAS MY HOME.
AMERICAN JEWS OFTEN FEEL THAT WAY WHEN THEY FIRST VISIT THE HOLY LAND, BUT BELIEVE ME...
I DON'T WANT TO ARGUE WITH YOU, POPPY. I KNOW HOW IT FEELS TO HAVE SOMEONE YOU LOVE IN THE MIDDLE OF A WAR. I REMEMBER THE FRUSTRATION OF KNOWING THERE'S NOTHING YOU CAN DO ABOUT IT.
OUR ARGUMENT WAS CUT SHORT BY THE SPINE-CHILLING WAIL OF AN AIR RAID SIREN.
IS THERE AN AIR RAID SHELTER NEARBY?
WE'RE ONLY ABOUT TEN MINUTES FROM HOME. HANG ON, WE'LL MAKE A RUN FOR IT.
WHAT'S THE FLIGHT TIME OF A SCUD MISSILE?

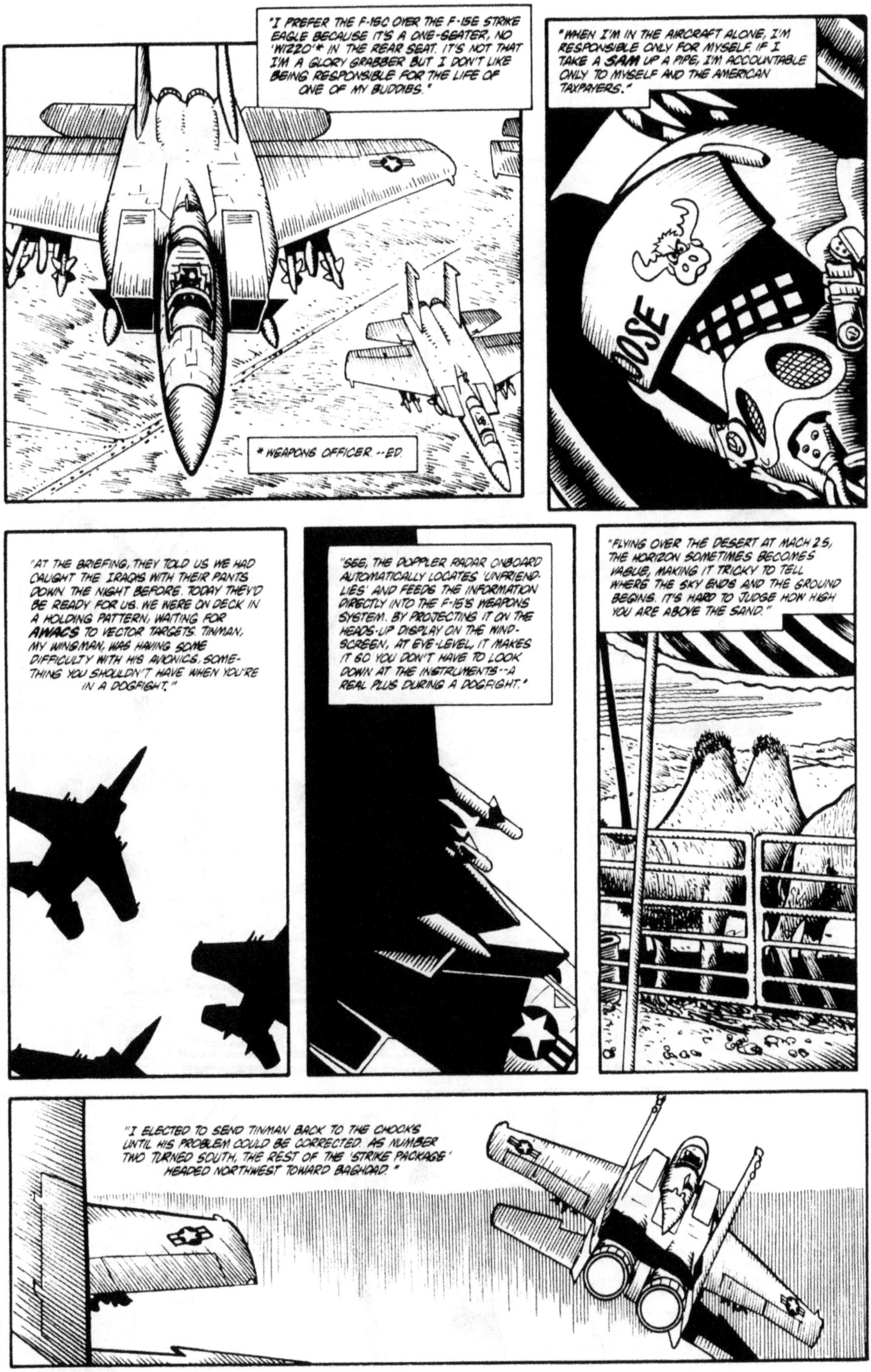
"I PREFER THE F-15C OVER THE F-15E STRIKE EAGLE BECAUSE IT'S A ONE-SEATER, NO 'WIZZO'* IN THE REAR SEAT. IT'S NOT THAT I'M A GLORY GRABBER BUT I DON'T LIKE BEING RESPONSIBLE FOR THE LIFE OF ONE OF MY BUDDIES."
* WEAPONS OFFICER. --ED.
"WHEN I'M IN THE AIRCRAFT ALONE, I'M RESPONSIBLE ONLY FOR MYSELF. IF I TAKE A SAM UP A PIPE, I'M ACCOUNTABLE ONLY TO MYSELF AND THE AMERICAN TAXPAYERS."
OOSE
"AT THE BRIEFING, THEY TOLD US WE HAD CAUGHT THE IRAQIS WITH THEIR PANTS DOWN THE NIGHT BEFORE. TODAY THEY'D BE READY FOR US. WE WERE ON DECK IN A HOLDING PATTERN, WAITING FOR AWACS TO VECTOR TARGETS. TINMAN, MY WINGMAN, WAS HAVING SOME DIFFICULTY WITH HIS AVIONICS, SOMETHING YOU SHOULDN'T HAVE WHEN YOU'RE IN A DOGFIGHT."
"SEE, THE DOPPLER RADAR ONBOARD AUTOMATICALLY LOCATES 'UNFRIENDLIES' AND FEEDS THE INFORMATION DIRECTLY INTO THE F-15'S WEAPONS SYSTEM. BY PROJECTING IT ON THE HEADS-UP DISPLAY ON THE WINDSCREEN, AT EYE-LEVEL, IT MAKES IT SO YOU DON'T HAVE TO LOOK DOWN AT THE INSTRUMENTS--A REAL PLUS DURING A DOGFIGHT."
"FLYING OVER THE DESERT AT MACH 2.5, THE HORIZON SOMETIMES BECOMES VAGUE, MAKING IT TRICKY TO TELL WHERE THE SKY ENDS AND THE GROUND BEGINS. IT'S HARD TO JUDGE HOW HIGH YOU ARE ABOVE THE SAND."
"I ELECTED TO SEND TINMAN BACK TO THE CHOCKS UNTIL HIS PROBLEM COULD BE CORRECTED. AS NUMBER TWO TURNED SOUTH, THE REST OF THE 'STRIKE PACKAGE' HEADED NORTHWEST TOWARD BAGHDAD."

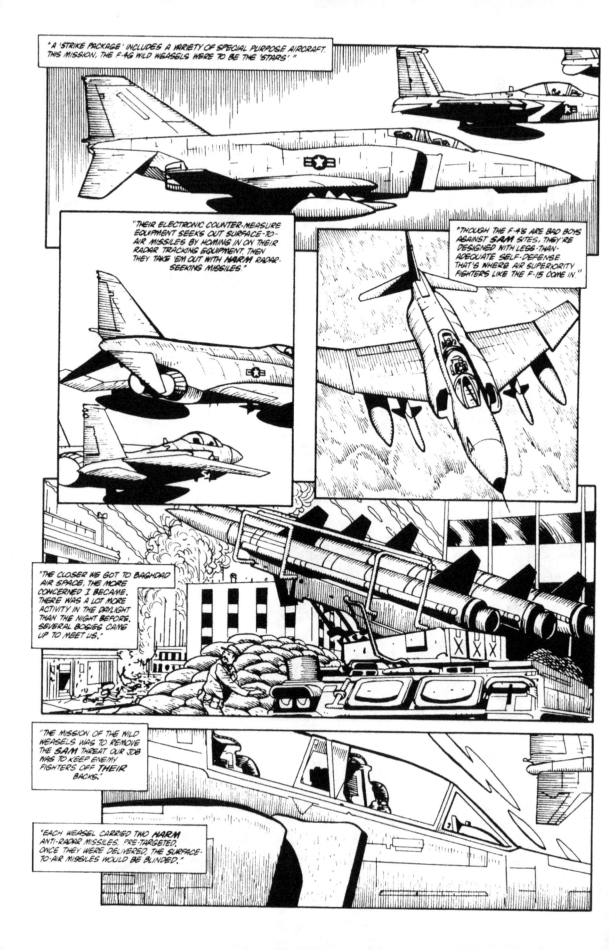

"A 'STRIKE PACKAGE' INCLUDES A VARIETY OF SPECIAL PURPOSE AIRCRAFT. THIS MISSION, THE F-4G WILD WEASELS WERE TO BE THE 'STARS'."

"THEIR ELECTRONIC COUNTER-MEASURE EQUIPMENT SEEKS OUT SURFACE-TO-AIR MISSILES BY HOMING IN ON THEIR RADAR TRACKING EQUIPMENT, THEN THEY TAKE 'EM OUT WITH *HARM* RADAR-SEEKING MISSILES."

"THOUGH THE F-4'S ARE BAD BOYS AGAINST *SAM* SITES, THEY'RE DESIGNED WITH LESS-THAN-ADEQUATE SELF-DEFENSE. THAT'S WHERE AIR SUPERIORITY FIGHTERS LIKE THE F-15 COME IN."

"THE CLOSER WE GOT TO BAGHDAD AIR SPACE, THE MORE CONCERNED I BECAME. THERE WAS A LOT MORE ACTIVITY IN THE DAYLIGHT THAN THE NIGHT BEFORE. SEVERAL BOGIES CAME UP TO MEET US."

"THE MISSION OF THE WILD WEASELS WAS TO REMOVE THE *SAM* THREAT. OUR JOB WAS TO KEEP ENEMY FIGHTERS OFF *THEIR* BACKS."

"EACH WEASEL CARRIED TWO *HARM* ANTI-RADAR MISSILES, PRE-TARGETED. ONCE THEY WERE DELIVERED, THE SURFACE-TO-AIR MISSILES WOULD BE BLINDED."

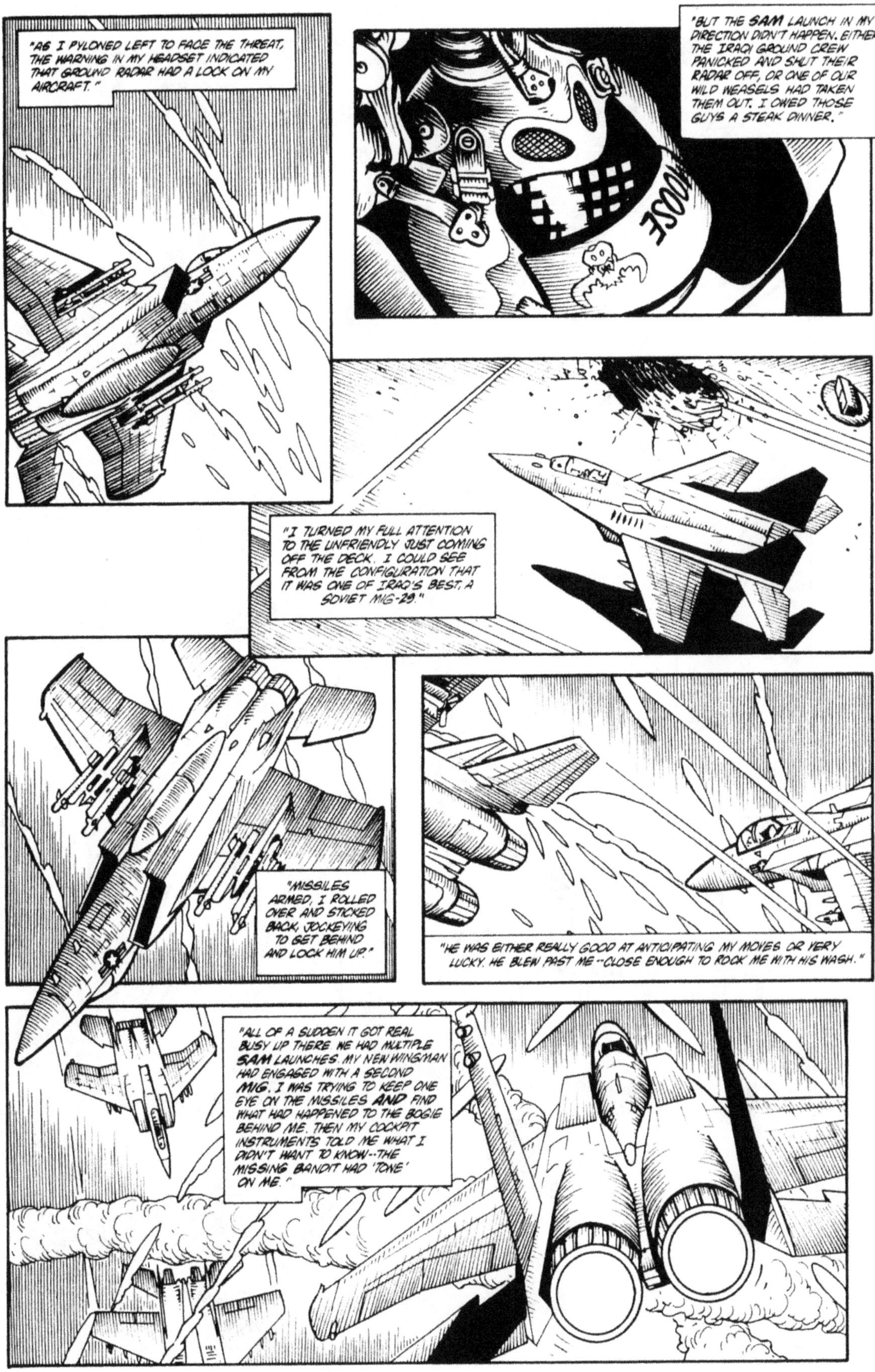
"AS I PYLONED LEFT TO FACE THE THREAT, THE WARNING IN MY HEADSET INDICATED THAT GROUND RADAR HAD A LOCK ON MY AIRCRAFT."
"BUT THE SAM LAUNCH IN MY DIRECTION DIDN'T HAPPEN. EITHER THE IRAQI GROUND CREW PANICKED AND SHUT THEIR RADAR OFF, OR ONE OF OUR WILD WEASELS HAD TAKEN THEM OUT. I OWED THOSE GUYS A STEAK DINNER."
"I TURNED MY FULL ATTENTION TO THE UNFRIENDLY JUST COMING OFF THE DECK. I COULD SEE FROM THE CONFIGURATION THAT IT WAS ONE OF IRAQ'S BEST, A SOVIET MIG-29."
"MISSILES ARMED, I ROLLED OVER AND STICKED BACK, JOCKEYING TO GET BEHIND AND LOCK HIM UP."
"HE WAS EITHER REALLY GOOD AT ANTICIPATING MY MOVES OR VERY LUCKY. HE BLEW PAST ME--CLOSE ENOUGH TO ROCK ME WITH HIS WASH."
"ALL OF A SUDDEN IT GOT REAL BUSY UP THERE. WE HAD MULTIPLE SAM LAUNCHES. MY NEW WINGMAN HAD ENGAGED WITH A SECOND MIG. I WAS TRYING TO KEEP ONE EYE ON THE MISSILES AND FIND WHAT HAD HAPPENED TO THE BOGIE BEHIND ME. THEN MY COCKPIT INSTRUMENTS TOLD ME WHAT I DIDN'T WANT TO KNOW--THE MISSING BANDIT HAD 'TONE' ON ME."

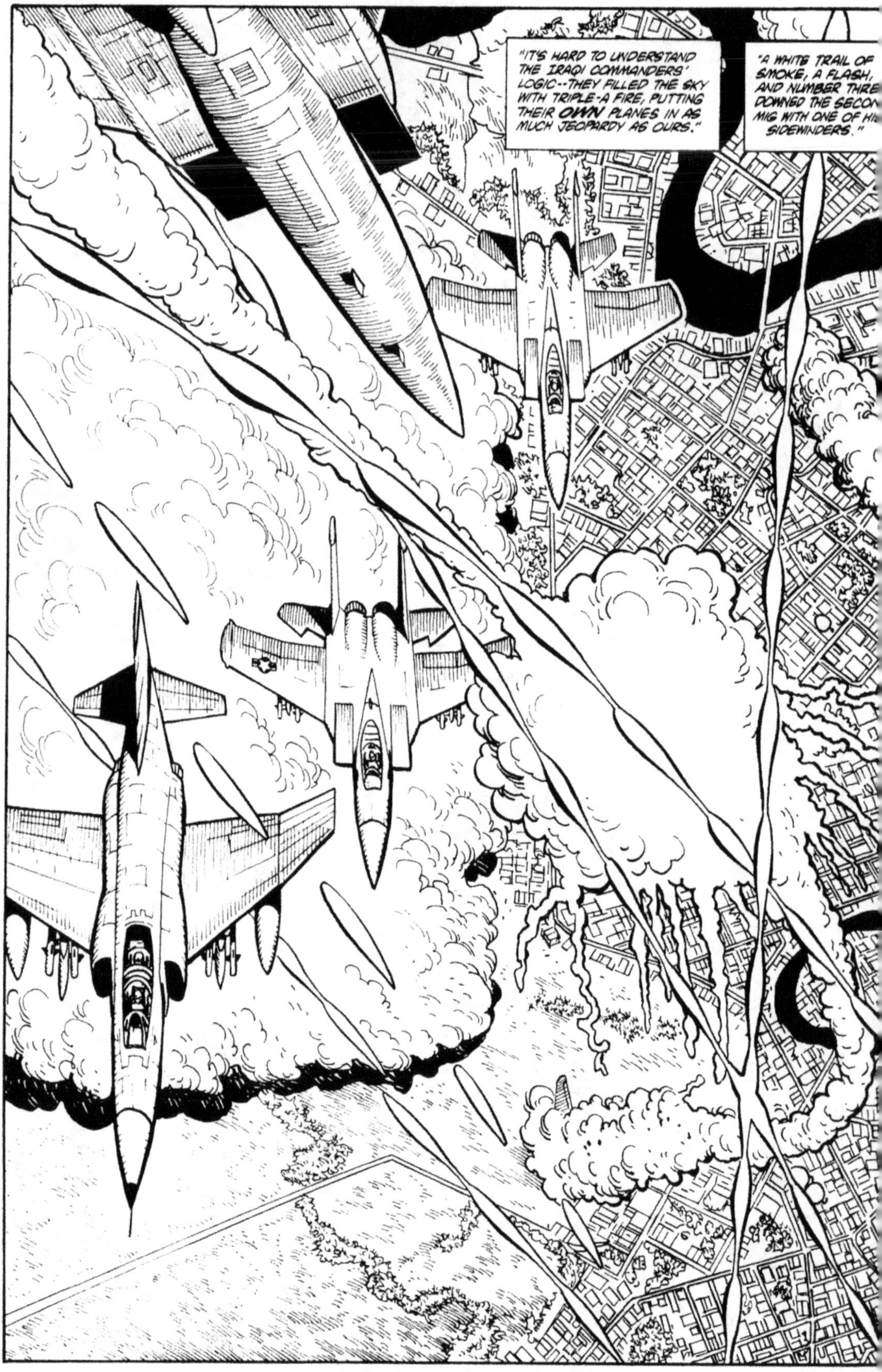
"IT'S HARD TO UNDERSTAND THE IRAQI COMMANDERS' LOGIC--THEY FILLED THE SKY WITH TRIPLE-A FIRE, PUTTING THEIR **OWN** PLANES IN AS MUCH JEOPARDY AS OURS."
"A WHITE TRAIL OF SMOKE, A FLASH, AND NUMBER THRE DOWNED THE SECON MIG WITH ONE OF HI SIDEWINDERS."

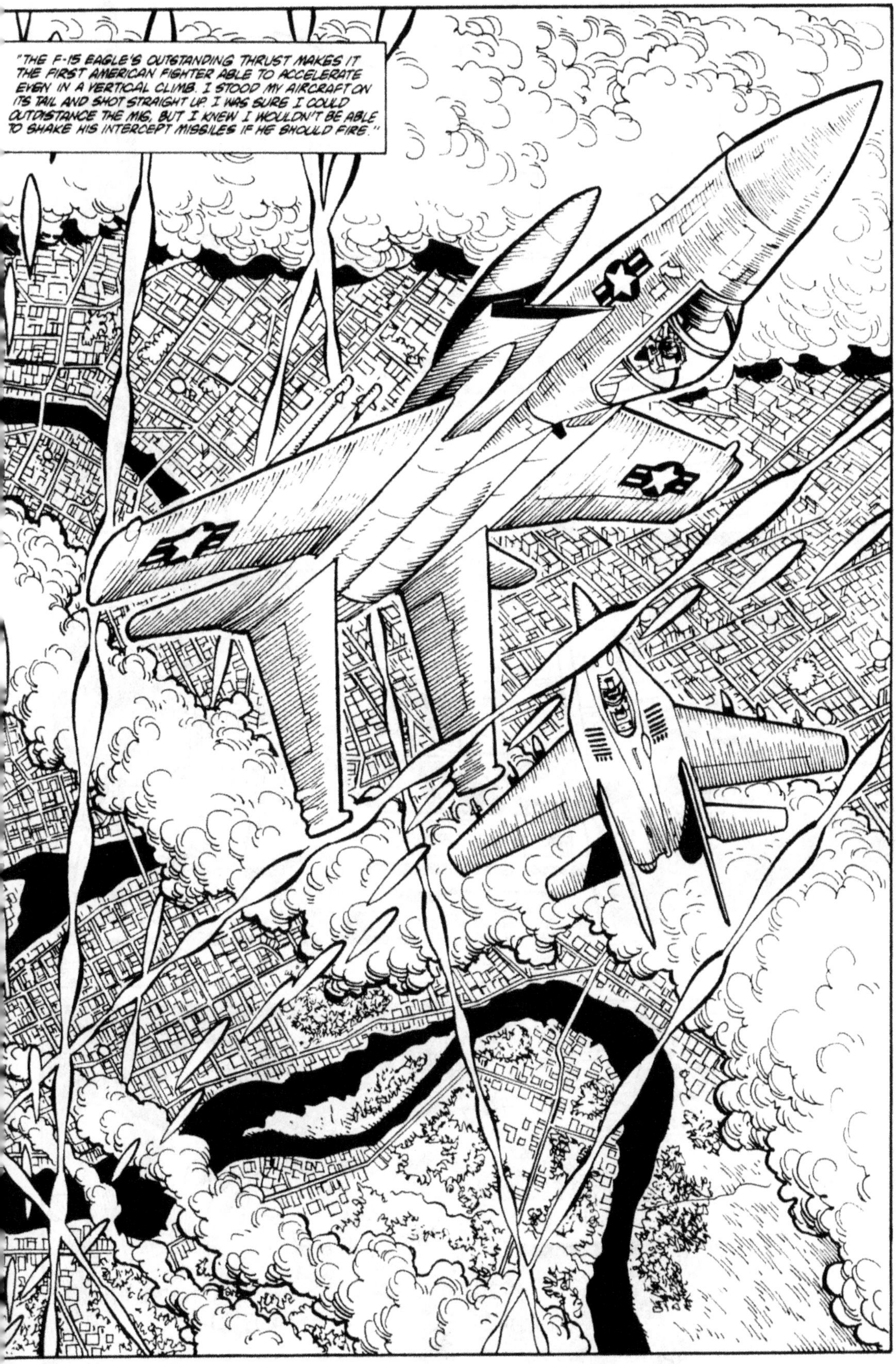
"THE F-15 EAGLE'S OUTSTANDING THRUST MAKES IT THE FIRST AMERICAN FIGHTER ABLE TO ACCELERATE EVEN IN A VERTICAL CLIMB. I STOOD MY AIRCRAFT ON ITS TAIL AND SHOT STRAIGHT UP. I WAS SURE I COULD OUTDISTANCE THE MIG, BUT I KNEW I WOULDN'T BE ABLE TO SHAKE HIS INTERCEPT MISSILES IF HE SHOULD FIRE."

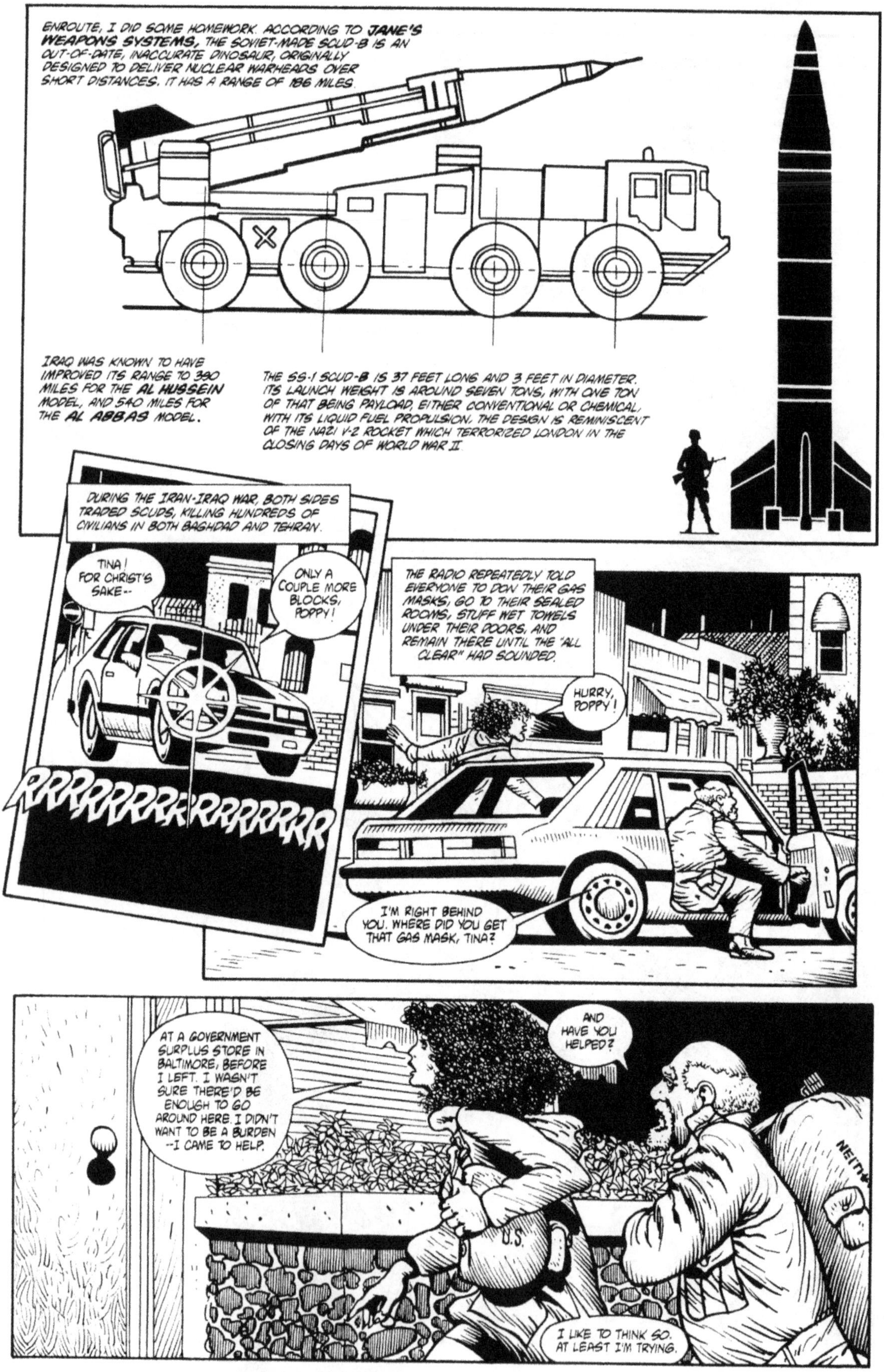
ENROUTE, I DID SOME HOMEWORK. ACCORDING TO JANE'S WEAPONS SYSTEMS, THE SOVIET-MADE SCUD-B IS AN OUT-OF-DATE, INACCURATE DINOSAUR, ORIGINALLY DESIGNED TO DELIVER NUCLEAR WARHEADS OVER SHORT DISTANCES. IT HAS A RANGE OF 186 MILES.
IRAQ WAS KNOWN TO HAVE IMPROVED ITS RANGE TO 390 MILES FOR THE AL HUSSEIN MODEL, AND 540 MILES FOR THE AL ABBAS MODEL.
THE SS-1 SCUD-B IS 37 FEET LONG AND 3 FEET IN DIAMETER. ITS LAUNCH WEIGHT IS AROUND SEVEN TONS, WITH ONE TON OF THAT BEING PAYLOAD, EITHER CONVENTIONAL OR CHEMICAL, WITH ITS LIQUID FUEL PROPULSION. THE DESIGN IS REMINISCENT OF THE NAZI V-2 ROCKET WHICH TERRORIZED LONDON IN THE CLOSING DAYS OF WORLD WAR II.
DURING THE IRAN-IRAQ WAR, BOTH SIDES TRADED SCUDS, KILLING HUNDREDS OF CIVILIANS IN BOTH BAGHDAD AND TEHRAN.
TINA! FOR CHRIST'S SAKE--
ONLY A COUPLE MORE BLOCKS, POPPY!
RRRRRRRRRRRRRRRRR
THE RADIO REPEATEDLY TOLD EVERYONE TO DON THEIR GAS MASKS, GO TO THEIR SEALED ROOMS, STUFF WET TOWELS UNDER THEIR DOORS, AND REMAIN THERE UNTIL THE "ALL CLEAR" HAD SOUNDED.
HURRY, POPPY!
I'M RIGHT BEHIND YOU. WHERE DID YOU GET THAT GAS MASK, TINA?
AT A GOVERNMENT SURPLUS STORE IN BALTIMORE, BEFORE I LEFT. I WASN'T SURE THERE'D BE ENOUGH TO GO AROUND HERE. I DIDN'T WANT TO BE A BURDEN --I CAME TO HELP.
AND HAVE YOU HELPED?
I LIKE TO THINK SO. AT LEAST I'M TRYING.

BIG AL'S, PEORIA, ILLINOIS.

WHADDA YA CALL THREE IRAQI WOMEN COMIN' INTO A BAR?

BEATS ME.

A SCUD ATTACK-- GET IT? A SCUD ATTACK! OH, JEEZ, THAT'S FUNNY!

DRAW ME ANOTHER ONE, BUTCH--AND A SET OF EAR PLUGS.

HMMM. WOULD THAT I COULD.

OKAY, POPPY, I'LL ADMIT I CAME OVER HERE WITH STARS IN MY EYES, THINKING MY LIFE WOULD BE FULFILLED. IT HASN'T BEEN.

I'D LIKE TO INTRODUCE YOU TO THE FAMILY I'M STAYING WITH, THE GEITHEIMS.

PLEASED TO MEET YOU.

THE GEITHEIMS SEEMED NICE. I SAW NO SIGNS OF PANIC--THEY SEEMED AS MENTALLY PREPARED AS ONE COULD BE WITH MISSILES--POSSIBLY CARRYING POISON GAS--HURTLING TOWARD THEM.

WHEN I GOT HERE I FOUND OUT THAT TO WORK IN A HOSPITAL I'D HAVE TO BE RE-CERTIFIED--IN HEBREW. SO I CAN ONLY DO UNSKILLED VOLUNTEER WORK RIGHT NOW, AND THE COUNTRY'S FULL OF DO-GOODERS.

THINGS TAKE TIME, SWEETHEART. YOU CAN'T...

I RECOGNIZED THE FAINT, DULL THUD IN THE DISTANCE. I HAD HEARD IT TOO MANY TIMES BEFORE.

WHAT IS IT?

SOMETHING INCOMING JUST IMPACTED.

MY GOD!

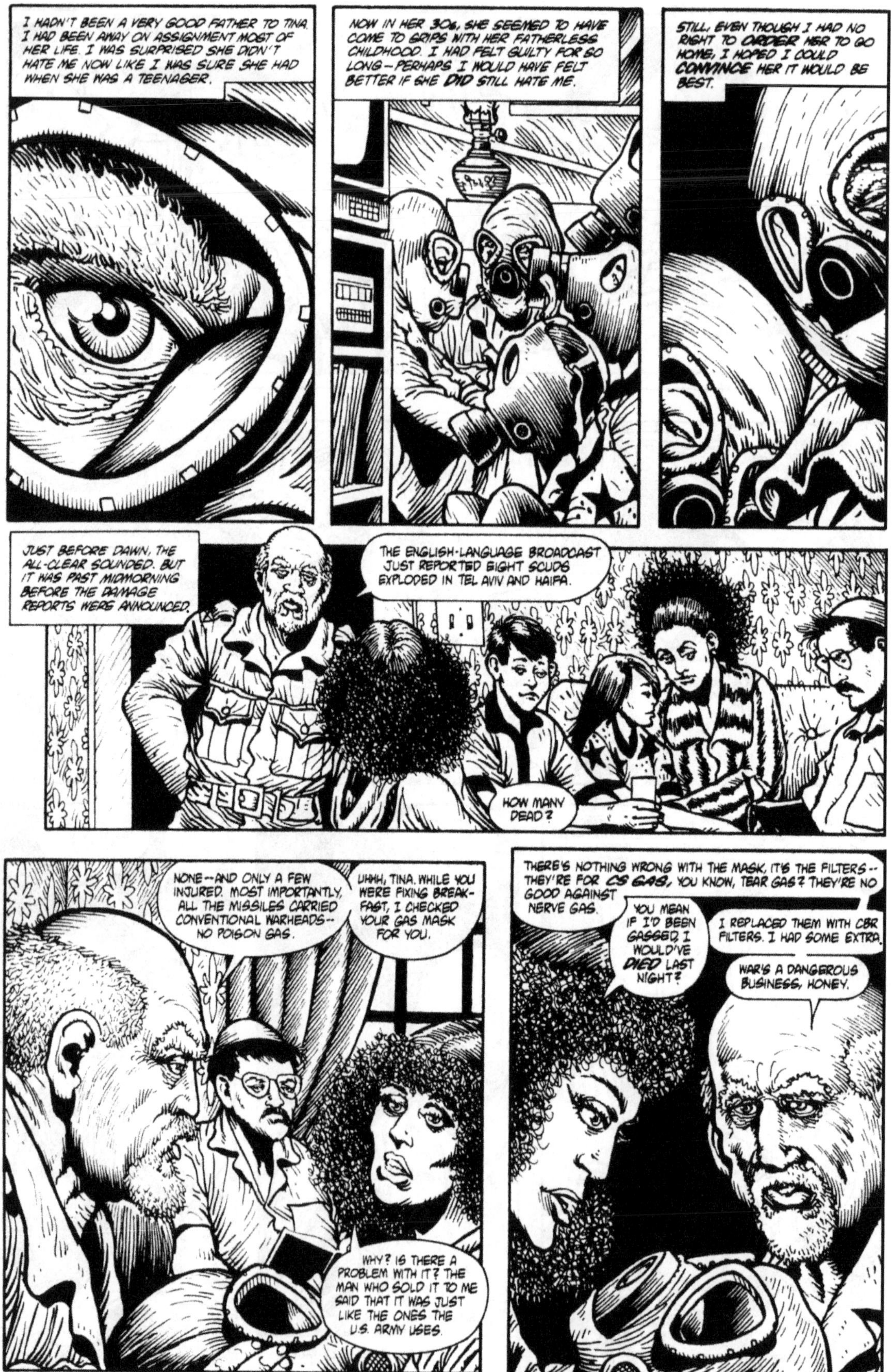
I HADN'T BEEN A VERY GOOD FATHER TO TINA. I HAD BEEN AWAY ON ASSIGNMENT MOST OF HER LIFE. I WAS SURPRISED SHE DIDN'T HATE ME NOW LIKE I WAS SURE SHE HAD WHEN SHE WAS A TEENAGER.
NOW IN HER 30s, SHE SEEMED TO HAVE COME TO GRIPS WITH HER FATHERLESS CHILDHOOD. I HAD FELT GUILTY FOR SO LONG--PERHAPS I WOULD HAVE FELT BETTER IF SHE DID STILL HATE ME.
STILL, EVEN THOUGH I HAD NO RIGHT TO ORDER HER TO GO HOME, I HOPED I COULD CONVINCE HER IT WOULD BE BEST.
JUST BEFORE DAWN, THE ALL-CLEAR SOUNDED. BUT IT WAS PAST MIDMORNING BEFORE THE DAMAGE REPORTS WERE ANNOUNCED.
THE ENGLISH-LANGUAGE BROADCAST JUST REPORTED EIGHT SCUDS EXPLODED IN TEL AVIV AND HAIFA.
HOW MANY DEAD?
NONE--AND ONLY A FEW INJURED. MOST IMPORTANTLY, ALL THE MISSILES CARRIED CONVENTIONAL WARHEADS--NO POISON GAS.
UHHH, TINA. WHILE YOU WERE FIXING BREAKFAST, I CHECKED YOUR GAS MASK FOR YOU.
WHY? IS THERE A PROBLEM WITH IT? THE MAN WHO SOLD IT TO ME SAID THAT IT WAS JUST LIKE THE ONES THE U.S. ARMY USES.
THERE'S NOTHING WRONG WITH THE MASK, IT'S THE FILTERS--THEY'RE FOR CS GAS, YOU KNOW, TEAR GAS? THEY'RE NO GOOD AGAINST NERVE GAS.
YOU MEAN IF I'D BEEN GASSED, I WOULD'VE DIED LAST NIGHT?
I REPLACED THEM WITH CBR FILTERS. I HAD SOME EXTRA.
WAR'S A DANGEROUS BUSINESS, HONEY.

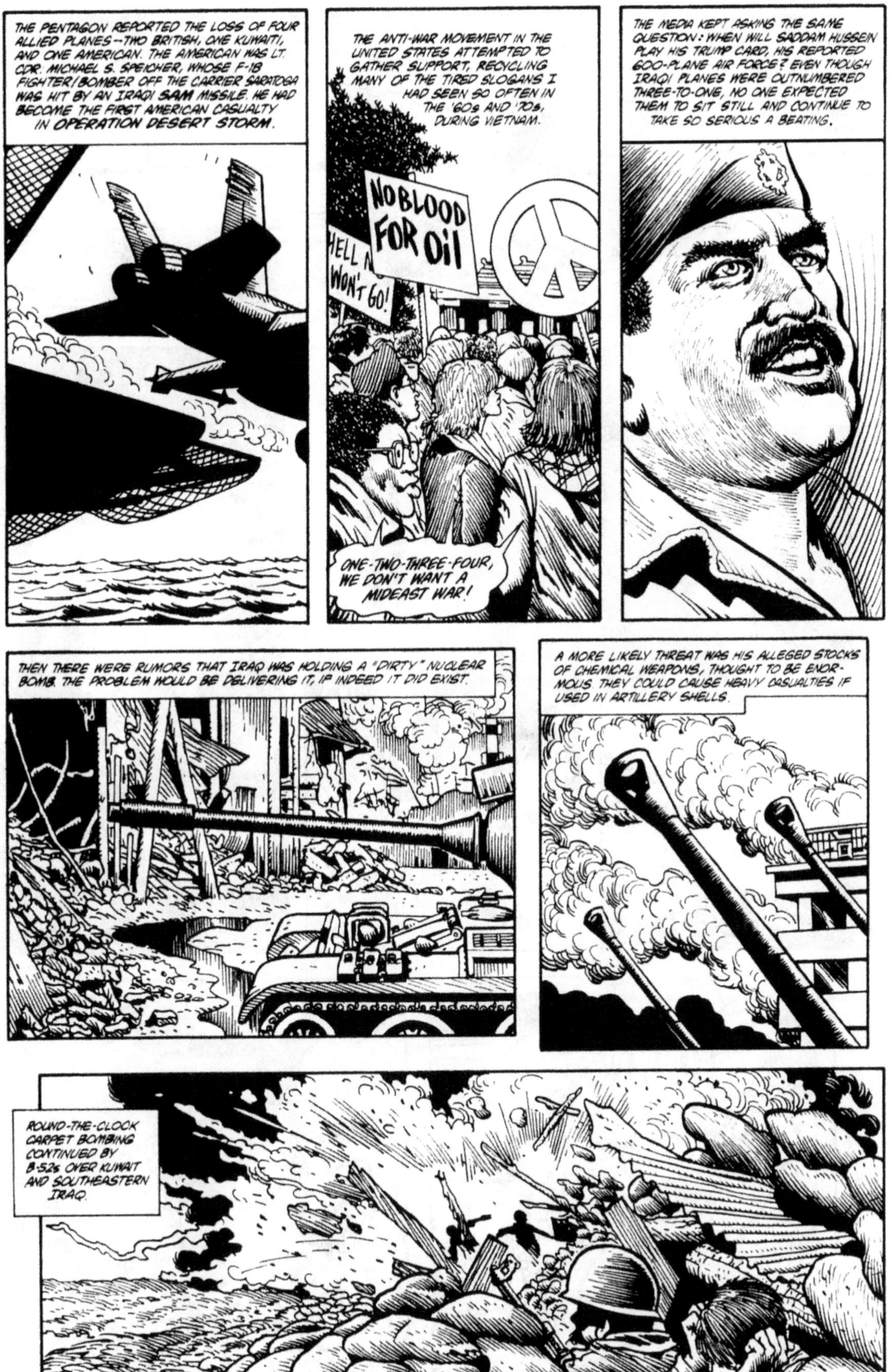
THE PENTAGON REPORTED THE LOSS OF FOUR ALLIED PLANES--TWO BRITISH, ONE KUWAITI, AND ONE AMERICAN. THE AMERICAN WAS LT. CDR. MICHAEL S. SPEICHER, WHOSE F-18 FIGHTER/BOMBER OFF THE CARRIER SARATOGA WAS HIT BY AN IRAQI SAM MISSILE. HE HAD BECOME THE FIRST AMERICAN CASUALTY IN OPERATION DESERT STORM.
THE ANTI-WAR MOVEMENT IN THE UNITED STATES ATTEMPTED TO GATHER SUPPORT, RECYCLING MANY OF THE TIRED SLOGANS I HAD SEEN SO OFTEN IN THE '60s AND '70s, DURING VIETNAM.
NO BLOOD FOR Oil
WON'T GO!
ONE-TWO-THREE-FOUR, WE DON'T WANT A MIDEAST WAR!
THE MEDIA KEPT ASKING THE SAME QUESTION: WHEN WILL SADDAM HUSSEIN PLAY HIS TRUMP CARD, HIS REPORTED 600-PLANE AIR FORCE? EVEN THOUGH IRAQI PLANES WERE OUTNUMBERED THREE-TO-ONE, NO ONE EXPECTED THEM TO SIT STILL AND CONTINUE TO TAKE SO SERIOUS A BEATING.
THEN THERE WERE RUMORS THAT IRAQ WAS HOLDING A "DIRTY" NUCLEAR BOMB. THE PROBLEM WOULD BE DELIVERING IT, IF INDEED IT DID EXIST.
A MORE LIKELY THREAT WAS HIS ALLEGED STOCKS OF CHEMICAL WEAPONS, THOUGHT TO BE ENORMOUS. THEY COULD CAUSE HEAVY CASUALTIES IF USED IN ARTILLERY SHELLS.
ROUND-THE-CLOCK CARPET BOMBING CONTINUED BY B-52s OVER KUWAIT AND SOUTHEASTERN IRAQ.

MORE RUMORS--ALLIED GROUND FORCES WERE REPORTED MOVING NORTH, TOWARD IRAQ, AND NAVAL FORCES WERE SAID TO BE PREPARING FOR AN AMPHIBIOUS INVASION OF KUWAIT CITY.

ANOTHER SIGNIFICANT EVENT ON FRIDAY WAS THE INTERCEPTION OF A SCUD-B MISSILE AIMED AT THE ALLIED STAGING AREAS NEAR DHAHRAN.

AMERICA'S MUCH-CRITICIZED, MULTI-BILLION DOLLAR SMART MISSILE, THE *PATRIOT*, ACTUALLY WORKED IN COMBAT--

U.S. ARMY

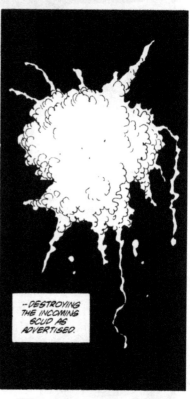

--DESTROYING THE INCOMING SCUD AS ADVERTISED.

BIG AL'S, PEORIA, ILLINOIS.

D'YA KNOW WHAT SADDAM HUSSEIN AND HIS DADDY HAVE IN COMMON?

BEER ON DRAFT

UNH-UH.

NEITHER ONE WITHDREW IN TIME !

Mötley Crüe DR FEEL GOOD

NOW THAT'S FUNNY! WHATCHA THINK, BUTCH?

7.5 ON A SCALE OF 10.

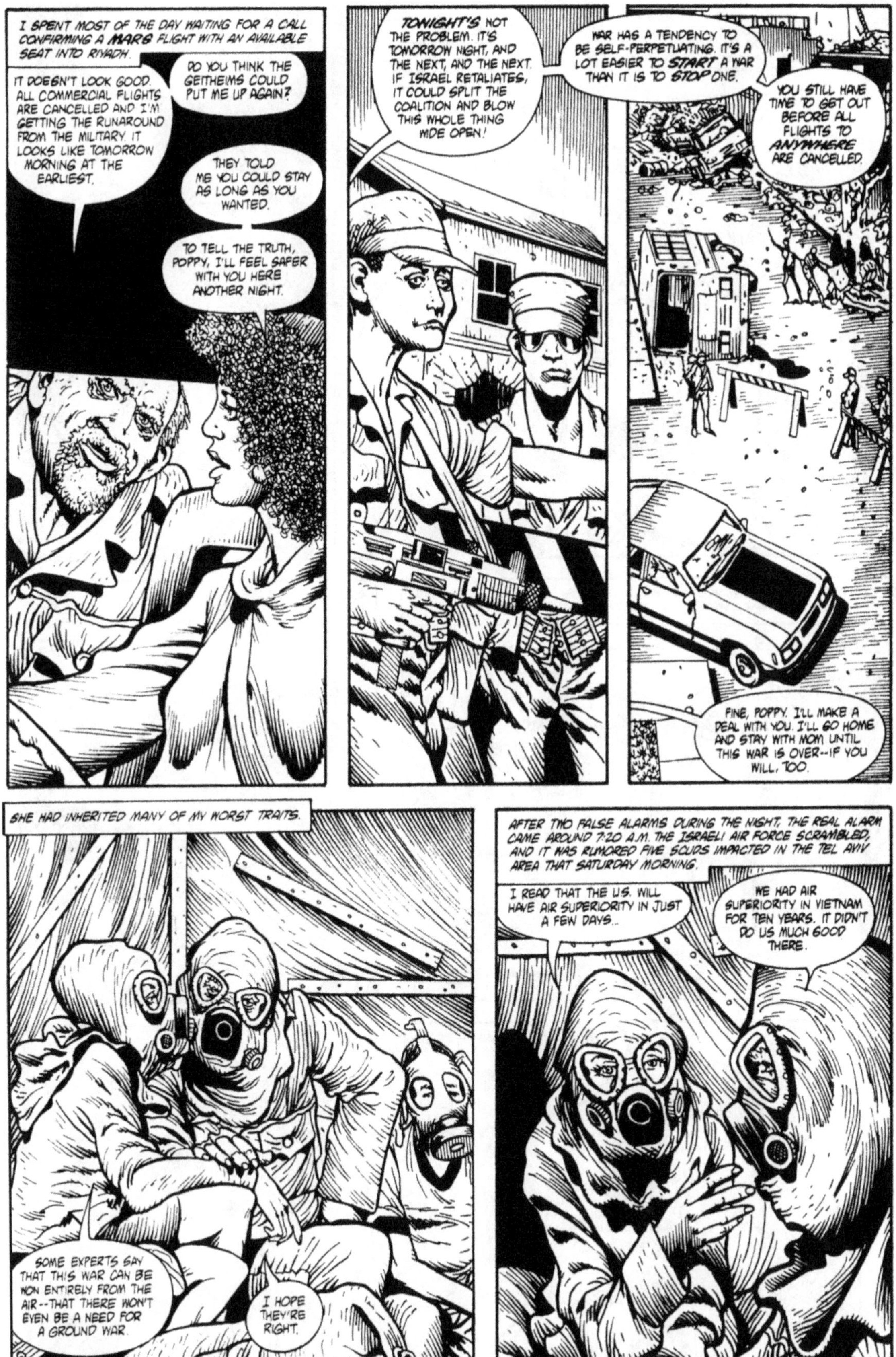
I SPENT MOST OF THE DAY WAITING FOR A CALL CONFIRMING A MARS FLIGHT WITH AN AVAILABLE SEAT INTO RIYADH.
IT DOESN'T LOOK GOOD. ALL COMMERCIAL FLIGHTS ARE CANCELLED AND I'M GETTING THE RUNAROUND FROM THE MILITARY. IT LOOKS LIKE TOMORROW MORNING AT THE EARLIEST.
DO YOU THINK THE GEITHEIMS COULD PUT ME UP AGAIN?
THEY TOLD ME YOU COULD STAY AS LONG AS YOU WANTED.
TO TELL THE TRUTH, POPPY, I'LL FEEL SAFER WITH YOU HERE ANOTHER NIGHT.
TONIGHT'S NOT THE PROBLEM. IT'S TOMORROW NIGHT, AND THE NEXT, AND THE NEXT. IF ISRAEL RETALIATES, IT COULD SPLIT THE COALITION AND BLOW THIS WHOLE THING WIDE OPEN!
WAR HAS A TENDENCY TO BE SELF-PERPETUATING. IT'S A LOT EASIER TO START A WAR THAN IT IS TO STOP ONE.
YOU STILL HAVE TIME TO GET OUT BEFORE ALL FLIGHTS TO ANYWHERE ARE CANCELLED.
FINE, POPPY. I'LL MAKE A DEAL WITH YOU. I'LL GO HOME AND STAY WITH MOM UNTIL THIS WAR IS OVER--IF YOU WILL, TOO.
SHE HAD INHERITED MANY OF MY WORST TRAITS.
SOME EXPERTS SAY THAT THIS WAR CAN BE WON ENTIRELY FROM THE AIR--THAT THERE WON'T EVEN BE A NEED FOR A GROUND WAR.
I HOPE THEY'RE RIGHT.
AFTER TWO FALSE ALARMS DURING THE NIGHT, THE REAL ALARM CAME AROUND 7:20 A.M. THE ISRAELI AIR FORCE SCRAMBLED, AND IT WAS RUMORED FIVE SCUDS IMPACTED IN THE TEL AVIV AREA THAT SATURDAY MORNING.
I READ THAT THE U.S. WILL HAVE AIR SUPERIORITY IN JUST A FEW DAYS...
WE HAD AIR SUPERIORITY IN VIETNAM FOR TEN YEARS. IT DIDN'T DO US MUCH GOOD THERE.

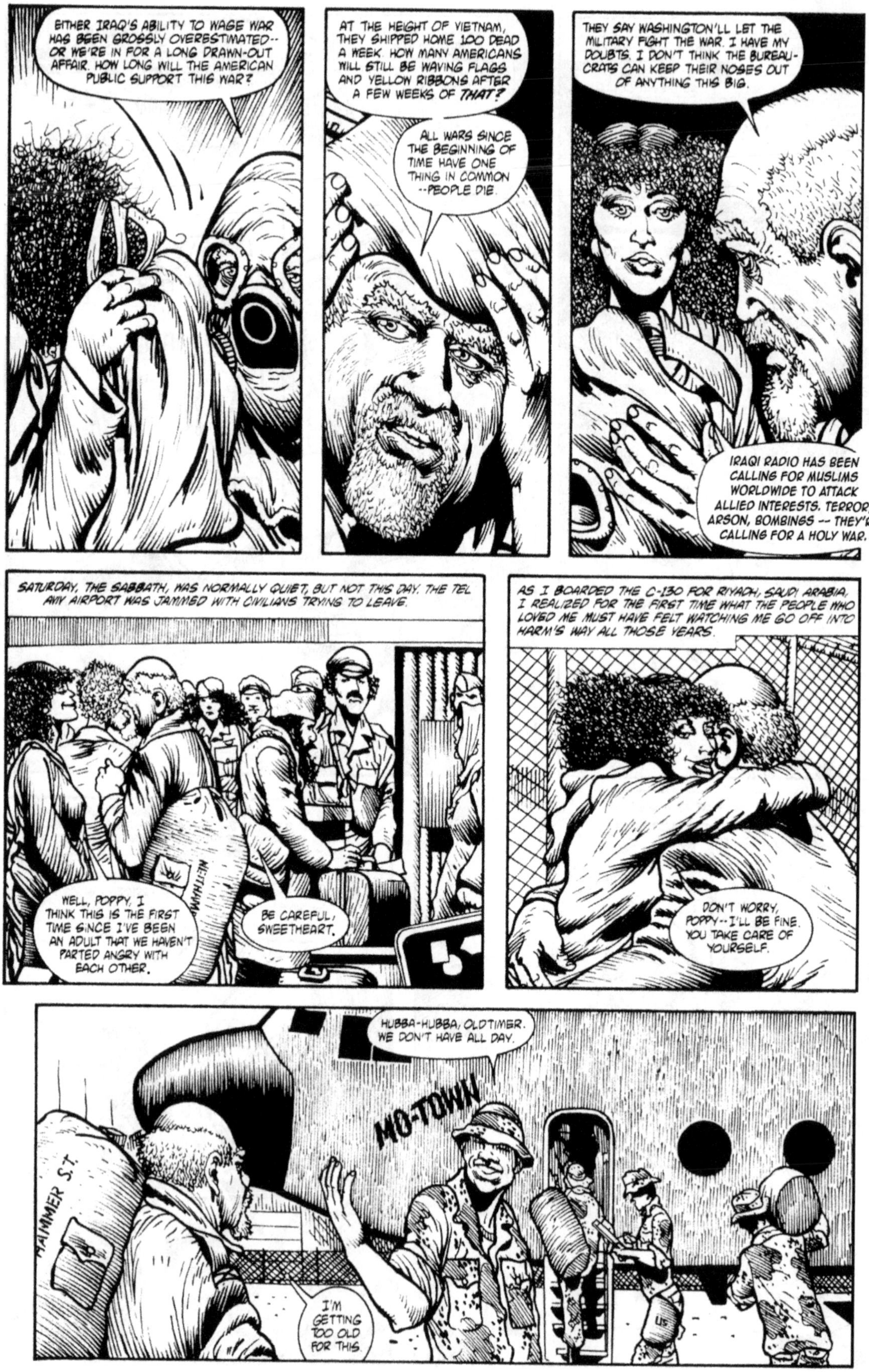
EITHER IRAQ'S ABILITY TO WAGE WAR HAS BEEN GROSSLY OVERESTIMATED-- OR WE'RE IN FOR A LONG DRAWN-OUT AFFAIR. HOW LONG WILL THE AMERICAN PUBLIC SUPPORT THIS WAR?
AT THE HEIGHT OF VIETNAM, THEY SHIPPED HOME 100 DEAD A WEEK. HOW MANY AMERICANS WILL STILL BE WAVING FLAGS AND YELLOW RIBBONS AFTER A FEW WEEKS OF THAT?
ALL WARS SINCE THE BEGINNING OF TIME HAVE ONE THING IN COMMON --PEOPLE DIE.
THEY SAY WASHINGTON'LL LET THE MILITARY FIGHT THE WAR. I HAVE MY DOUBTS. I DON'T THINK THE BUREAUCRATS CAN KEEP THEIR NOSES OUT OF ANYTHING THIS BIG.
IRAQI RADIO HAS BEEN CALLING FOR MUSLIMS WORLDWIDE TO ATTACK ALLIED INTERESTS. TERROR, ARSON, BOMBINGS -- THEY'RE CALLING FOR A HOLY WAR.
SATURDAY, THE SABBATH, WAS NORMALLY QUIET, BUT NOT THIS DAY. THE TEL AVIV AIRPORT WAS JAMMED WITH CIVILIANS TRYING TO LEAVE.
NEITHAMMER
WELL, POPPY, I THINK THIS IS THE FIRST TIME SINCE I'VE BEEN AN ADULT THAT WE HAVEN'T PARTED ANGRY WITH EACH OTHER.
BE CAREFUL, SWEETHEART.
AS I BOARDED THE C-130 FOR RIYADH, SAUDI ARABIA, I REALIZED FOR THE FIRST TIME WHAT THE PEOPLE WHO LOVED ME MUST HAVE FELT WATCHING ME GO OFF INTO HARM'S WAY ALL THOSE YEARS.
DON'T WORRY, POPPY--I'LL BE FINE. YOU TAKE CARE OF YOURSELF.
HUBBA-HUBBA, OLDTIMER. WE DON'T HAVE ALL DAY.
MO-TOWN
HAMMER S.T.
I'M GETTING TOO OLD FOR THIS.
US

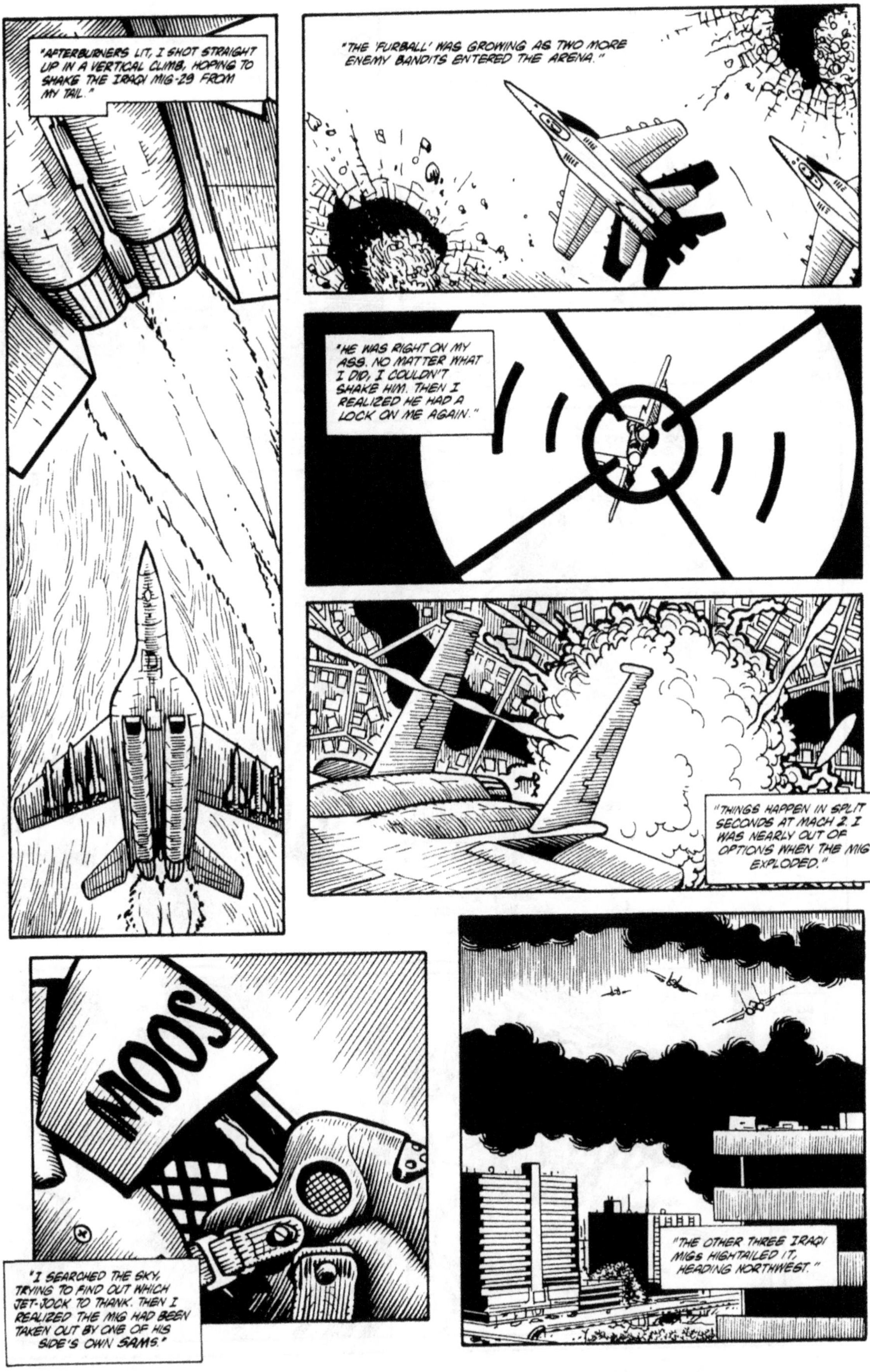
"AFTERBURNERS LIT, I SHOT STRAIGHT UP IN A VERTICAL CLIMB, HOPING TO SHAKE THE IRAQI MIG-29 FROM MY TAIL."
"THE 'FURBALL' WAS GROWING AS TWO MORE ENEMY BANDITS ENTERED THE ARENA."
"HE WAS RIGHT ON MY ASS. NO MATTER WHAT I DID, I COULDN'T SHAKE HIM. THEN I REALIZED HE HAD A LOCK ON ME AGAIN."
"THINGS HAPPEN IN SPLIT SECONDS AT MACH 2. I WAS NEARLY OUT OF OPTIONS WHEN THE MIG EXPLODED."
MOOS
"I SEARCHED THE SKY, TRYING TO FIND OUT WHICH JET-JOCK TO THANK. THEN I REALIZED THE MIG HAD BEEN TAKEN OUT BY ONE OF HIS SIDE'S OWN SAMS."
"THE OTHER THREE IRAQI MIGS HIGHTAILED IT, HEADING NORTHWEST."

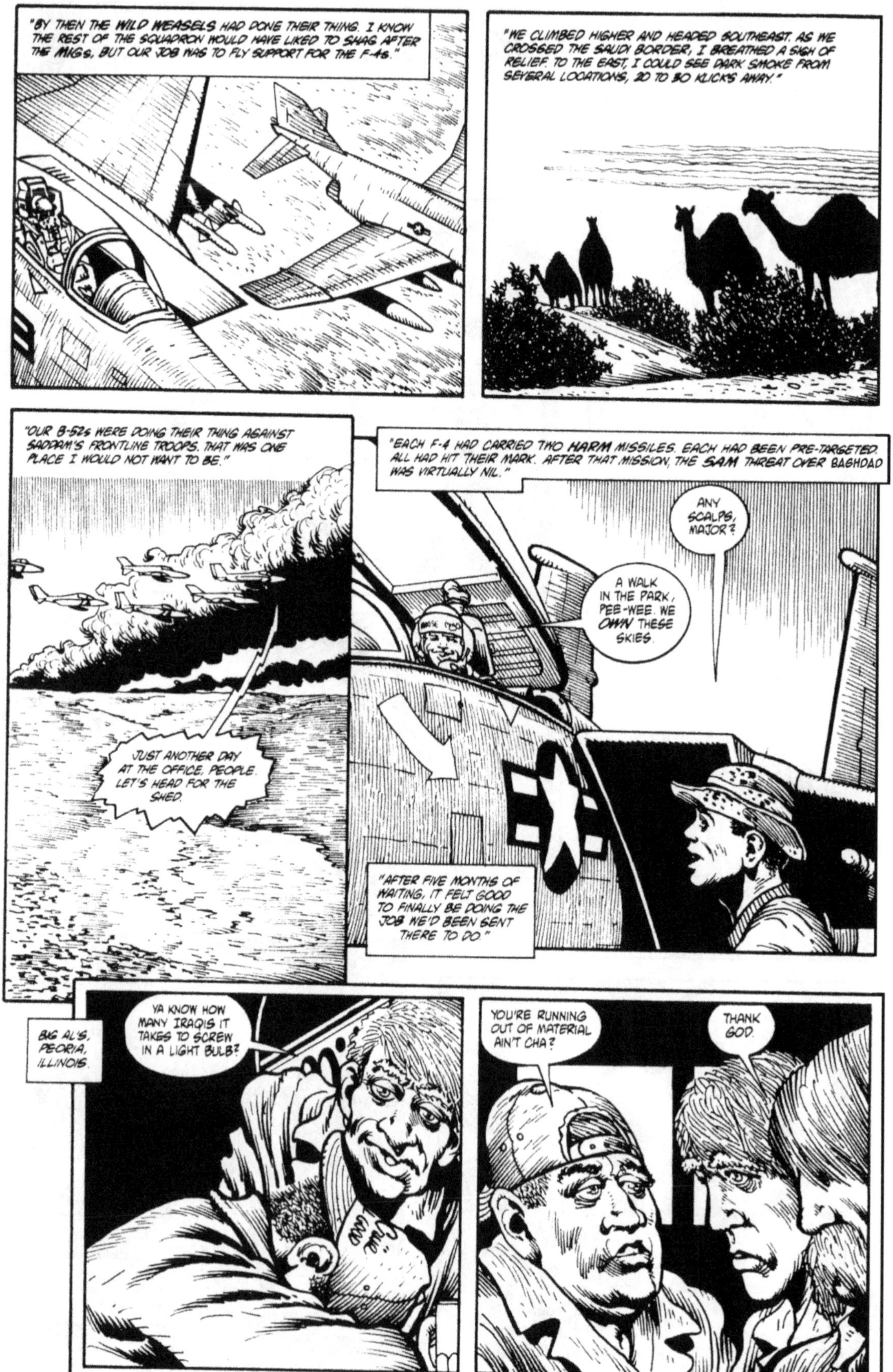
"BY THEN THE WILD WEASELS HAD DONE THEIR THING. I KNOW THE REST OF THE SQUADRON WOULD HAVE LIKED TO SHAG AFTER THE MIGs, BUT OUR JOB WAS TO FLY SUPPORT FOR THE F-4s."
"WE CLIMBED HIGHER AND HEADED SOUTHEAST. AS WE CROSSED THE SAUDI BORDER, I BREATHED A SIGH OF RELIEF. TO THE EAST, I COULD SEE DARK SMOKE FROM SEVERAL LOCATIONS, 20 TO 30 KLICKS AWAY."
"OUR B-52s WERE DOING THEIR THING AGAINST SADDAM'S FRONTLINE TROOPS. THAT WAS ONE PLACE I WOULD NOT WANT TO BE."
JUST ANOTHER DAY AT THE OFFICE, PEOPLE. LET'S HEAD FOR THE SHED.
"EACH F-4 HAD CARRIED TWO HARM MISSILES. EACH HAD BEEN PRE-TARGETED. ALL HAD HIT THEIR MARK. AFTER THAT MISSION, THE SAM THREAT OVER BAGHDAD WAS VIRTUALLY NIL."
ANY SCALPS, MAJOR?
A WALK IN THE PARK, PEE-WEE. WE OWN THESE SKIES.
"AFTER FIVE MONTHS OF WAITING, IT FELT GOOD TO FINALLY BE DOING THE JOB WE'D BEEN SENT THERE TO DO."
BIG AL'S, PEORIA, ILLINOIS.
YA KNOW HOW MANY IRAQIS IT TAKES TO SCREW IN A LIGHT BULB?
YOU'RE RUNNING OUT OF MATERIAL AIN'T CHA?
THANK GOD.

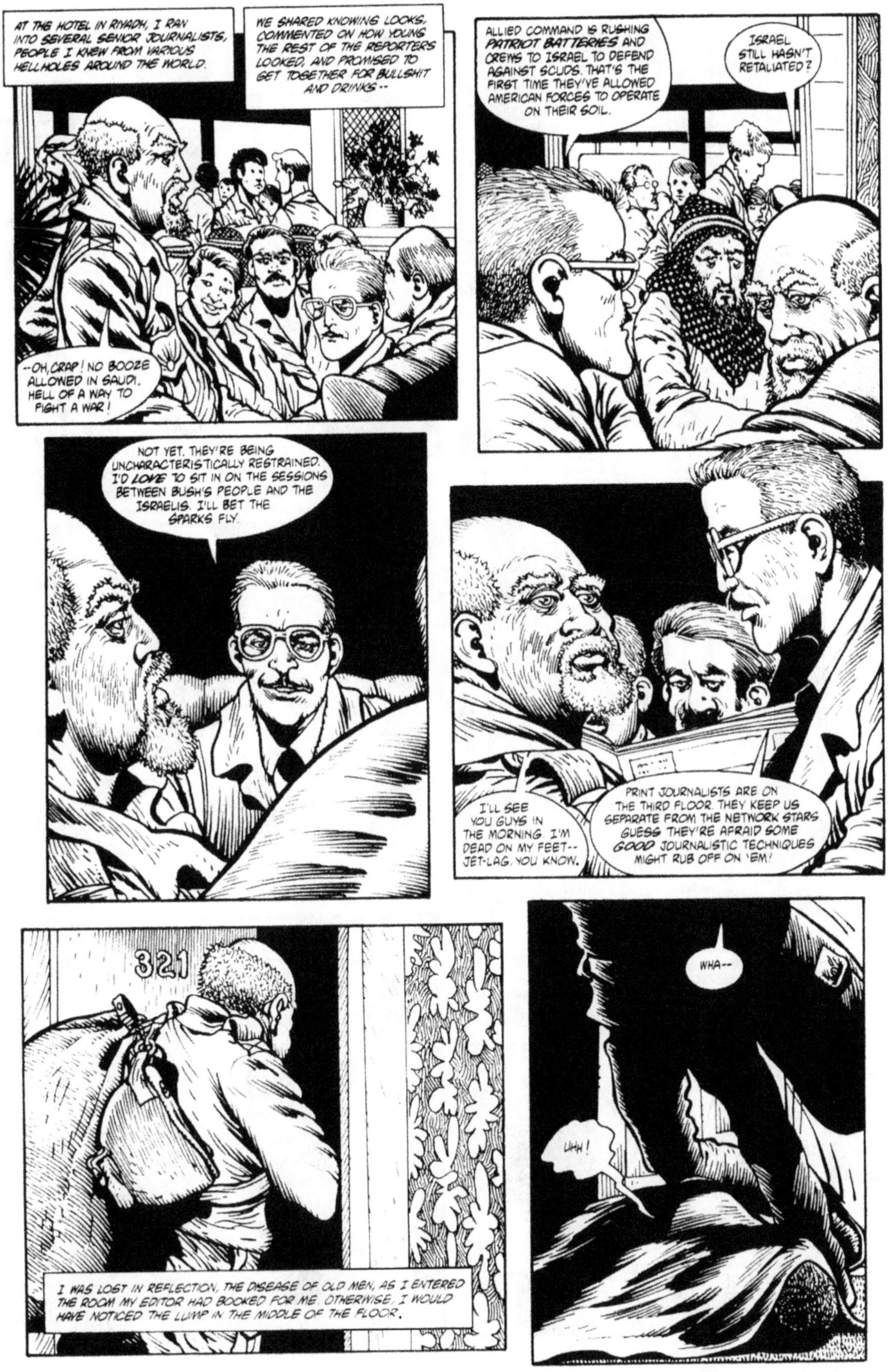

AT THE HOTEL IN RIYADH, I RAN INTO SEVERAL SENIOR JOURNALISTS, PEOPLE I KNEW FROM VARIOUS HELLHOLES AROUND THE WORLD.
WE SHARED KNOWING LOOKS, COMMENTED ON HOW YOUNG THE REST OF THE REPORTERS LOOKED, AND PROMISED TO GET TOGETHER FOR BULLSHIT AND DRINKS --
--OH, CRAP! NO BOOZE ALLOWED IN SAUDI. HELL OF A WAY TO FIGHT A WAR!
ALLIED COMMAND IS RUSHING PATRIOT BATTERIES AND CREWS TO ISRAEL TO DEFEND AGAINST SCUDS. THAT'S THE FIRST TIME THEY'VE ALLOWED AMERICAN FORCES TO OPERATE ON THEIR SOIL.
ISRAEL STILL HASN'T RETALIATED?
NOT YET. THEY'RE BEING UNCHARACTERISTICALLY RESTRAINED. I'D LOVE TO SIT IN ON THE SESSIONS BETWEEN BUSH'S PEOPLE AND THE ISRAELIS. I'LL BET THE SPARKS FLY.
I'LL SEE YOU GUYS IN THE MORNING. I'M DEAD ON MY FEET-- JET-LAG, YOU KNOW.
PRINT JOURNALISTS ARE ON THE THIRD FLOOR. THEY KEEP US SEPARATE FROM THE NETWORK STARS. GUESS THEY'RE AFRAID SOME GOOD JOURNALISTIC TECHNIQUES MIGHT RUB OFF ON 'EM!
321
I WAS LOST IN REFLECTION, THE DISEASE OF OLD MEN, AS I ENTERED THE ROOM MY EDITOR HAD BOOKED FOR ME. OTHERWISE, I WOULD HAVE NOTICED THE LUMP IN THE MIDDLE OF THE FLOOR.
WHA--
UHH!

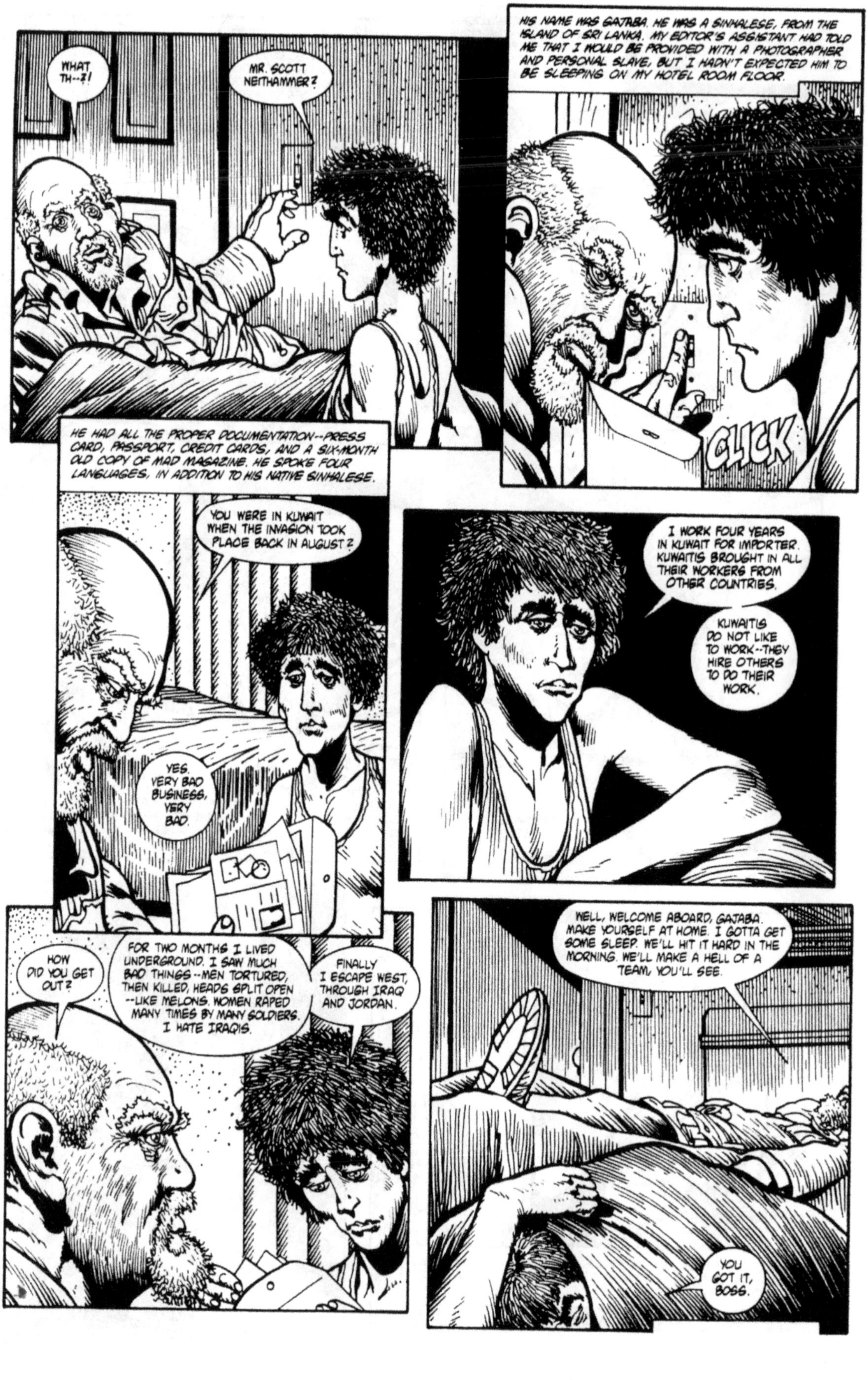
WHAT TH--?!
MR. SCOTT NEITHAMMER?
HIS NAME WAS GAJABA. HE WAS A SINHALESE, FROM THE ISLAND OF SRI LANKA. MY EDITOR'S ASSISTANT HAD TOLD ME THAT I WOULD BE PROVIDED WITH A PHOTOGRAPHER AND PERSONAL SLAVE, BUT I HADN'T EXPECTED HIM TO BE SLEEPING ON MY HOTEL ROOM FLOOR.
CLICK
HE HAD ALL THE PROPER DOCUMENTATION--PRESS CARD, PASSPORT, CREDIT CARDS, AND A SIX-MONTH OLD COPY OF MAD MAGAZINE. HE SPOKE FOUR LANGUAGES, IN ADDITION TO HIS NATIVE SINHALESE.
YOU WERE IN KUWAIT WHEN THE INVASION TOOK PLACE BACK IN AUGUST?
YES. VERY BAD BUSINESS, VERY BAD.
I WORK FOUR YEARS IN KUWAIT FOR IMPORTER. KUWAITIS BROUGHT IN ALL THEIR WORKERS FROM OTHER COUNTRIES.
KUWAITIS DO NOT LIKE TO WORK--THEY HIRE OTHERS TO DO THEIR WORK.
HOW DID YOU GET OUT?
FOR TWO MONTHS I LIVED UNDERGROUND. I SAW MUCH BAD THINGS--MEN TORTURED, THEN KILLED, HEADS SPLIT OPEN --LIKE MELONS. WOMEN RAPED MANY TIMES BY MANY SOLDIERS. I HATE IRAQIS.
FINALLY I ESCAPE WEST, THROUGH IRAQ AND JORDAN.
WELL, WELCOME ABOARD, GAJABA. MAKE YOURSELF AT HOME. I GOTTA GET SOME SLEEP. WE'LL HIT IT HARD IN THE MORNING. WE'LL MAKE A HELL OF A TEAM, YOU'LL SEE.
YOU GOT IT, BOSS.

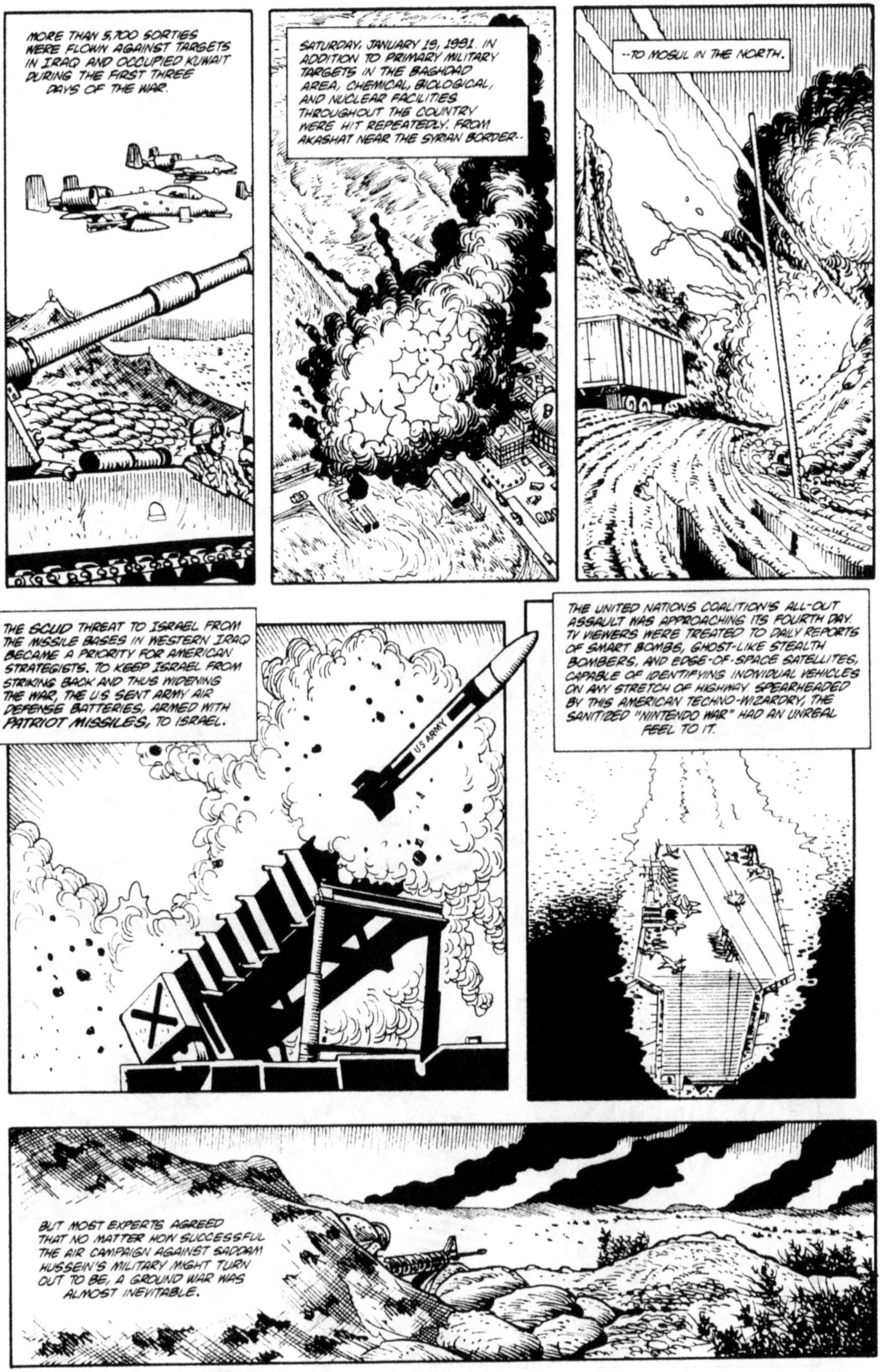
MORE THAN 5,700 SORTIES WERE FLOWN AGAINST TARGETS IN IRAQ AND OCCUPIED KUWAIT DURING THE FIRST THREE DAYS OF THE WAR.
SATURDAY, JANUARY 19, 1991. IN ADDITION TO PRIMARY MILITARY TARGETS IN THE BAGHDAD AREA, CHEMICAL, BIOLOGICAL, AND NUCLEAR FACILITIES THROUGHOUT THE COUNTRY WERE HIT REPEATEDLY. FROM AKASHAT NEAR THE SYRIAN BORDER--
--TO MOSUL IN THE NORTH.
THE SCUD THREAT TO ISRAEL FROM THE MISSILE BASES IN WESTERN IRAQ BECAME A PRIORITY FOR AMERICAN STRATEGISTS. TO KEEP ISRAEL FROM STRIKING BACK AND THUS WIDENING THE WAR, THE U.S. SENT ARMY AIR DEFENSE BATTERIES, ARMED WITH PATRIOT MISSILES, TO ISRAEL.
U.S. ARMY
THE UNITED NATIONS COALITION'S ALL-OUT ASSAULT WAS APPROACHING ITS FOURTH DAY. TV VIEWERS WERE TREATED TO DAILY REPORTS OF SMART BOMBS, GHOST-LIKE STEALTH BOMBERS, AND EDGE-OF-SPACE SATELLITES, CAPABLE OF IDENTIFYING INDIVIDUAL VEHICLES ON ANY STRETCH OF HIGHWAY. SPEARHEADED BY THIS AMERICAN TECHNO-WIZARDRY, THE SANITIZED "NINTENDO WAR" HAD AN UNREAL FEEL TO IT.
BUT MOST EXPERTS AGREED THAT NO MATTER HOW SUCCESSFUL THE AIR CAMPAIGN AGAINST SADDAM HUSSEIN'S MILITARY MIGHT TURN OUT TO BE, A GROUND WAR WAS ALMOST INEVITABLE.

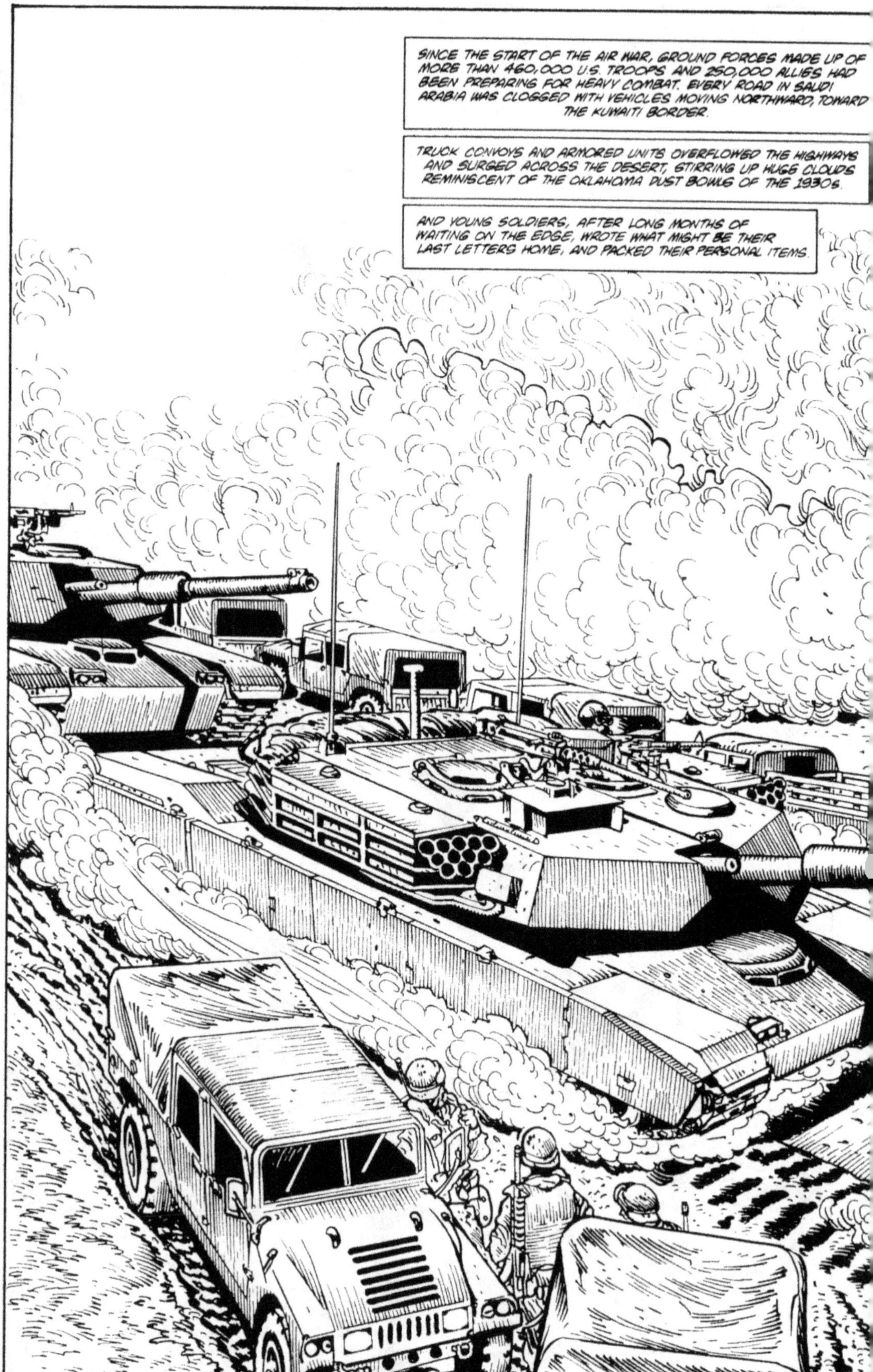
SINCE THE START OF THE AIR WAR, GROUND FORCES MADE UP OF MORE THAN 460,000 U.S. TROOPS AND 250,000 ALLIES HAD BEEN PREPARING FOR HEAVY COMBAT. EVERY ROAD IN SAUDI ARABIA WAS CLOGGED WITH VEHICLES MOVING NORTHWARD, TOWARD THE KUWAITI BORDER.
TRUCK CONVOYS AND ARMORED UNITS OVERFLOWED THE HIGHWAYS AND SURGED ACROSS THE DESERT, STIRRING UP HUGE CLOUDS REMINISCENT OF THE OKLAHOMA DUST BOWLS OF THE 1930s.
AND YOUNG SOLDIERS, AFTER LONG MONTHS OF WAITING ON THE EDGE, WROTE WHAT MIGHT BE THEIR LAST LETTERS HOME, AND PACKED THEIR PERSONAL ITEMS.

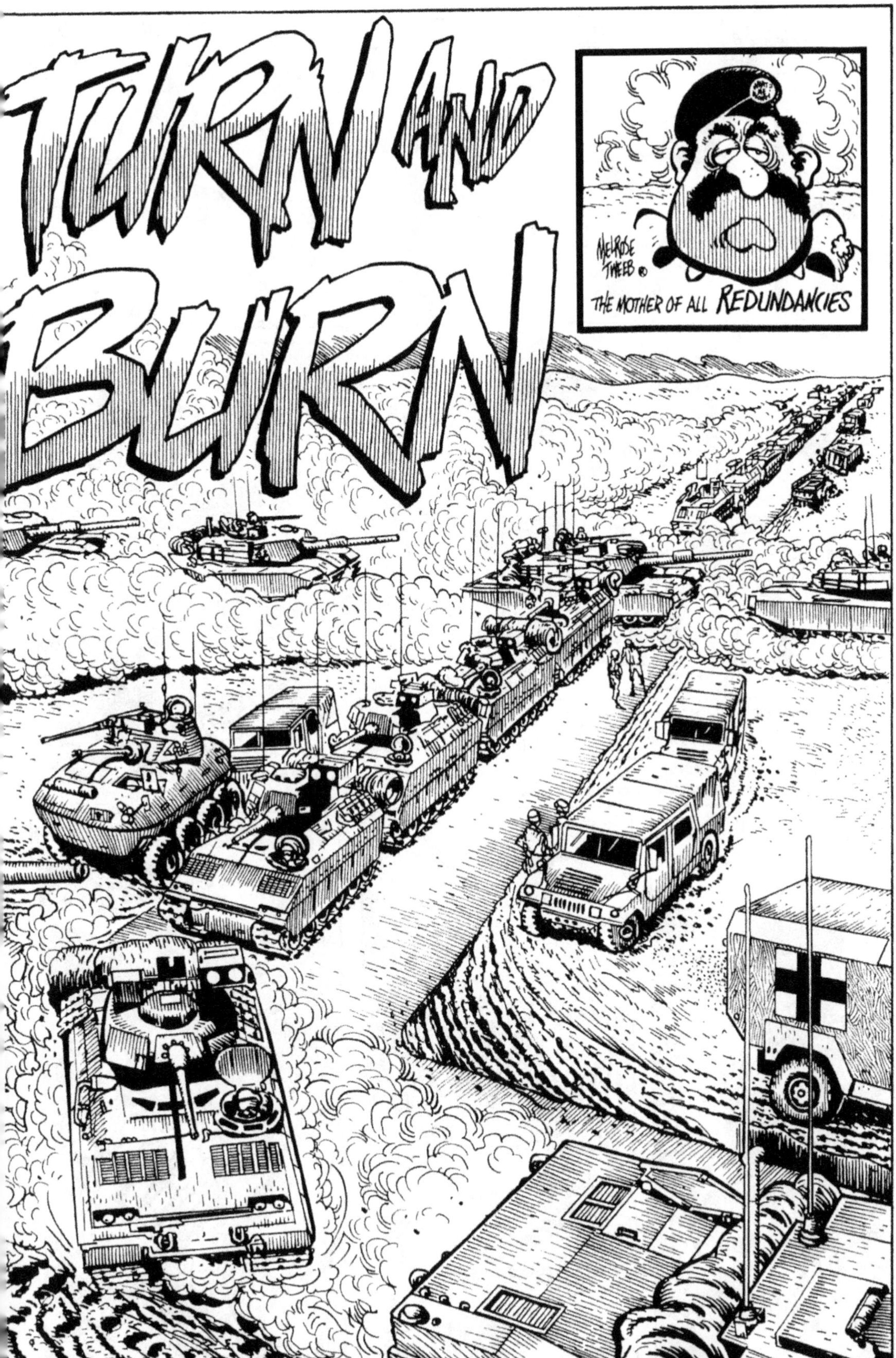
TURN AND BURN
MELROSE TWEEB ®
THE MOTHER OF ALL REDUNDANCIES

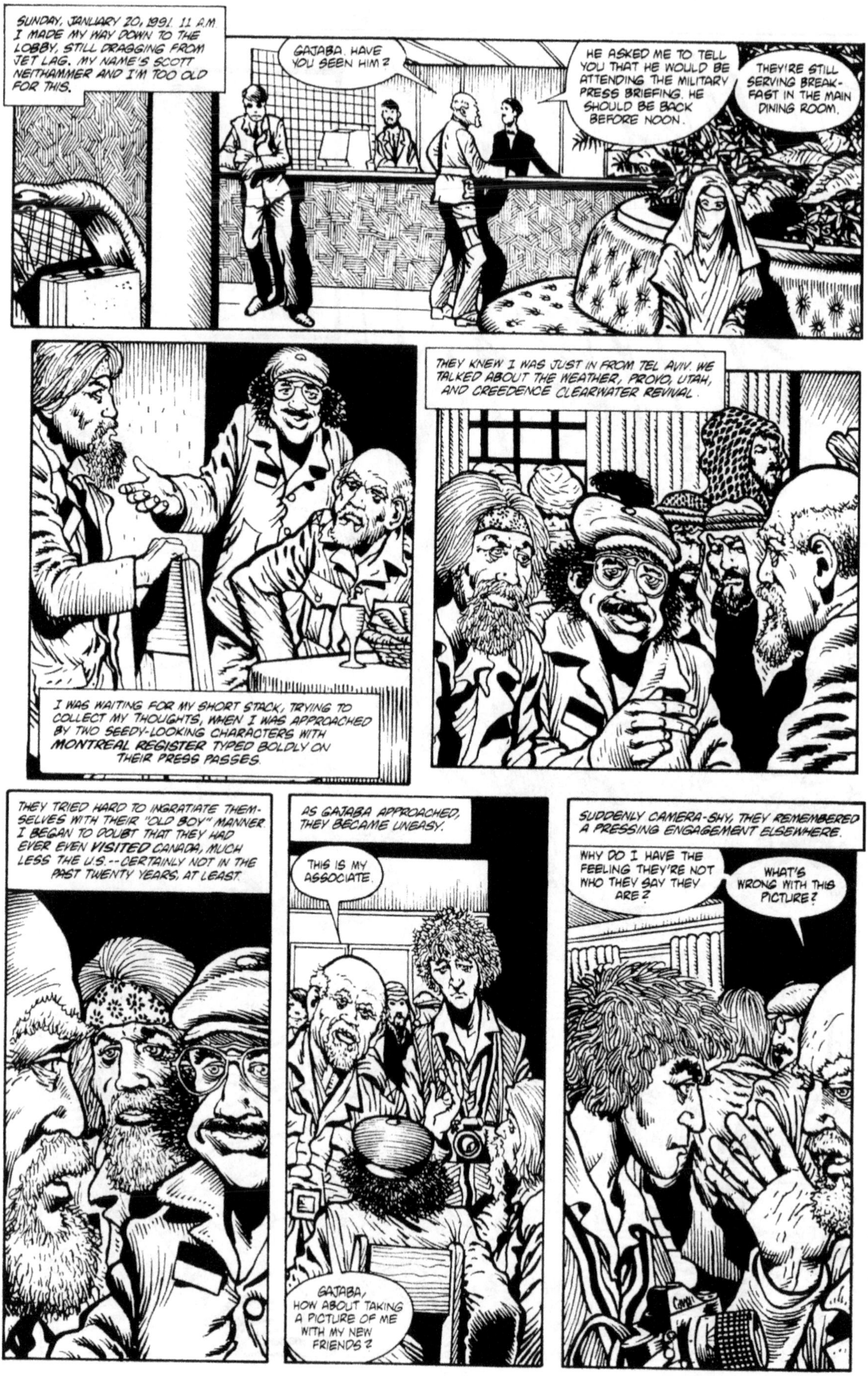
SUNDAY, JANUARY 20, 1991. 11 A.M. I MADE MY WAY DOWN TO THE LOBBY, STILL DRAGGING FROM JET LAG. MY NAME'S SCOTT NEITHAMMER AND I'M TOO OLD FOR THIS.
GAJABA. HAVE YOU SEEN HIM?
HE ASKED ME TO TELL YOU THAT HE WOULD BE ATTENDING THE MILITARY PRESS BRIEFING. HE SHOULD BE BACK BEFORE NOON.
THEY'RE STILL SERVING BREAKFAST IN THE MAIN DINING ROOM.
I WAS WAITING FOR MY SHORT STACK, TRYING TO COLLECT MY THOUGHTS, WHEN I WAS APPROACHED BY TWO SEEDY-LOOKING CHARACTERS WITH MONTREAL REGISTER TYPED BOLDLY ON THEIR PRESS PASSES.
THEY KNEW I WAS JUST IN FROM TEL AVIV. WE TALKED ABOUT THE WEATHER, PROVO, UTAH, AND CREEDENCE CLEARWATER REVIVAL.
THEY TRIED HARD TO INGRATIATE THEMSELVES WITH THEIR "OLD BOY" MANNER. I BEGAN TO DOUBT THAT THEY HAD EVER EVEN VISITED CANADA, MUCH LESS THE U.S.--CERTAINLY NOT IN THE PAST TWENTY YEARS, AT LEAST.
AS GAJABA APPROACHED, THEY BECAME UNEASY.
THIS IS MY ASSOCIATE.
GAJABA, HOW ABOUT TAKING A PICTURE OF ME WITH MY NEW FRIENDS?
SUDDENLY CAMERA-SHY, THEY REMEMBERED A PRESSING ENGAGEMENT ELSEWHERE.
WHY DO I HAVE THE FEELING THEY'RE NOT WHO THEY SAY THEY ARE?
WHAT'S WRONG WITH THIS PICTURE?

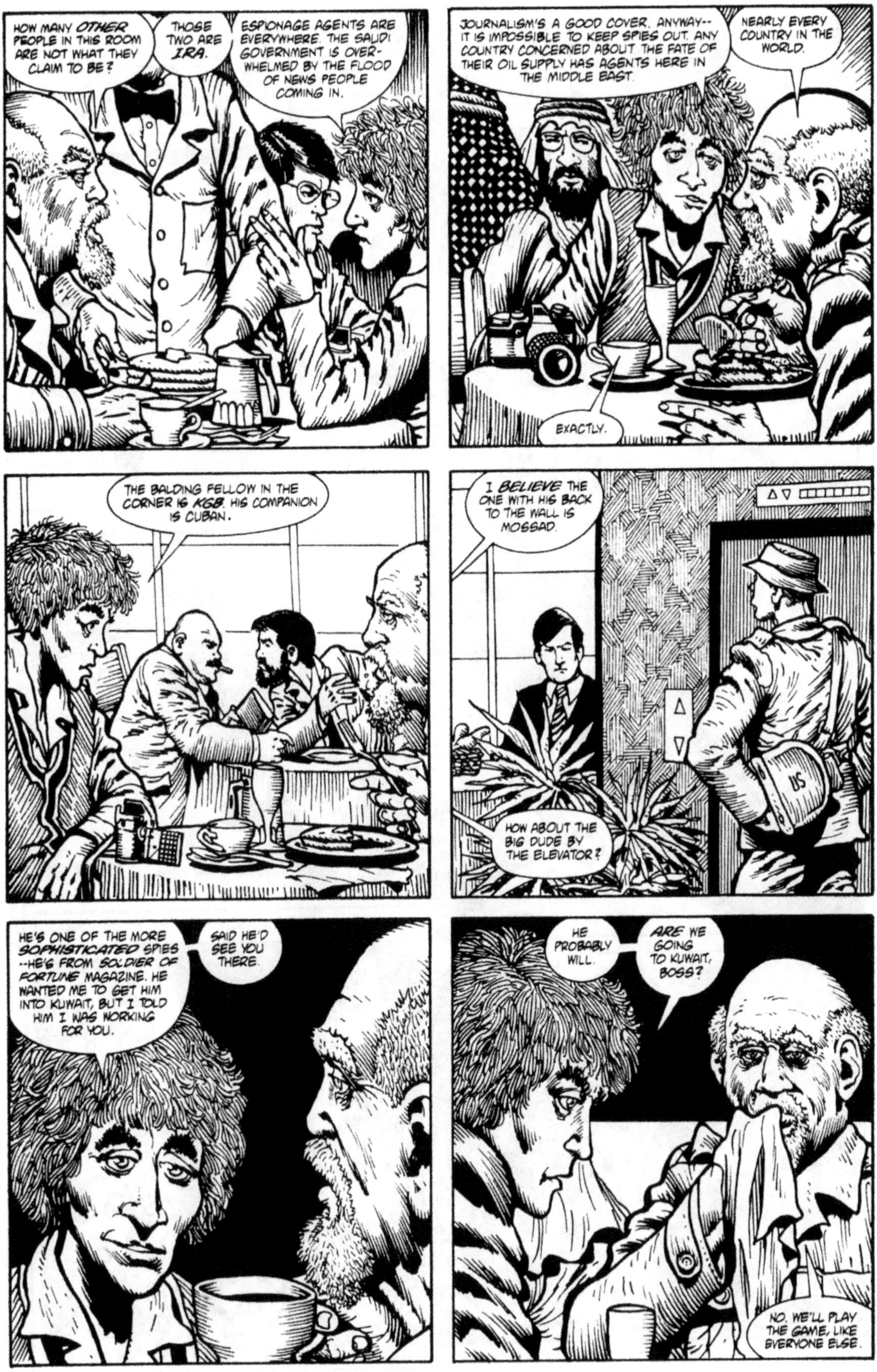
HOW MANY OTHER PEOPLE IN THIS ROOM ARE NOT WHAT THEY CLAIM TO BE?
THOSE TWO ARE IRA.
ESPIONAGE AGENTS ARE EVERYWHERE. THE SAUDI GOVERNMENT IS OVER-WHELMED BY THE FLOOD OF NEWS PEOPLE COMING IN.
JOURNALISM'S A GOOD COVER, ANYWAY-- IT IS IMPOSSIBLE TO KEEP SPIES OUT. ANY COUNTRY CONCERNED ABOUT THE FATE OF THEIR OIL SUPPLY HAS AGENTS HERE IN THE MIDDLE EAST.
NEARLY EVERY COUNTRY IN THE WORLD.
EXACTLY.
THE BALDING FELLOW IN THE CORNER IS KGB. HIS COMPANION IS CUBAN.
I BELIEVE THE ONE WITH HIS BACK TO THE WALL IS MOSSAD.
HOW ABOUT THE BIG DUDE BY THE ELEVATOR?
US
HE'S ONE OF THE MORE SOPHISTICATED SPIES --HE'S FROM SOLDIER OF FORTUNE MAGAZINE. HE WANTED ME TO GET HIM INTO KUWAIT, BUT I TOLD HIM I WAS WORKING FOR YOU.
SAID HE'D SEE YOU THERE.
HE PROBABLY WILL.
ARE WE GOING TO KUWAIT, BOSS?
NO. WE'LL PLAY THE GAME, LIKE EVERYONE ELSE.

YOU'LL HAVE TO GET USED TO BEING APPROACHED BY FOREIGN AGENTS.

THESE CENSORED, SEALED, AND DECLARED INFORMATION PACKETS ARE IDEAL FOR GETTING ILLICIT INFORMATION OUT OF THE COUNTRY.

GAJABA PRESENTED ME WITH A COMPLETE SET OF NOTES FROM THE NEWS BRIEFING, IN LONGHAND. NOT JUST THE ANSWERS, BUT THE QUESTIONS TOO, INCLUDING WHICH REPORTER ASKED WHAT, AND FOOTNOTES.

I'M IMPRESSED.

I TOOK THREE ROLLS OF FILM. THE PRINTS WILL BE READY AFTER 3:30.

I HAD A LOT TO CATCH UP ON.

BY THIS TIME, THE CONCENTRATION OF BOMBING RAIDS HAD SHIFTED FROM THE AIRFIELDS AND DEFENSE COMPLEXES IN THE BAGHDAD AREA TO THE ESTIMATED 110,000-MAN REPUBLICAN GUARD, REPORTEDLY WELL ENTRENCHED JUST INSIDE IRAQ.

WITH OVER A THOUSAND B-52 SORTIES EXPECTED BY THE END OF THE DAY, THE SOFTENING-UP HAD BEGUN.

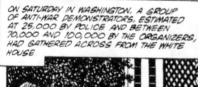

ON SATURDAY IN WASHINGTON, A GROUP OF ANTI-WAR DEMONSTRATORS, ESTIMATED AT 25,000 BY POLICE AND BETWEEN 70,000 AND 100,000 BY THE ORGANIZERS, HAD GATHERED ACROSS FROM THE WHITE HOUSE.

NOT ALL AMERICANS WERE BUSY TYING YELLOW RIBBONS.

NO MORE WAR

GET OUT OF THE

NO BLOOD FOR OIL

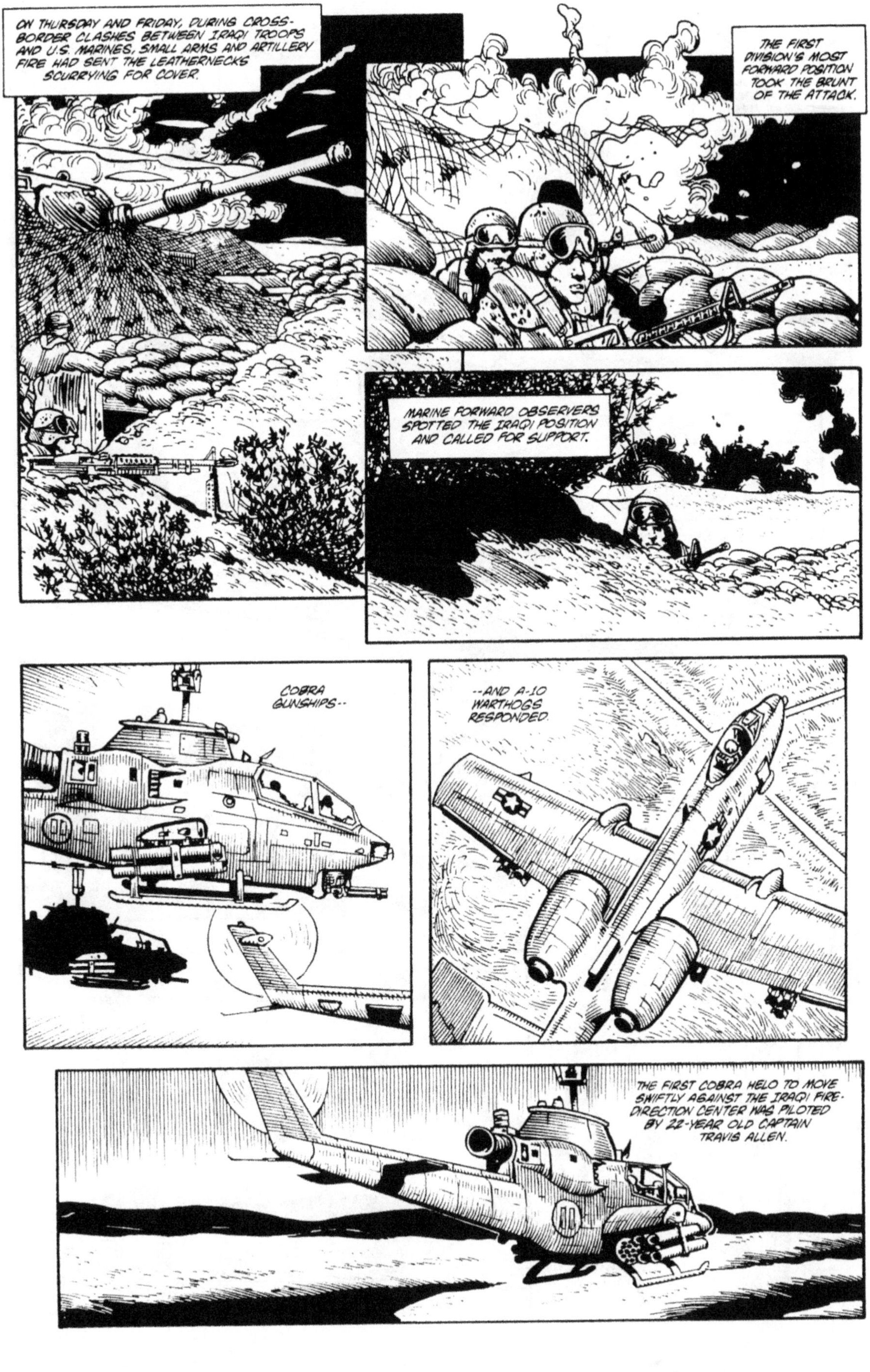
ON THURSDAY AND FRIDAY, DURING CROSS-BORDER CLASHES BETWEEN IRAQI TROOPS AND U.S. MARINES, SMALL ARMS AND ARTILLERY FIRE HAD SENT THE LEATHERNECKS SCURRYING FOR COVER.
THE FIRST DIVISION'S MOST FORWARD POSITION TOOK THE BRUNT OF THE ATTACK.
MARINE FORWARD OBSERVERS SPOTTED THE IRAQI POSITION AND CALLED FOR SUPPORT.
COBRA GUNSHIPS--
--AND A-10 WARTHOGS RESPONDED.
THE FIRST COBRA HELO TO MOVE SWIFTLY AGAINST THE IRAQI FIRE-DIRECTION CENTER WAS PILOTED BY 22-YEAR OLD CAPTAIN TRAVIS ALLEN.

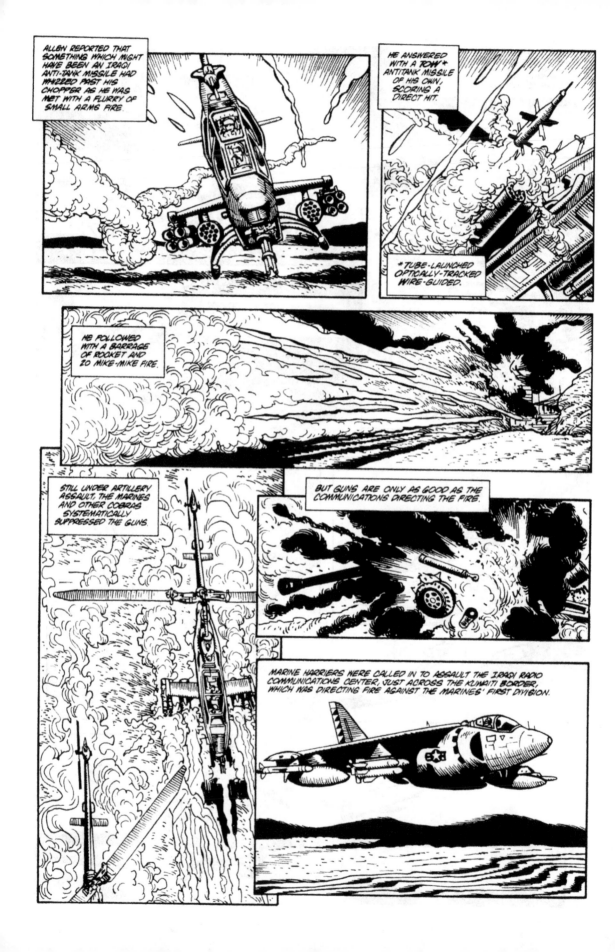

ALLEN REPORTED THAT SOMETHING WHICH MIGHT HAVE BEEN AN IRAQI ANTI-TANK MISSILE HAD WHIZZED PAST HIS CHOPPER AS HE WAS MET WITH A FLURRY OF SMALL ARMS FIRE.

HE ANSWERED WITH A TOW* ANTITANK MISSILE OF HIS OWN, SCORING A DIRECT HIT.

*TUBE-LAUNCHED OPTICALLY-TRACKED WIRE-GUIDED.

HE FOLLOWED WITH A BARRAGE OF ROCKET AND 20 MIKE-MIKE FIRE.

STILL UNDER ARTILLERY ASSAULT, THE MARINES AND OTHER COBRAS SYSTEMATICALLY SUPPRESSED THE GUNS.

BUT GUNS ARE ONLY AS GOOD AS THE COMMUNICATIONS DIRECTING THE FIRE.

MARINE HARRIERS WERE CALLED IN TO ASSAULT THE IRAQI RADIO COMMUNICATIONS CENTER, JUST ACROSS THE KUWAITI BORDER, WHICH WAS DIRECTING FIRE AGAINST THE MARINES' FIRST DIVISION.

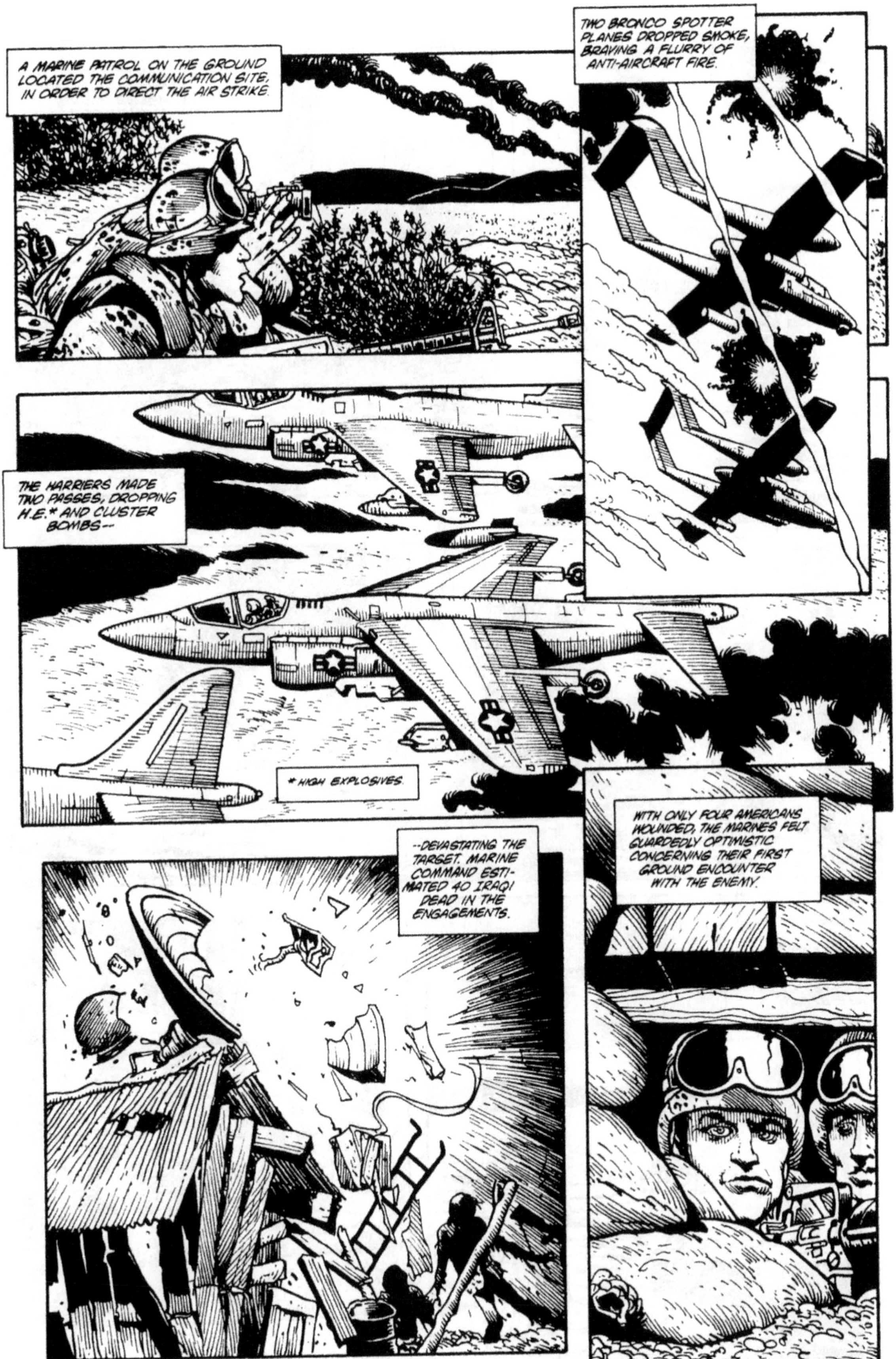
A MARINE PATROL ON THE GROUND LOCATED THE COMMUNICATION SITE, IN ORDER TO DIRECT THE AIR STRIKE.
TWO BRONCO SPOTTER PLANES DROPPED SMOKE, BRAVING A FLURRY OF ANTI-AIRCRAFT FIRE.
THE HARRIERS MADE TWO PASSES, DROPPING H.E.* AND CLUSTER BOMBS--
* HIGH EXPLOSIVES.
--DEVASTATING THE TARGET. MARINE COMMAND ESTIMATED 40 IRAQI DEAD IN THE ENGAGEMENTS.
WITH ONLY FOUR AMERICANS WOUNDED, THE MARINES FELT GUARDEDLY OPTIMISTIC CONCERNING THEIR FIRST GROUND ENCOUNTER WITH THE ENEMY.

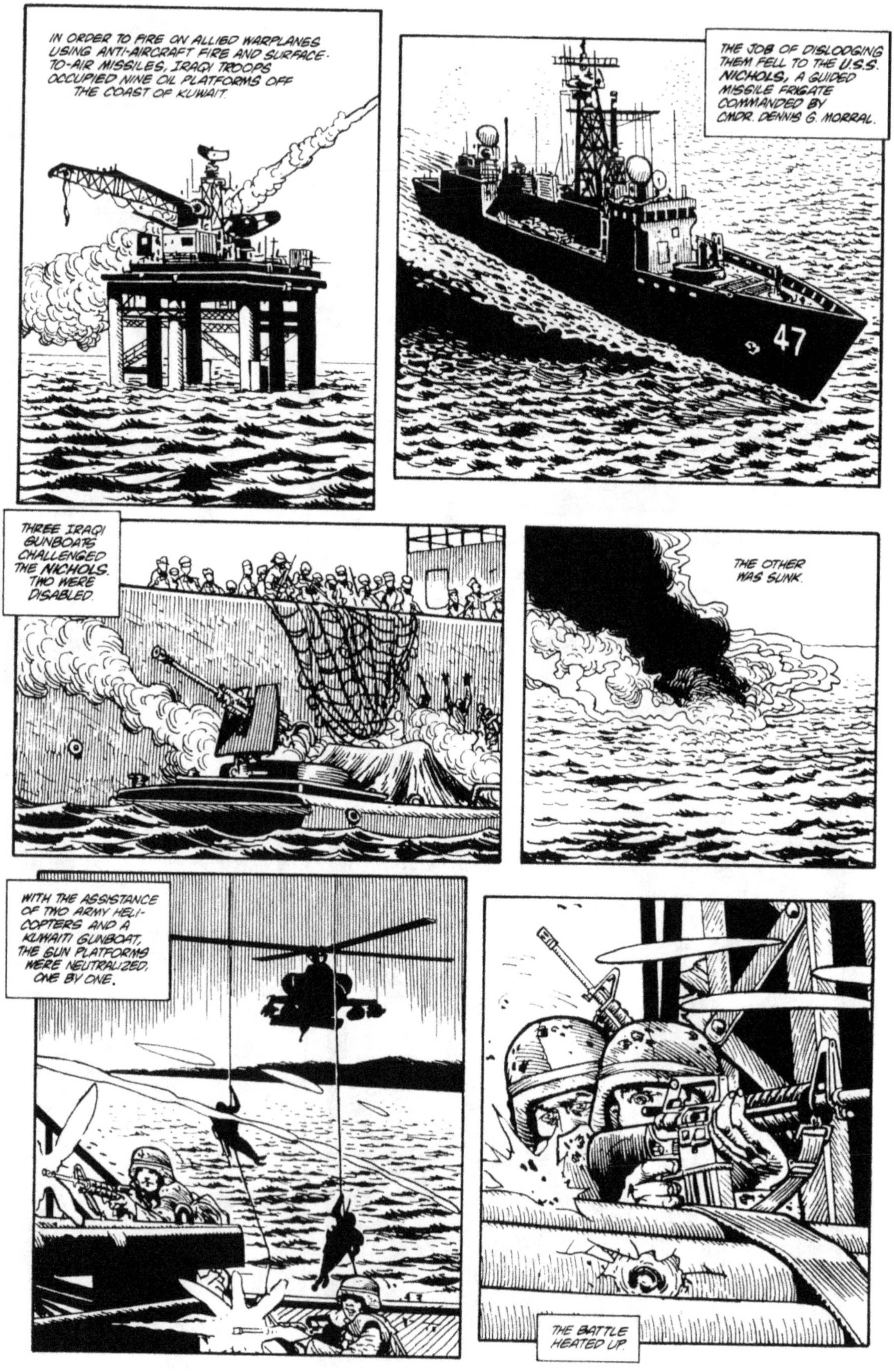
IN ORDER TO FIRE ON ALLIED WARPLANES USING ANTI-AIRCRAFT FIRE AND SURFACE-TO-AIR MISSILES, IRAQI TROOPS OCCUPIED NINE OIL PLATFORMS OFF THE COAST OF KUWAIT.
THE JOB OF DISLODGING THEM FELL TO THE U.S.S. NICHOLS, A GUIDED MISSILE FRIGATE COMMANDED BY CMDR. DENNIS G. MORRAL.
47
THREE IRAQI GUNBOATS CHALLENGED THE NICHOLS. TWO WERE DISABLED.
THE OTHER WAS SUNK.
WITH THE ASSISTANCE OF TWO ARMY HELI-COPTERS AND A KUWAITI GUNBOAT, THE GUN PLATFORMS WERE NEUTRALIZED, ONE BY ONE.
THE BATTLE HEATED UP.

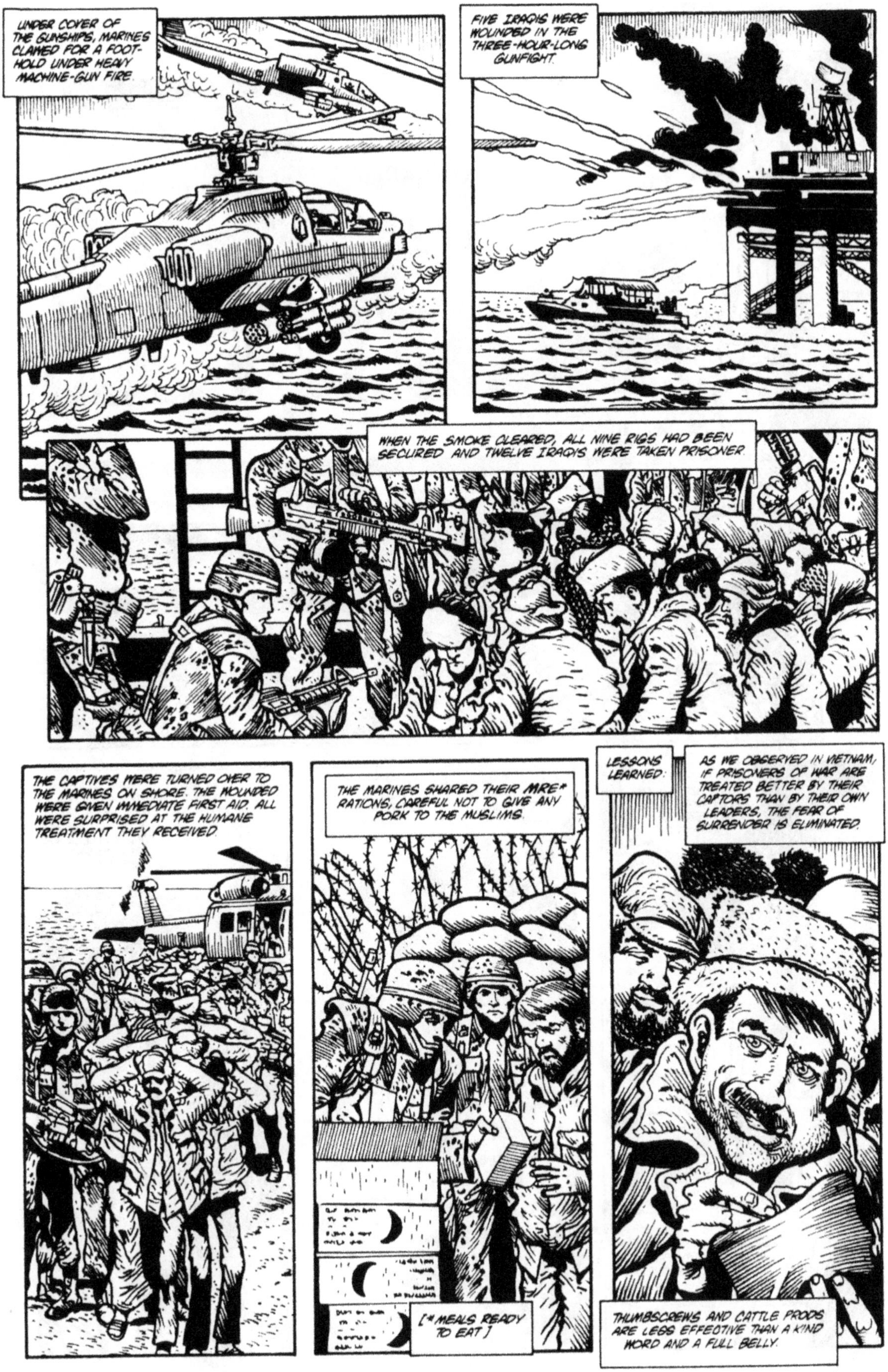
UNDER COVER OF THE GUNSHIPS, MARINES CLAWED FOR A FOOT-HOLD UNDER HEAVY MACHINE-GUN FIRE.
FIVE IRAQIS WERE WOUNDED IN THE THREE-HOUR-LONG GUNFIGHT.
WHEN THE SMOKE CLEARED, ALL NINE RIGS HAD BEEN SECURED AND TWELVE IRAQIS WERE TAKEN PRISONER.
THE CAPTIVES WERE TURNED OVER TO THE MARINES ON SHORE. THE WOUNDED WERE GIVEN IMMEDIATE FIRST AID. ALL WERE SURPRISED AT THE HUMANE TREATMENT THEY RECEIVED.
THE MARINES SHARED THEIR MRE* RATIONS, CAREFUL NOT TO GIVE ANY PORK TO THE MUSLIMS.
[* MEALS READY TO EAT]
LESSONS LEARNED:
AS WE OBSERVED IN VIETNAM, IF PRISONERS OF WAR ARE TREATED BETTER BY THEIR CAPTORS THAN BY THEIR OWN LEADERS, THE FEAR OF SURRENDER IS ELIMINATED.
THUMBSCREWS AND CATTLE PRODS ARE LESS EFFECTIVE THAN A KIND WORD AND A FULL BELLY.

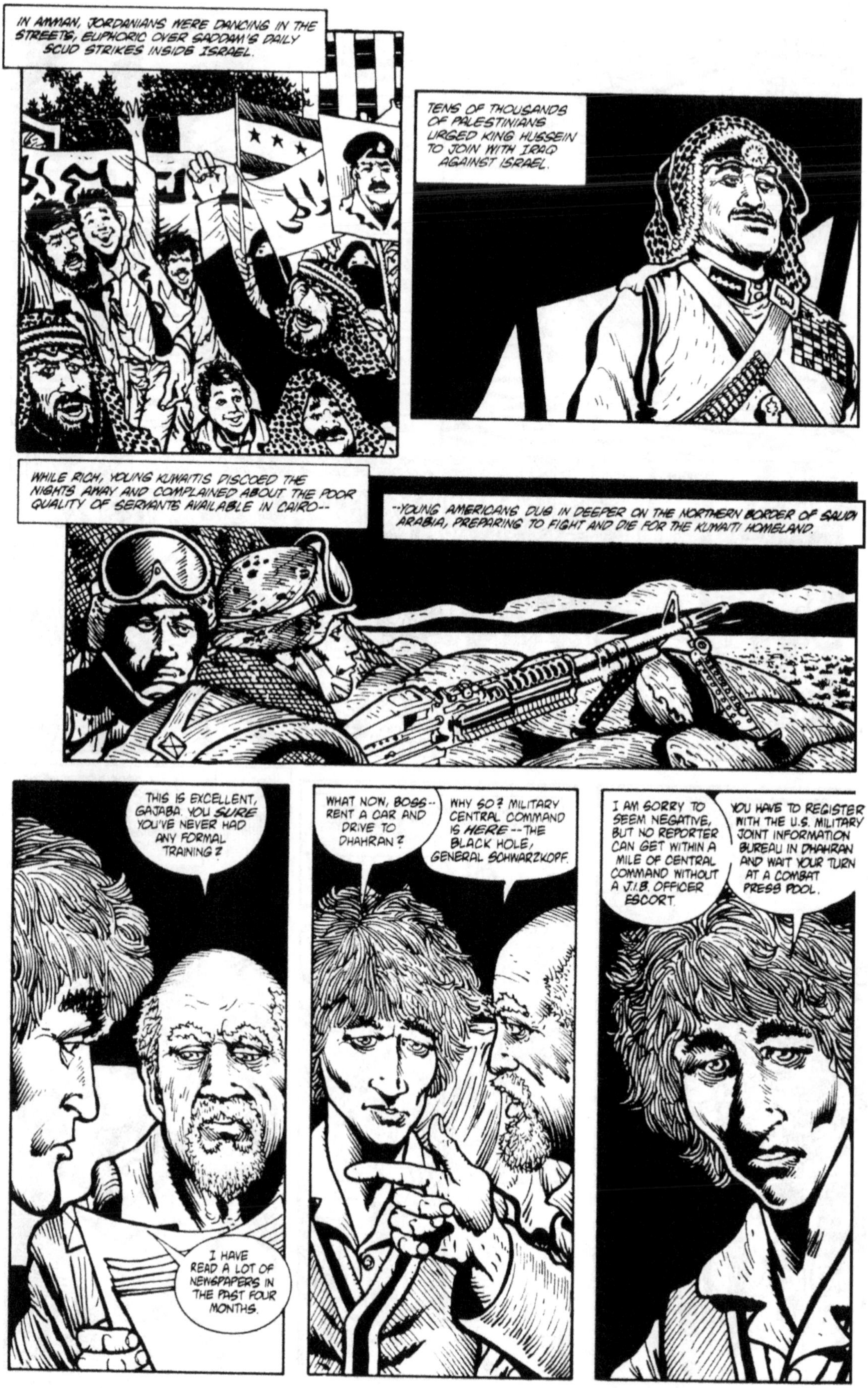
IN AMMAN, JORDANIANS WERE DANCING IN THE STREETS, EUPHORIC OVER SADDAM'S DAILY SCUD STRIKES INSIDE ISRAEL.
TENS OF THOUSANDS OF PALESTINIANS URGED KING HUSSEIN TO JOIN WITH IRAQ AGAINST ISRAEL.
WHILE RICH, YOUNG KUWAITIS DISCOED THE NIGHTS AWAY AND COMPLAINED ABOUT THE POOR QUALITY OF SERVANTS AVAILABLE IN CAIRO--
--YOUNG AMERICANS DUG IN DEEPER ON THE NORTHERN BORDER OF SAUDI ARABIA, PREPARING TO FIGHT AND DIE FOR THE KUWAITI HOMELAND.
THIS IS EXCELLENT, GAJABA. YOU SURE YOU'VE NEVER HAD ANY FORMAL TRAINING?
I HAVE READ A LOT OF NEWSPAPERS IN THE PAST FOUR MONTHS.
WHAT NOW, BOSS-- RENT A CAR AND DRIVE TO DHAHRAN?
WHY SO? MILITARY CENTRAL COMMAND IS HERE --THE BLACK HOLE, GENERAL SCHWARZKOPF.
I AM SORRY TO SEEM NEGATIVE, BUT NO REPORTER CAN GET WITHIN A MILE OF CENTRAL COMMAND WITHOUT A J.I.B. OFFICER ESCORT.
YOU HAVE TO REGISTER WITH THE U.S. MILITARY JOINT INFORMATION BUREAU IN DHAHRAN AND WAIT YOUR TURN AT A COMBAT PRESS POOL.

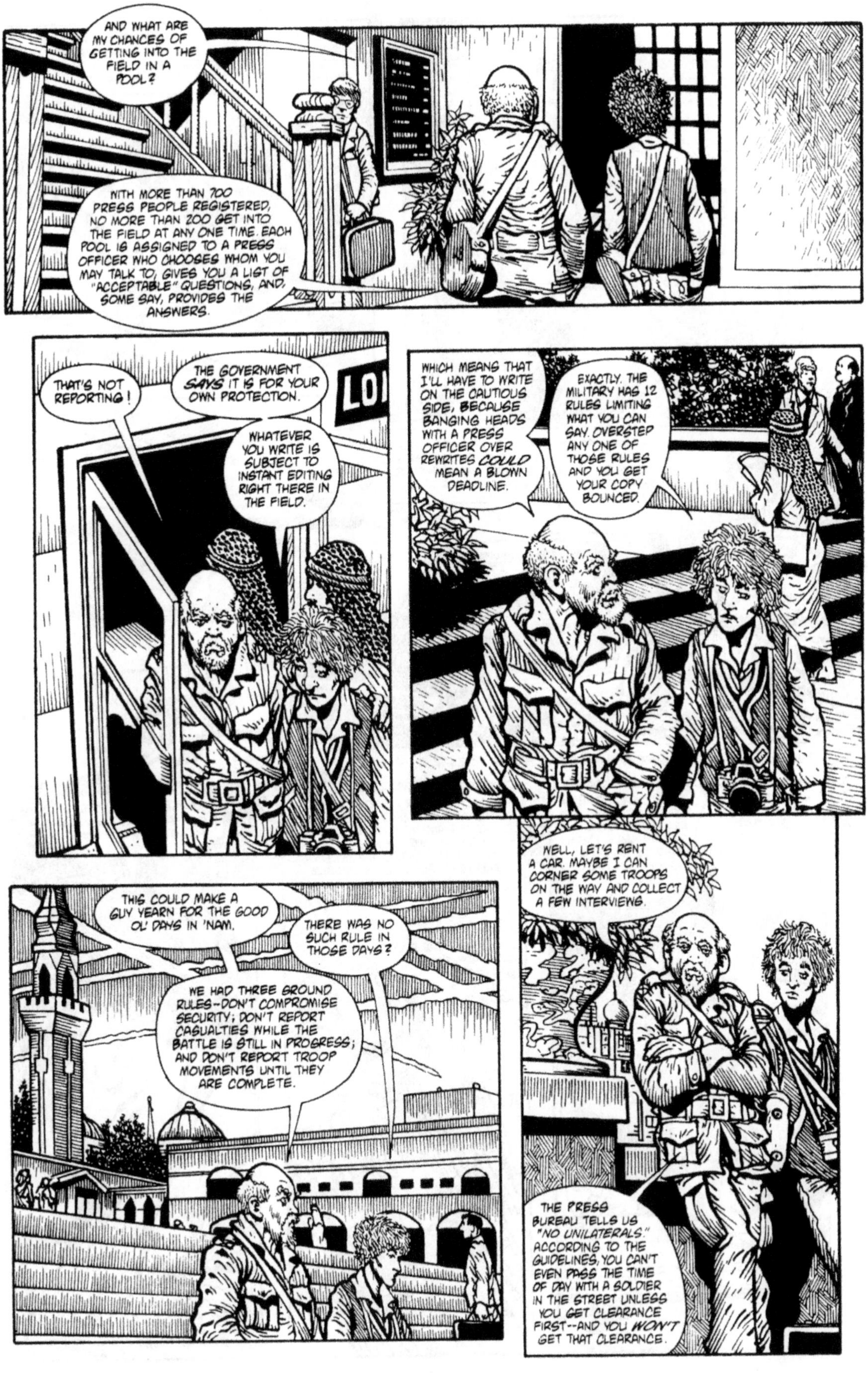
AND WHAT ARE MY CHANCES OF GETTING INTO THE FIELD IN A POOL?
WITH MORE THAN 700 PRESS PEOPLE REGISTERED, NO MORE THAN 200 GET INTO THE FIELD AT ANY ONE TIME. EACH POOL IS ASSIGNED TO A PRESS OFFICER WHO CHOOSES WHOM YOU MAY TALK TO, GIVES YOU A LIST OF "ACCEPTABLE" QUESTIONS, AND, SOME SAY, PROVIDES THE ANSWERS.
THAT'S NOT REPORTING!
THE GOVERNMENT *SAYS* IT IS FOR YOUR OWN PROTECTION.
WHATEVER YOU WRITE IS SUBJECT TO INSTANT EDITING RIGHT THERE IN THE FIELD.
WHICH MEANS THAT I'LL HAVE TO WRITE ON THE CAUTIOUS SIDE, BECAUSE BANGING HEADS WITH A PRESS OFFICER OVER REWRITES *COULD* MEAN A BLOWN DEADLINE.
EXACTLY. THE MILITARY HAS 12 RULES LIMITING WHAT YOU CAN SAY. OVERSTEP ANY ONE OF THOSE RULES AND YOU GET YOUR COPY BOUNCED.
THIS COULD MAKE A GUY YEARN FOR THE GOOD OL' DAYS IN 'NAM.
THERE WAS NO SUCH RULE IN THOSE DAYS?
WE HAD THREE GROUND RULES--DON'T COMPROMISE SECURITY; DON'T REPORT CASUALTIES WHILE THE BATTLE IS STILL IN PROGRESS; AND DON'T REPORT TROOP MOVEMENTS UNTIL THEY ARE COMPLETE.
WELL, LET'S RENT A CAR. MAYBE I CAN CORNER SOME TROOPS ON THE WAY AND COLLECT A FEW INTERVIEWS.
THE PRESS BUREAU TELLS US *"NO UNILATERALS."* ACCORDING TO THE GUIDELINES, YOU CAN'T EVEN PASS THE TIME OF DAY WITH A SOLDIER IN THE STREET UNLESS YOU GET CLEARANCE FIRST--AND YOU *WON'T* GET THAT CLEARANCE.

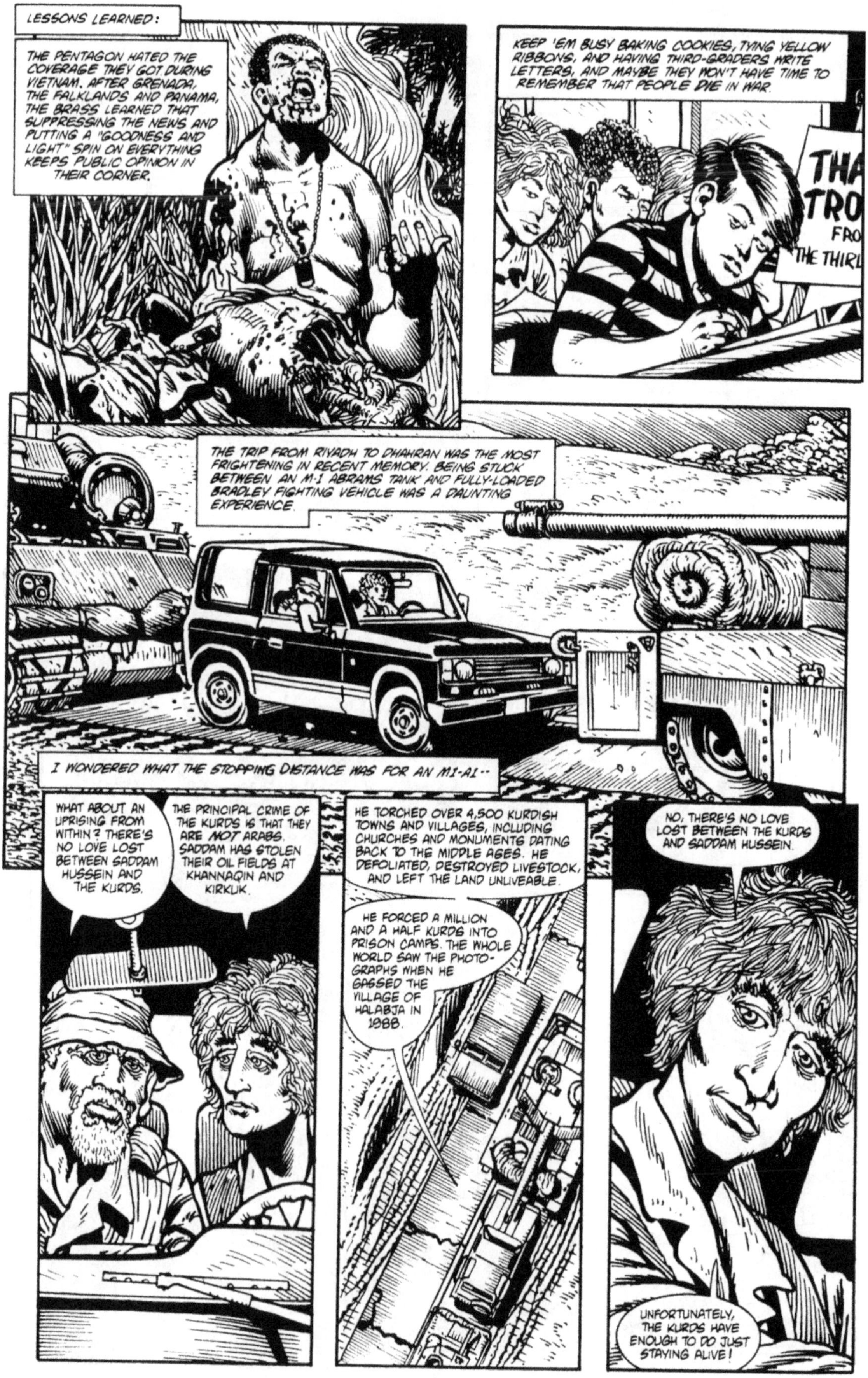
LESSONS LEARNED:
THE PENTAGON HATED THE COVERAGE THEY GOT DURING VIETNAM. AFTER GRENADA, THE FALKLANDS AND PANAMA, THE BRASS LEARNED THAT SUPPRESSING THE NEWS AND PUTTING A "GOODNESS AND LIGHT" SPIN ON EVERYTHING KEEPS PUBLIC OPINION IN THEIR CORNER.
KEEP 'EM BUSY BAKING COOKIES, TYING YELLOW RIBBONS, AND HAVING THIRD-GRADERS WRITE LETTERS, AND MAYBE THEY WON'T HAVE TIME TO REMEMBER THAT PEOPLE DIE IN WAR.
THA
TRO
FRO
THE THIRI
THE TRIP FROM RIYADH TO DHAHRAN WAS THE MOST FRIGHTENING IN RECENT MEMORY. BEING STUCK BETWEEN AN M-1 ABRAMS TANK AND FULLY-LOADED BRADLEY FIGHTING VEHICLE WAS A DAUNTING EXPERIENCE.
I WONDERED WHAT THE STOPPING DISTANCE WAS FOR AN M1-A1--
WHAT ABOUT AN UPRISING FROM WITHIN? THERE'S NO LOVE LOST BETWEEN SADDAM HUSSEIN AND THE KURDS.
THE PRINCIPAL CRIME OF THE KURDS IS THAT THEY ARE NOT ARABS. SADDAM HAS STOLEN THEIR OIL FIELDS AT KHANNAQIN AND KIRKUK.
HE TORCHED OVER 4,500 KURDISH TOWNS AND VILLAGES, INCLUDING CHURCHES AND MONUMENTS DATING BACK TO THE MIDDLE AGES. HE DEFOLIATED, DESTROYED LIVESTOCK, AND LEFT THE LAND UNLIVEABLE.
HE FORCED A MILLION AND A HALF KURDS INTO PRISON CAMPS. THE WHOLE WORLD SAW THE PHOTOGRAPHS WHEN HE GASSED THE VILLAGE OF HALABJA IN 1988.
NO, THERE'S NO LOVE LOST BETWEEN THE KURDS AND SADDAM HUSSEIN.
UNFORTUNATELY, THE KURDS HAVE ENOUGH TO DO JUST STAYING ALIVE!

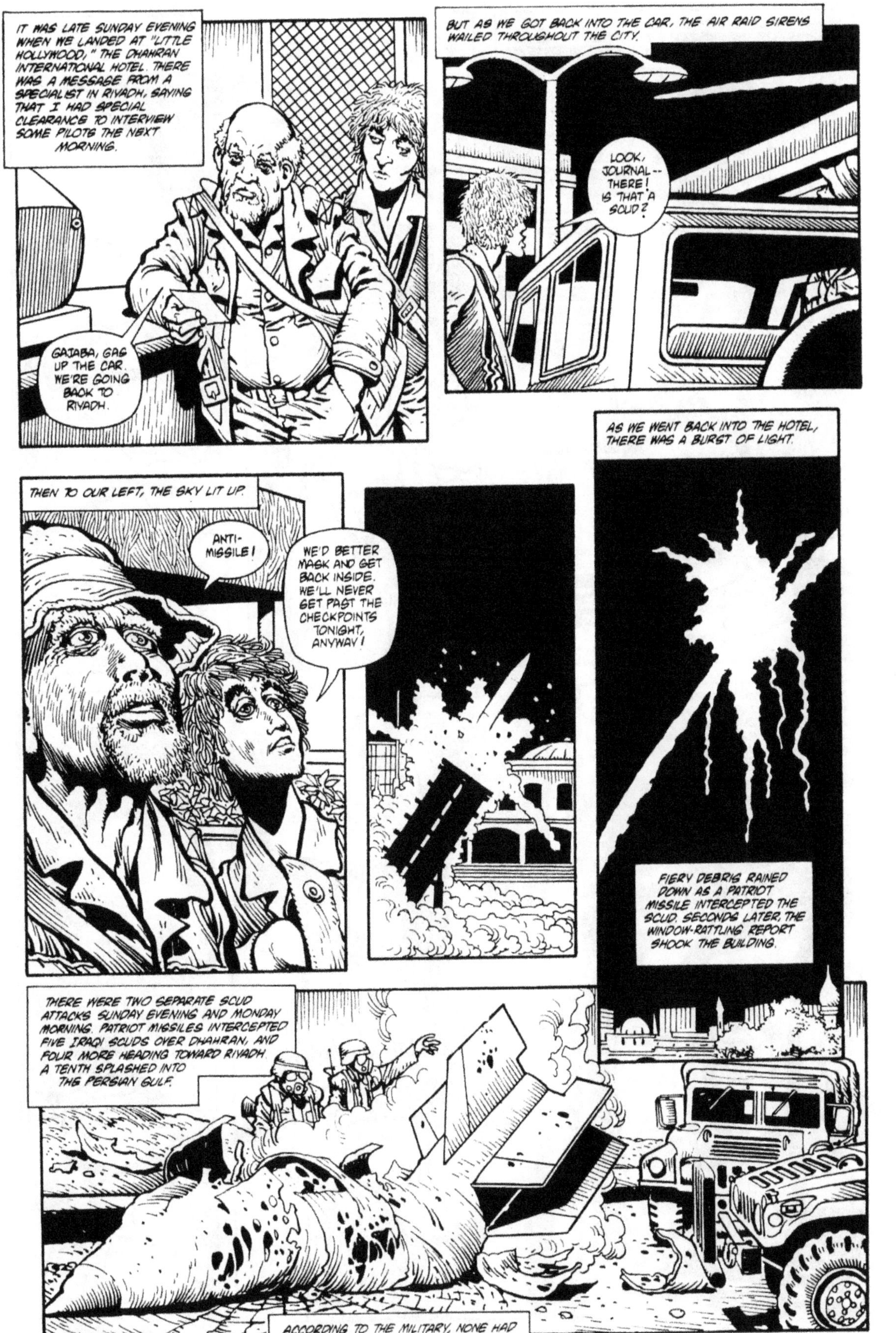
IT WAS LATE SUNDAY EVENING WHEN WE LANDED AT "LITTLE HOLLYWOOD," THE DHAHRAN INTERNATIONAL HOTEL. THERE WAS A MESSAGE FROM A SPECIALIST IN RIYADH, SAYING THAT I HAD SPECIAL CLEARANCE TO INTERVIEW SOME PILOTS THE NEXT MORNING.
GAJABA, GAS UP THE CAR. WE'RE GOING BACK TO RIYADH.
BUT AS WE GOT BACK INTO THE CAR, THE AIR RAID SIRENS WAILED THROUGHOUT THE CITY.
LOOK, JOURNAL -- THERE! IS THAT A SCUD?
THEN TO OUR LEFT, THE SKY LIT UP.
ANTI-MISSILE!
WE'D BETTER MASK AND GET BACK INSIDE. WE'LL NEVER GET PAST THE CHECKPOINTS TONIGHT, ANYWAY!
AS WE WENT BACK INTO THE HOTEL, THERE WAS A BURST OF LIGHT.
FIERY DEBRIS RAINED DOWN AS A PATRIOT MISSILE INTERCEPTED THE SCUD. SECONDS LATER, THE WINDOW-RATTLING REPORT SHOOK THE BUILDING.
THERE WERE TWO SEPARATE SCUD ATTACKS SUNDAY EVENING AND MONDAY MORNING. PATRIOT MISSILES INTERCEPTED FIVE IRAQI SCUDS OVER DHAHRAN, AND FOUR MORE HEADING TOWARD RIYADH. A TENTH SPLASHED INTO THE PERSIAN GULF.
ACCORDING TO THE MILITARY, NONE HAD CARRIED CHEMICAL OR NERVE AGENTS.

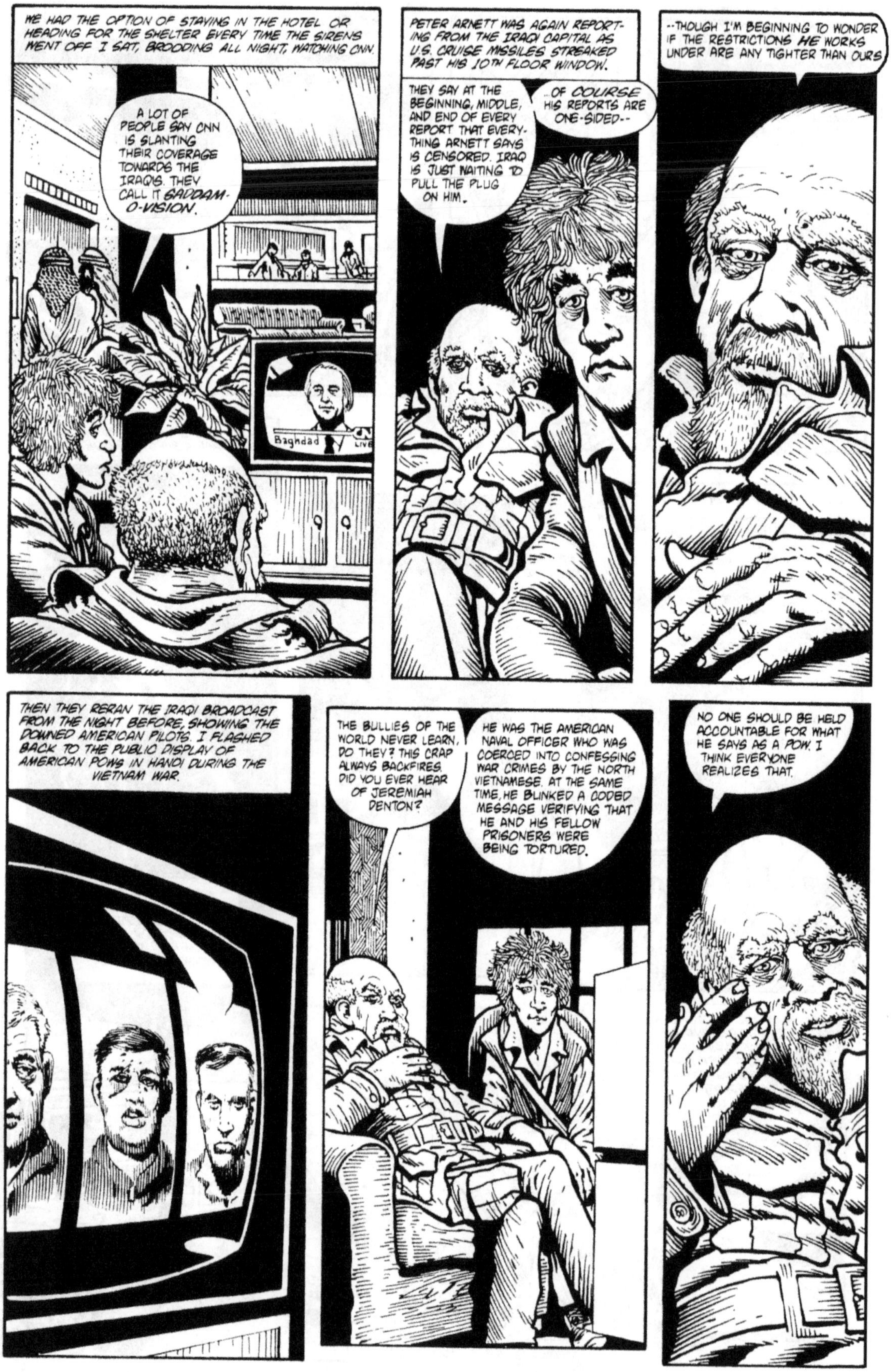
WE HAD THE OPTION OF STAYING IN THE HOTEL OR HEADING FOR THE SHELTER EVERY TIME THE SIRENS WENT OFF I SAT, BROODING ALL NIGHT, WATCHING CNN.
A LOT OF PEOPLE SAY CNN IS SLANTING THEIR COVERAGE TOWARDS THE IRAQIS. THEY CALL IT SADDAM-O-VISION.
Baghdad
LIVE
PETER ARNETT WAS AGAIN REPORTING FROM THE IRAQI CAPITAL AS U.S. CRUISE MISSILES STREAKED PAST HIS 10TH FLOOR WINDOW.
THEY SAY AT THE BEGINNING, MIDDLE, AND END OF EVERY REPORT THAT EVERYTHING ARNETT SAYS IS CENSORED. IRAQ IS JUST WAITING TO PULL THE PLUG ON HIM.
...OF COURSE HIS REPORTS ARE ONE-SIDED--
--THOUGH I'M BEGINNING TO WONDER IF THE RESTRICTIONS HE WORKS UNDER ARE ANY TIGHTER THAN OURS
THEN THEY RERAN THE IRAQI BROADCAST FROM THE NIGHT BEFORE, SHOWING THE DOWNED AMERICAN PILOTS. I FLASHED BACK TO THE PUBLIC DISPLAY OF AMERICAN POWS IN HANOI DURING THE VIETNAM WAR.
THE BULLIES OF THE WORLD NEVER LEARN, DO THEY? THIS CRAP ALWAYS BACKFIRES. DID YOU EVER HEAR OF JEREMIAH DENTON?
HE WAS THE AMERICAN NAVAL OFFICER WHO WAS COERCED INTO CONFESSING WAR CRIMES BY THE NORTH VIETNAMESE. AT THE SAME TIME, HE BLINKED A CODED MESSAGE VERIFYING THAT HE AND HIS FELLOW PRISONERS WERE BEING TORTURED.
NO ONE SHOULD BE HELD ACCOUNTABLE FOR WHAT HE SAYS AS A POW. I THINK EVERYONE REALIZES THAT.

THE ARMY'S APACHE IS THE MOST SOPHISTICATED HELICOPTER IN THE PERSIAN GULF THEATER. I MANAGED AN INTERVIEW IN RIYADH THE FOLLOWING DAY WHICH HINTED AT ITS CAPABILITIES.

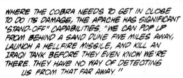

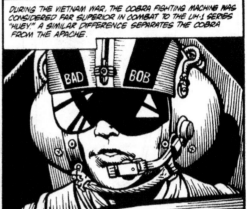

DURING THE VIETNAM WAR, THE COBRA FIGHTING MACHINE WAS CONSIDERED FAR SUPERIOR IN COMBAT TO THE UH-1 SERIES "HUEY." A SIMILAR DIFFERENCE SEPARATES THE COBRA FROM THE APACHE.

WHERE THE COBRA NEEDS TO GET IN CLOSE TO DO ITS DAMAGE, THE APACHE HAS SIGNIFICANT "STAND-OFF" CAPABILITIES. "WE CAN POP UP FROM BEHIND A SAND DUNE FIVE MILES AWAY, LAUNCH A HELLFIRE MISSILE, AND KILL AN IRAQI TANK BEFORE THEY EVEN KNOW WE'RE THERE. THEY HAVE NO WAY OF DETECTING US FROM THAT FAR AWAY."

WO-2 STEPHEN LANTZ, OF PITTSBURGH, PA, TOOK ME THROUGH A TYPICAL MISSION.

"WE WERE VECTORED INTO K-MART [KUWAIT] AFTER OUR SPECIAL FORCES FORWARD OBSERVERS HAD CHOSEN OUR TARGETS."

"THAT'S THE DEAL. WHEN THE UPPER ECHELONS CALL KUWAIT A 'TARGET-RICH ENVIRONMENT,' IT'S AN UNDERSTATEMENT. THE TARGETS ARE CHOSEN BY THE FO. SOMETIMES, THEY FEEL LIKE KIDS IN A CANDY SHOP--WHAT TO CHOOSE, WHAT TO CHOOSE.."

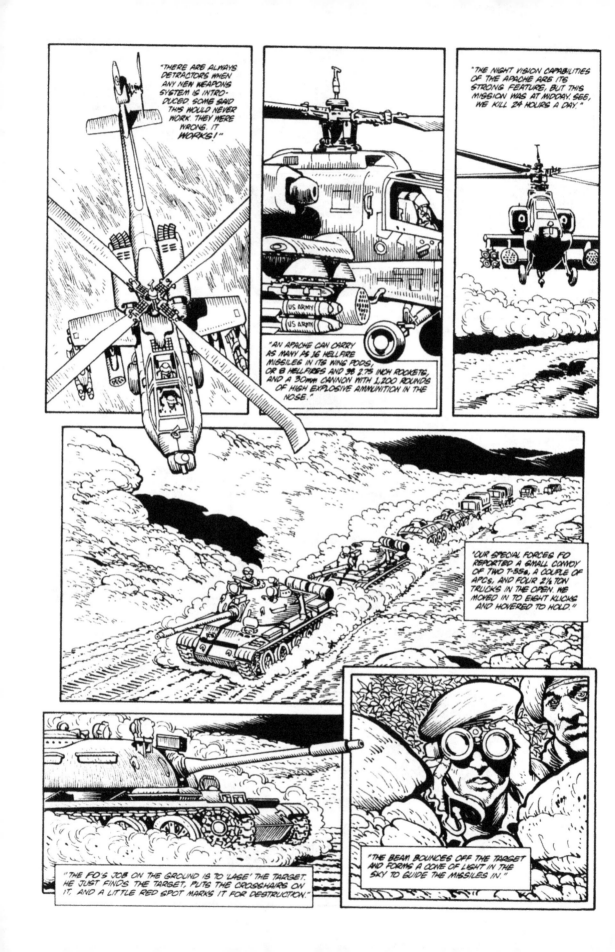

"THERE ARE ALWAYS DETRACTORS WHEN ANY NEW WEAPONS SYSTEM IS INTRODUCED. SOME SAID THIS WOULD NEVER WORK. THEY WERE WRONG. IT *WORKS!*"

"THE NIGHT VISION CAPABILITIES OF THE APACHE ARE ITS STRONG FEATURE, BUT THIS MISSION WAS AT MIDDAY. SEE, WE KILL 24 HOURS A DAY."

"AN APACHE CAN CARRY AS MANY AS 16 HELLFIRE MISSILES IN ITS WING PODS, OR 8 HELLFIRES AND 38 2.75 INCH ROCKETS, AND A 30mm CANNON WITH 1,200 ROUNDS OF HIGH EXPLOSIVE AMMUNITION IN THE NOSE."

"OUR SPECIAL FORCES FO REPORTED A SMALL CONVOY OF TWO T-55s, A COUPLE OF APCs, AND FOUR 2½ TON TRUCKS IN THE OPEN. WE MOVED IN TO EIGHT KLICKS AND HOVERED TO HOLD."

"THE FO'S JOB ON THE GROUND IS TO 'LASE' THE TARGET. HE JUST FINDS THE TARGET, PUTS THE CROSSHAIRS ON IT, AND A LITTLE RED SPOT MARKS IT FOR DESTRUCTION."

"THE BEAM BOUNCES OFF THE TARGET AND FORMS A CONE OF LIGHT IN THE SKY TO GUIDE THE MISSILES IN."

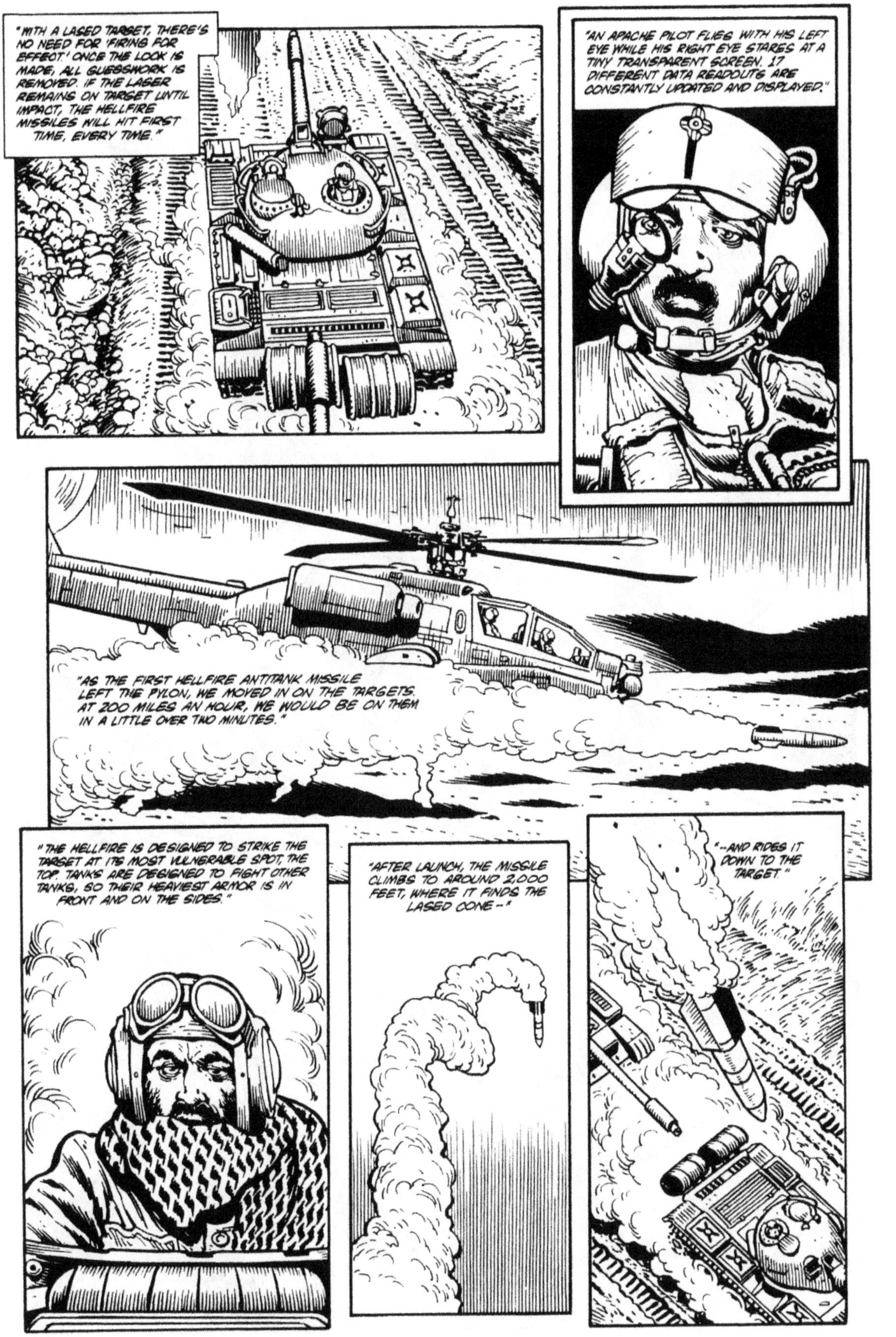
"WITH A LASED TARGET, THERE'S NO NEED FOR 'FIRING FOR EFFECT.' ONCE THE LOOK IS MADE, ALL GUESSWORK IS REMOVED. IF THE LASER REMAINS ON TARGET UNTIL IMPACT, THE HELLFIRE MISSILES WILL HIT FIRST TIME, EVERY TIME."
"AN APACHE PILOT FLIES WITH HIS LEFT EYE WHILE HIS RIGHT EYE STARES AT A TINY TRANSPARENT SCREEN. 17 DIFFERENT DATA READOUTS ARE CONSTANTLY UPDATED AND DISPLAYED."
"AS THE FIRST HELLFIRE ANTITANK MISSILE LEFT THE PYLON, WE MOVED IN ON THE TARGETS. AT 200 MILES AN HOUR, WE WOULD BE ON THEM IN A LITTLE OVER TWO MINUTES."
"THE HELLFIRE IS DESIGNED TO STRIKE THE TARGET AT ITS MOST VULNERABLE SPOT, THE TOP. TANKS ARE DESIGNED TO FIGHT OTHER TANKS, SO THEIR HEAVIEST ARMOR IS IN FRONT AND ON THE SIDES."
"AFTER LAUNCH, THE MISSILE CLIMBS TO AROUND 2,000 FEET, WHERE IT FINDS THE LASED CONE--"
"--AND RIDES IT DOWN TO THE TARGET."

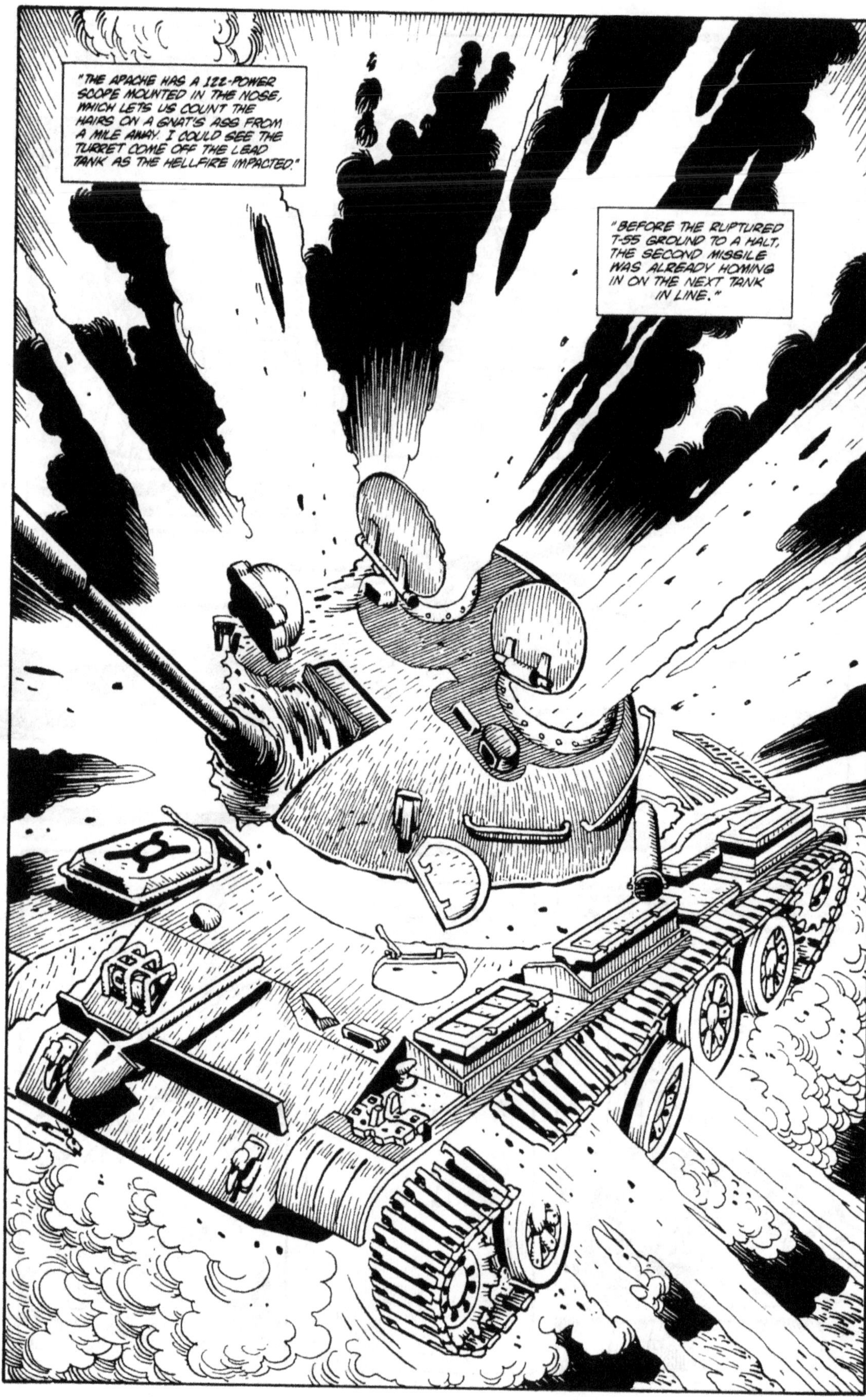
"THE APACHE HAS A 122-POWER SCOPE MOUNTED IN THE NOSE, WHICH LETS US COUNT THE HAIRS ON A GNAT'S ASS FROM A MILE AWAY. I COULD SEE THE TURRET COME OFF THE LEAD TANK AS THE HELLFIRE IMPACTED."
"BEFORE THE RUPTURED T-55 GROUND TO A HALT, THE SECOND MISSILE WAS ALREADY HOMING IN ON THE NEXT TANK IN LINE."

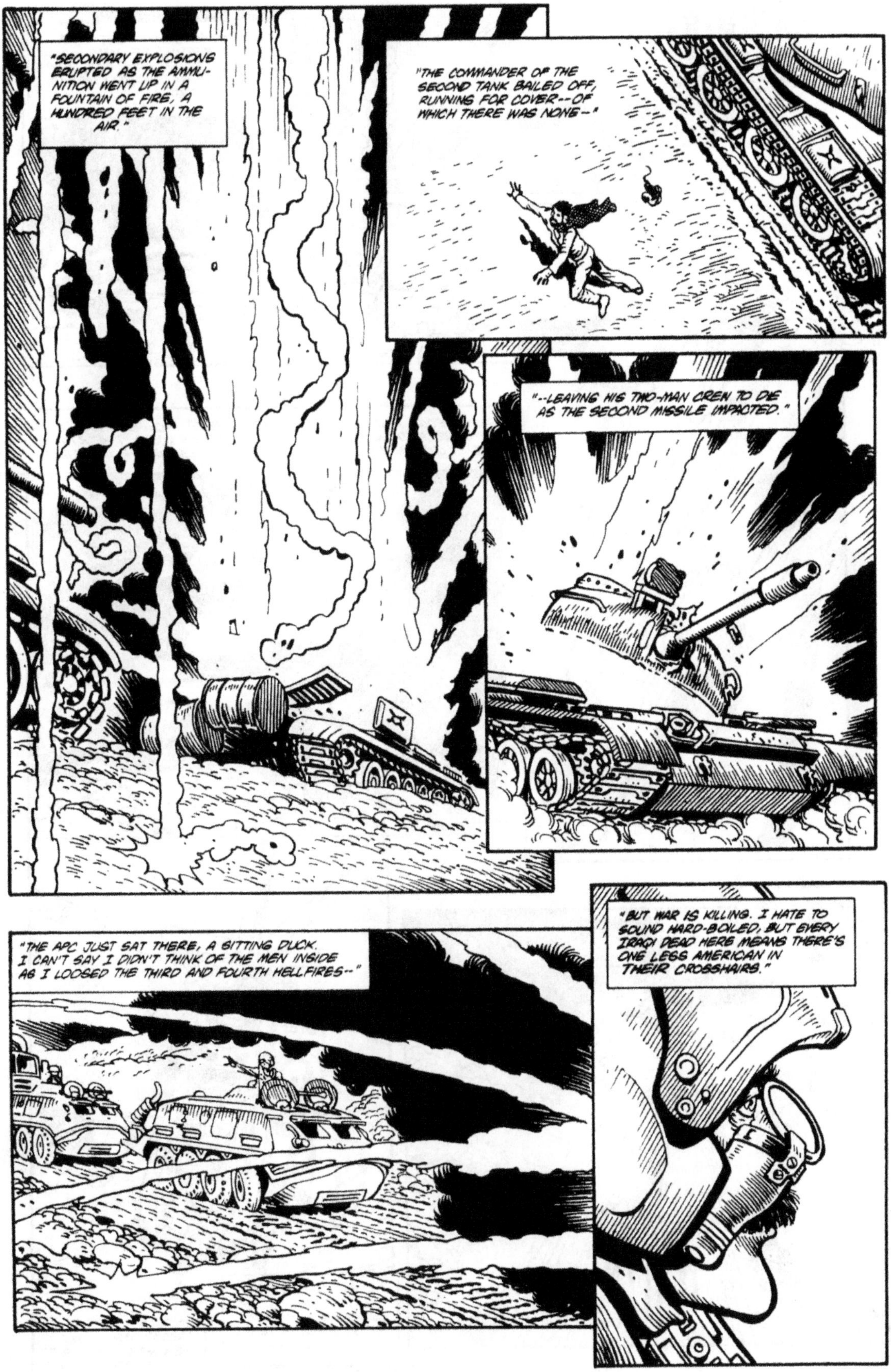
"SECONDARY EXPLOSIONS ERUPTED AS THE AMMUNITION WENT UP IN A FOUNTAIN OF FIRE, A HUNDRED FEET IN THE AIR."
"THE COMMANDER OF THE SECOND TANK BAILED OFF, RUNNING FOR COVER--OF WHICH THERE WAS NONE--"
"--LEAVING HIS TWO-MAN CREW TO DIE AS THE SECOND MISSILE IMPACTED."
"THE APC JUST SAT THERE, A SITTING DUCK. I CAN'T SAY I DIDN'T THINK OF THE MEN INSIDE AS I LOOSED THE THIRD AND FOURTH HELLFIRES--"
"BUT WAR IS KILLING. I HATE TO SOUND HARD-BOILED, BUT EVERY IRAQI DEAD HERE MEANS THERE'S ONE LESS AMERICAN IN THEIR CROSSHAIRS."

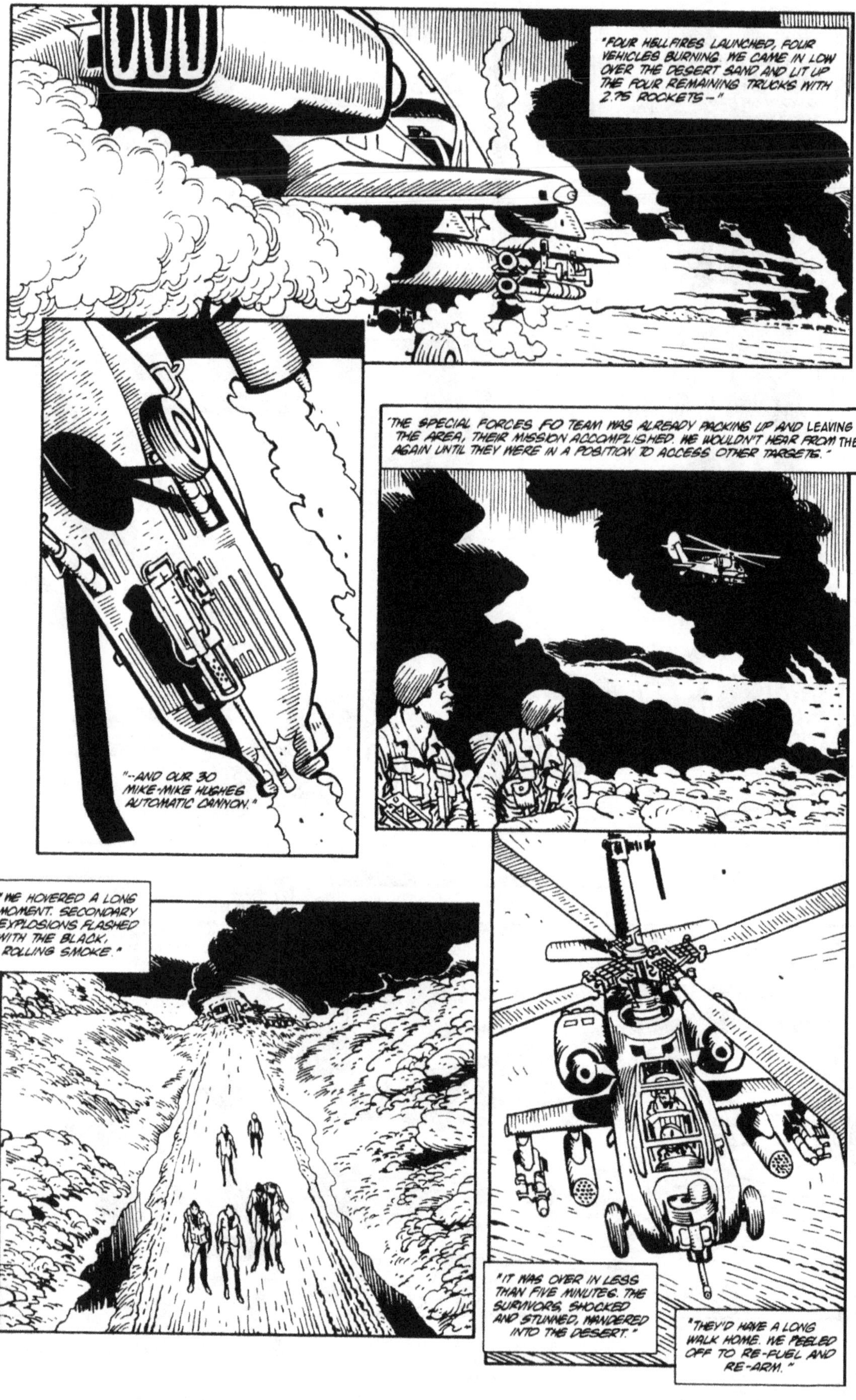
"FOUR HELLFIRES LAUNCHED, FOUR VEHICLES BURNING. WE CAME IN LOW OVER THE DESERT SAND AND LIT UP THE FOUR REMAINING TRUCKS WITH 2.75 ROCKETS--"
"--AND OUR 30 MIKE-MIKE HUGHES AUTOMATIC CANNON."
"THE SPECIAL FORCES FO TEAM WAS ALREADY PACKING UP AND LEAVING THE AREA, THEIR MISSION ACCOMPLISHED. WE WOULDN'T HEAR FROM THEM AGAIN UNTIL THEY WERE IN A POSITION TO ACCESS OTHER TARGETS."
"WE HOVERED A LONG MOMENT. SECONDARY EXPLOSIONS FLASHED WITH THE BLACK, ROLLING SMOKE."
"IT WAS OVER IN LESS THAN FIVE MINUTES. THE SURVIVORS, SHOCKED AND STUNNED, WANDERED INTO THE DESERT."
"THEY'D HAVE A LONG WALK HOME. WE PEELED OFF TO RE-FUEL AND RE-ARM."

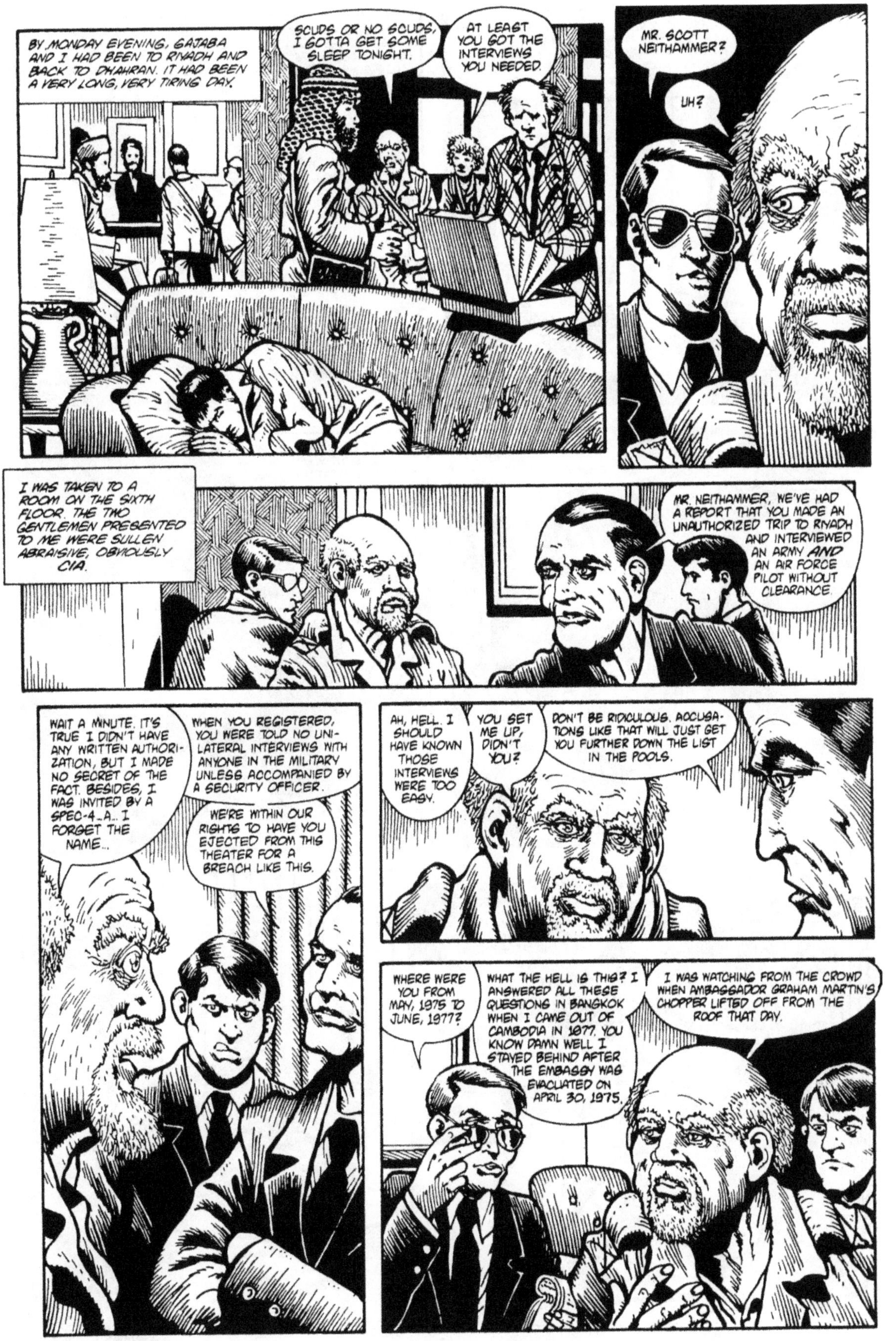
BY MONDAY EVENING, GAJABA AND I HAD BEEN TO RIYADH AND BACK TO DHAHRAN. IT HAD BEEN A VERY LONG, VERY TIRING DAY.
SCUDS OR NO SCUDS, I GOTTA GET SOME SLEEP TONIGHT.
AT LEAST YOU GOT THE INTERVIEWS YOU NEEDED.
MR. SCOTT NEITHAMMER?
UH?
I WAS TAKEN TO A ROOM ON THE SIXTH FLOOR. THE TWO GENTLEMEN PRESENTED TO ME WERE SULLEN ABRAISIVE, OBVIOUSLY CIA.
MR. NEITHAMMER, WE'VE HAD A REPORT THAT YOU MADE AN UNAUTHORIZED TRIP TO RIYADH AND INTERVIEWED AN ARMY AND AN AIR FORCE PILOT WITHOUT CLEARANCE.
WAIT A MINUTE. IT'S TRUE I DIDN'T HAVE ANY WRITTEN AUTHORIZATION, BUT I MADE NO SECRET OF THE FACT. BESIDES, I WAS INVITED BY A SPEC-4...A... I FORGET THE NAME...
WHEN YOU REGISTERED, YOU WERE TOLD NO UNILATERAL INTERVIEWS WITH ANYONE IN THE MILITARY UNLESS ACCOMPANIED BY A SECURITY OFFICER.
WE'RE WITHIN OUR RIGHTS TO HAVE YOU EJECTED FROM THIS THEATER FOR A BREACH LIKE THIS.
AH, HELL. I SHOULD HAVE KNOWN THOSE INTERVIEWS WERE TOO EASY.
YOU SET ME UP, DIDN'T YOU?
DON'T BE RIDICULOUS. ACCUSATIONS LIKE THAT WILL JUST GET YOU FURTHER DOWN THE LIST IN THE POOLS.
WHERE WERE YOU FROM MAY, 1975 TO JUNE, 1977?
WHAT THE HELL IS THIS? I ANSWERED ALL THESE QUESTIONS IN BANGKOK WHEN I CAME OUT OF CAMBODIA IN 1977. YOU KNOW DAMN WELL I STAYED BEHIND AFTER THE EMBASSY WAS EVACUATED ON APRIL 30, 1975.
I WAS WATCHING FROM THE CROWD WHEN AMBASSADOR GRAHAM MARTIN'S CHOPPER LIFTED OFF FROM THE ROOF THAT DAY.

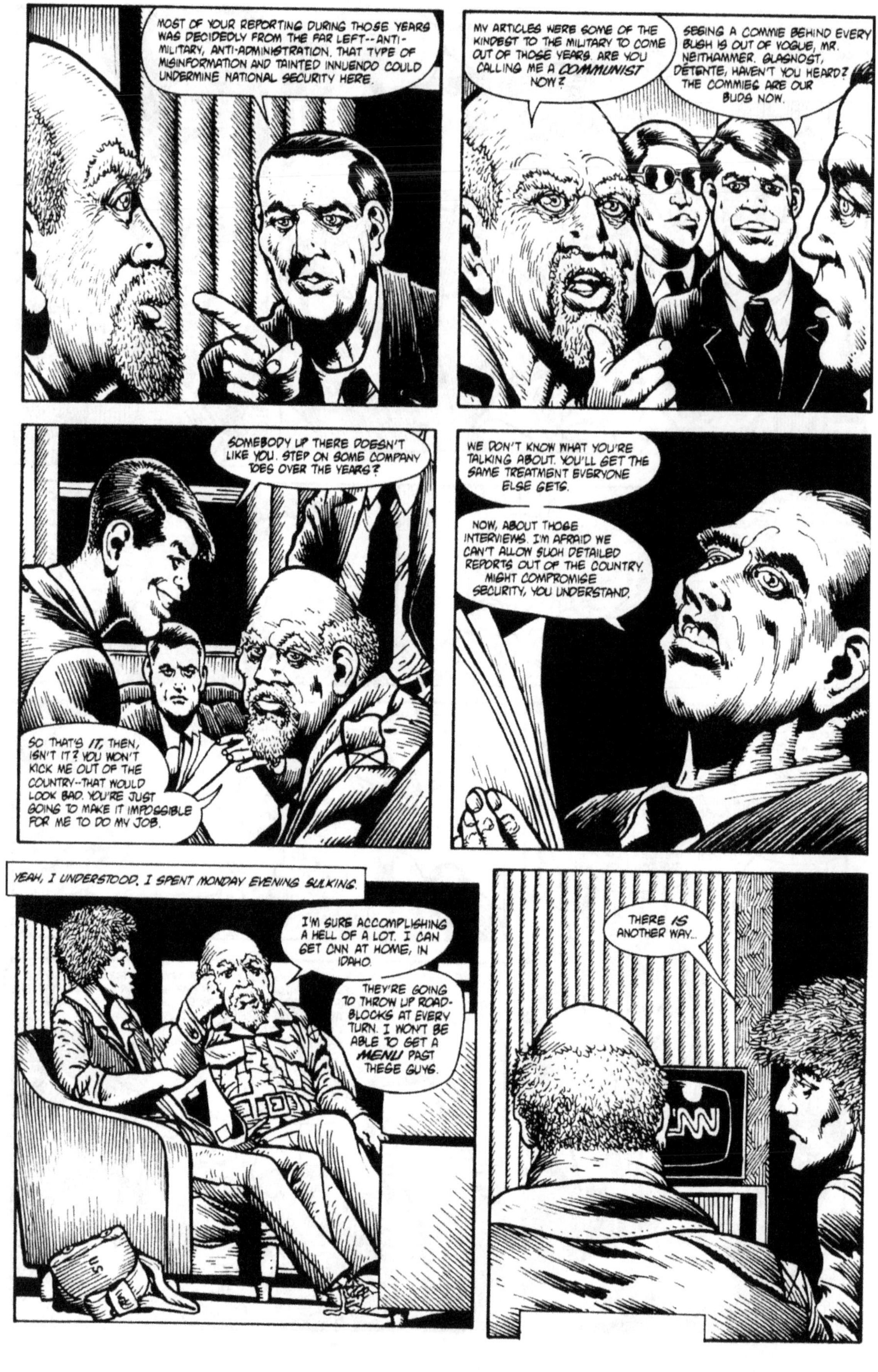
MOST OF YOUR REPORTING DURING THOSE YEARS WAS DECIDEDLY FROM THE FAR LEFT--ANTI-MILITARY, ANTI-ADMINISTRATION. THAT TYPE OF MISINFORMATION AND TAINTED INNUENDO COULD UNDERMINE NATIONAL SECURITY HERE.
MY ARTICLES WERE SOME OF THE KINDEST TO THE MILITARY TO COME OUT OF THOSE YEARS. ARE YOU CALLING ME A COMMUNIST NOW?
SEEING A COMMIE BEHIND EVERY BUSH IS OUT OF VOGUE, MR. NEITHAMMER. GLASNOST, DÉTENTE, HAVEN'T YOU HEARD? THE COMMIES ARE OUR BUDS NOW.
SOMEBODY UP THERE DOESN'T LIKE YOU. STEP ON SOME COMPANY TOES OVER THE YEARS?
SO THAT'S IT, THEN, ISN'T IT? YOU WON'T KICK ME OUT OF THE COUNTRY--THAT WOULD LOOK BAD. YOU'RE JUST GOING TO MAKE IT IMPOSSIBLE FOR ME TO DO MY JOB.
WE DON'T KNOW WHAT YOU'RE TALKING ABOUT. YOU'LL GET THE SAME TREATMENT EVERYONE ELSE GETS.
NOW, ABOUT THOSE INTERVIEWS. I'M AFRAID WE CAN'T ALLOW SUCH DETAILED REPORTS OUT OF THE COUNTRY. MIGHT COMPROMISE SECURITY, YOU UNDERSTAND.
YEAH, I UNDERSTOOD. I SPENT MONDAY EVENING SULKING.
I'M SURE ACCOMPLISHING A HELL OF A LOT. I CAN GET CNN AT HOME, IN IDAHO.
THEY'RE GOING TO THROW UP ROAD-BLOCKS AT EVERY TURN. I WON'T BE ABLE TO GET A MENU PAST THESE GUYS.
THERE IS ANOTHER WAY...

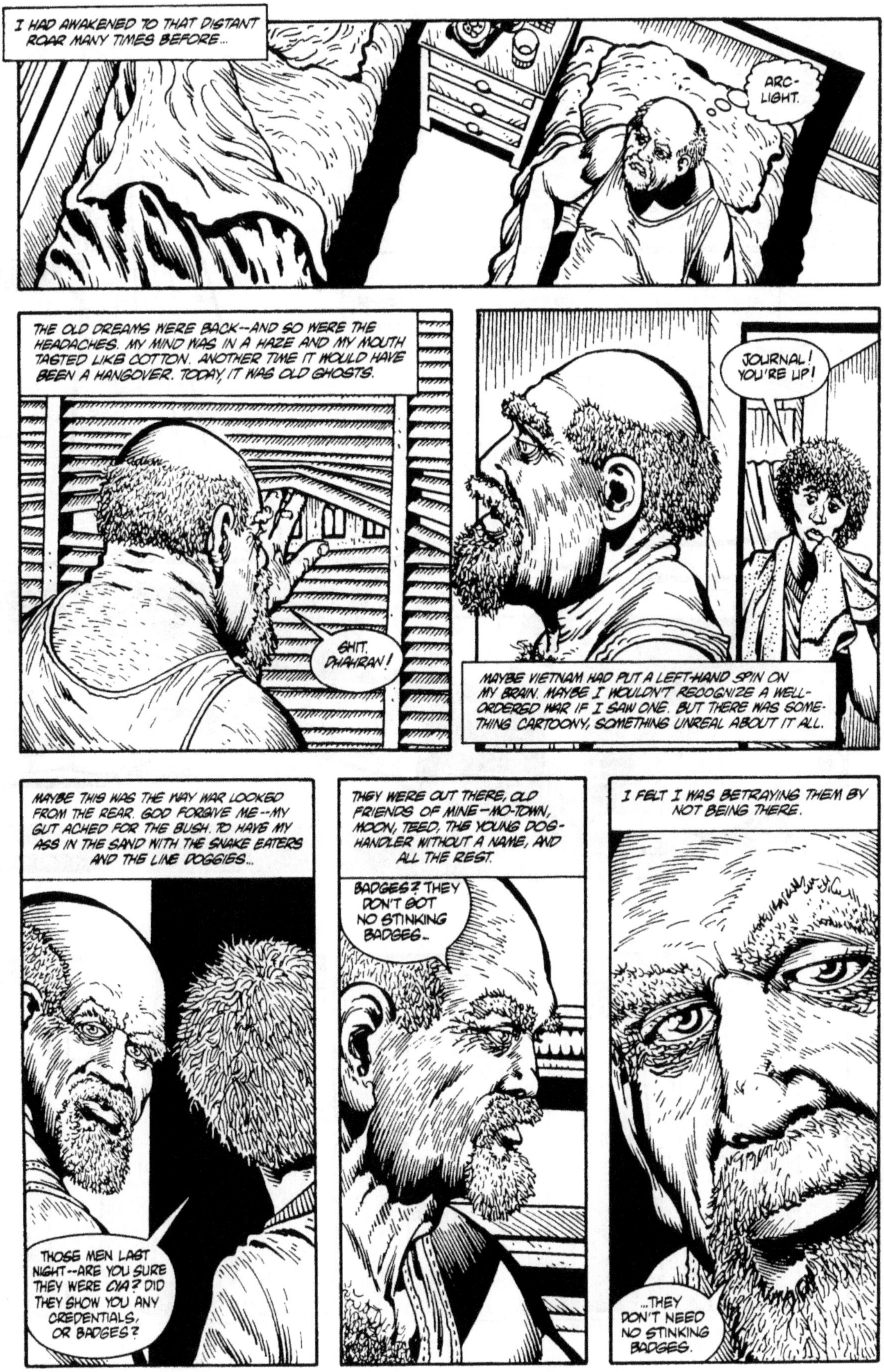
I HAD AWAKENED TO THAT DISTANT ROAR MANY TIMES BEFORE...
ARC-LIGHT.
THE OLD DREAMS WERE BACK--AND SO WERE THE HEADACHES. MY MIND WAS IN A HAZE AND MY MOUTH TASTED LIKE COTTON. ANOTHER TIME IT WOULD HAVE BEEN A HANGOVER. TODAY, IT WAS OLD GHOSTS.
SHIT. DHAHRAN!
JOURNAL! YOU'RE UP!
MAYBE VIETNAM HAD PUT A LEFT-HAND SPIN ON MY BRAIN. MAYBE I WOULDN'T RECOGNIZE A WELL-ORDERED WAR IF I SAW ONE. BUT THERE WAS SOMETHING CARTOONY, SOMETHING UNREAL ABOUT IT ALL.
MAYBE THIS WAS THE WAY WAR LOOKED FROM THE REAR. GOD FORGIVE ME--MY GUT ACHED FOR THE BUSH. TO HAVE MY ASS IN THE SAND WITH THE SNAKE EATERS AND THE LINE DOGGIES...
THOSE MEN LAST NIGHT--ARE YOU SURE THEY WERE CIA? DID THEY SHOW YOU ANY CREDENTIALS, OR BADGES?
THEY WERE OUT THERE, OLD FRIENDS OF MINE--MO-TOWN, MOON, TEED, THE YOUNG DOG-HANDLER WITHOUT A NAME, AND ALL THE REST.
BADGES? THEY DON'T GOT NO STINKING BADGES..
I FELT I WAS BETRAYING THEM BY NOT BEING THERE.
...THEY DON'T NEED NO STINKING BADGES.

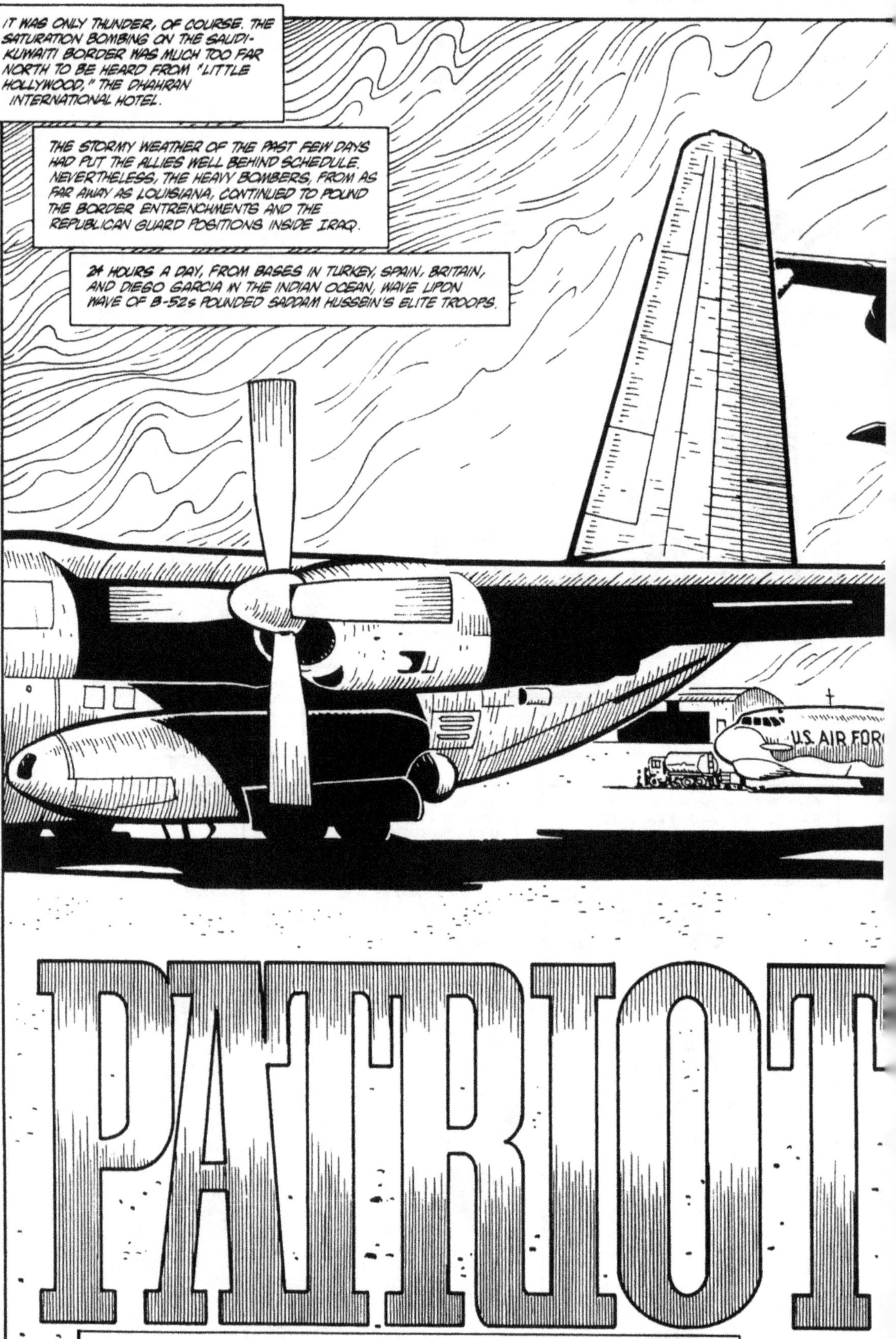
IT WAS ONLY THUNDER, OF COURSE. THE SATURATION BOMBING ON THE SAUDI-KUWAITI BORDER WAS MUCH TOO FAR NORTH TO BE HEARD FROM "LITTLE HOLLYWOOD," THE DHAHRAN INTERNATIONAL HOTEL.
THE STORMY WEATHER OF THE PAST FEW DAYS HAD PUT THE ALLIES WELL BEHIND SCHEDULE. NEVERTHELESS, THE HEAVY BOMBERS, FROM AS FAR AWAY AS LOUISIANA, CONTINUED TO POUND THE BORDER ENTRENCHMENTS AND THE REPUBLICAN GUARD POSITIONS INSIDE IRAQ.
24 HOURS A DAY, FROM BASES IN TURKEY, SPAIN, BRITAIN, AND DIEGO GARCIA IN THE INDIAN OCEAN, WAVE UPON WAVE OF B-52s POUNDED SADDAM HUSSEIN'S ELITE TROOPS.
U.S. AIR FORC
PATRIOT

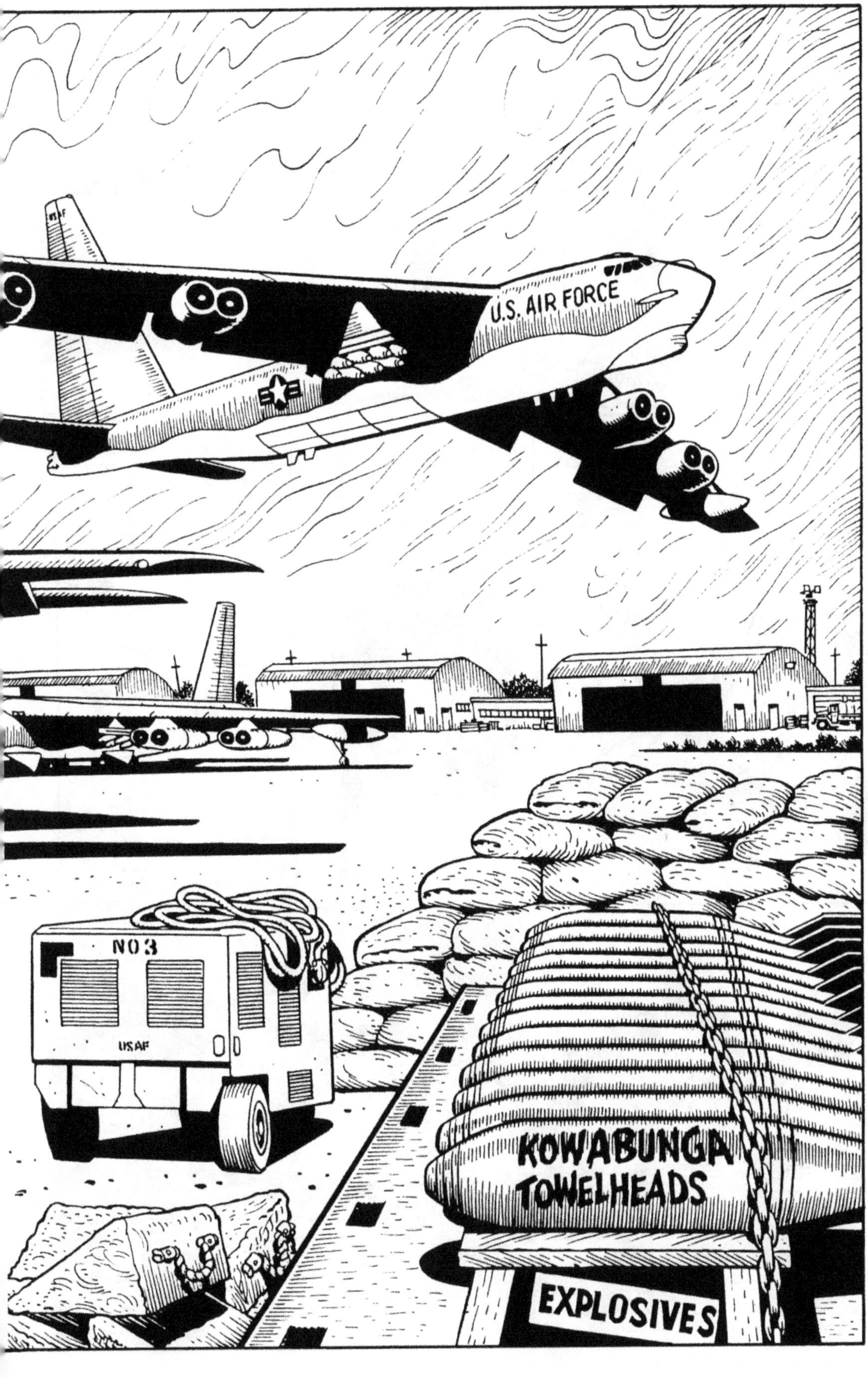
U.S. AIR FORCE
USAF
NO 3
USAF
KOWABUNGA
TOWELHEADS
EXPLOSIVES

THE B-52, WHICH WENT INTO PRODUCTION 36 YEARS AGO, HAS BEEN AROUND LONGER THAN MOST OF THE MEN WHO FLY THEM. THE PILOTS CALL THEM *BUFF* (BIG UGLY FAT FELLOW).

THE LAST B-52, DESIGNED TO DELIVER "THE BOMB" TO DOWNTOWN MOSCOW, ROLLED OFF THE ASSEMBLY LINE IN 1962, DURING THE HEIGHT OF THE COLD WAR.

RETROFITTED AND UPDATED MANY TIMES, THE B-52s IS HARDLY THE SAME AIRCRAFT FLOWN IN THE FIGHT AGAINST COMMUNIST FORCES IN VIETNAM, CAMBODIA, AND LAOS IN THE 60s AND EARLY 70s.

CODE-NAMED "ARC LIGHT," THE B-52D MODEL BECAME A LEGEND, WHISPERED ABOUT IN HUSHED TONES BY ANYONE WHO LIVED THROUGH ITS DEVASTATING ATTACKS.

WITH A RANGE OF 7,500 MILES BEFORE REFUELING, THE B-52 CAN BE BASED HOURS FROM THE COMBAT ZONE. FLYING IN FORMATIONS OF THREE--

--THEY DUMP THEIR LOADS OF "DUMB BOMBS" FROM ALTITUDES OF SIX OR SEVEN MILES. THE ENEMY DOESN'T EVEN KNOW THEY'RE THERE UNTIL THE GROUND ERUPTS IN "ROLLING THUNDER." LAYING A PATTERN HALF A MILE WIDE AND A MILE LONG, THEY REDUCE THE AREA TO A MOONSCAPE.

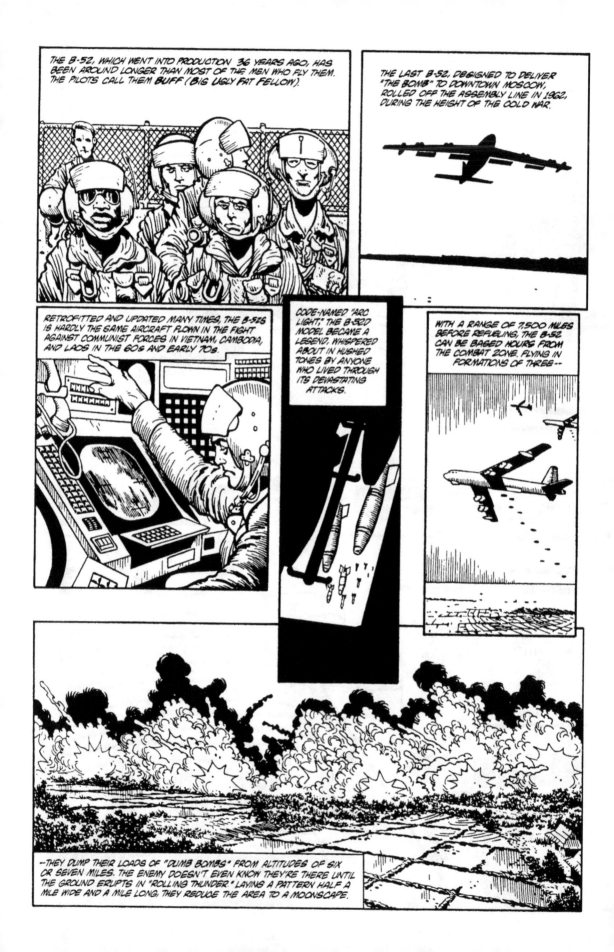

AFTER THE NORTH VIETNAMESE DELE-
GATES WITHDREW FROM THE PEACE
TABLES IN PARIS IN 1972, PRESIDENT
NIXON ORDERED THE RESUMPTION OF
BOMBING AGAINST TARGETS IN NORTH
VIETNAM, CODE NAMED *OPERATION
LINEBACKER II.*

DURING THE CHRISTMAS RAIDS THAT
YEAR, EXPLOSIVES ROUGHLY EQUIVA-
LENT TO THE BOMB DROPPED ON
HIROSHIMA WERE DUMPED ON 34
TARGETS IN NORTH VIETNAM IN
OVER 700 SORTIES--INCLUDING A
HORRENDOUS HAMMERING OF HANOI.

THE ELEVEN-DAY ONSLAUGHT IS
CREDITED BY MANY EXPERTS AS HAVING
PERSUADED THE NORTH VIETNAMESE
TO SIGN THE PARIS PEACE ACCORD.
SOME SAY THAT IF THE SAME INTENSITY
HAD BEEN USED SOONER IN THE WAR,
THE "CONFLICT" COULD HAVE BEEN
OVER TEN YEARS EARLIER.

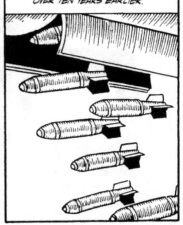

AGAINST AN ENTRENCHED ARMY WITH NO
RESUPPLY, THE B-52 COULD PROVE DEVASTATING.

THE "G" MODEL, WITH ITS BANKS OF COMPUTERS LIMITING THE
ORDNANCE CAPACITY TO ABOUT HALF THAT OF THE "D" MODEL,
HAS MORE PRECISE AND ACCURATE WEAPONS DELIVERY
SYSTEMS.

THE ALLIES REPORTED THAT THEY WERE HITTING
IRAQI POSITIONS EVERY THREE HOURS. THE CARPET
BOMBING WOULD HAVE TO BE DEMORALIZING, EVEN
TO HARDENED COMBAT VETERANS.

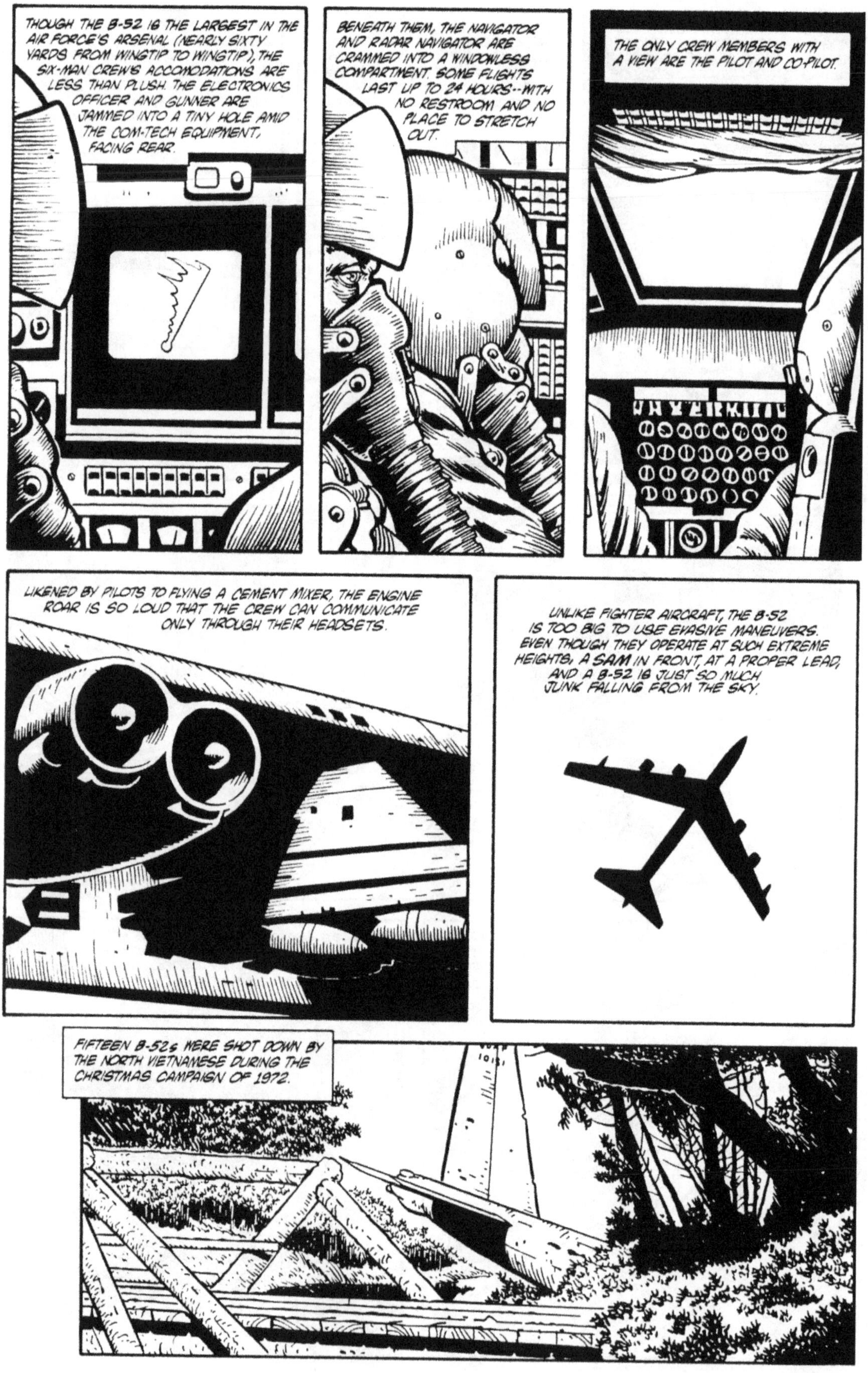
THOUGH THE B-52 IS THE LARGEST IN THE AIR FORCE'S ARSENAL (NEARLY SIXTY YARDS FROM WINGTIP TO WINGTIP), THE SIX-MAN CREW'S ACCOMODATIONS ARE LESS THAN PLUSH. THE ELECTRONICS OFFICER AND GUNNER ARE JAMMED INTO A TINY HOLE AMID THE COM-TECH EQUIPMENT, FACING REAR.
BENEATH THEM, THE NAVIGATOR AND RADAR NAVIGATOR ARE CRAMMED INTO A WINDOWLESS COMPARTMENT. SOME FLIGHTS LAST UP TO 24 HOURS--WITH NO RESTROOM AND NO PLACE TO STRETCH OUT.
THE ONLY CREW MEMBERS WITH A VIEW ARE THE PILOT AND CO-PILOT.
LIKENED BY PILOTS TO FLYING A CEMENT MIXER, THE ENGINE ROAR IS SO LOUD THAT THE CREW CAN COMMUNICATE ONLY THROUGH THEIR HEADSETS.
UNLIKE FIGHTER AIRCRAFT, THE B-52 IS TOO BIG TO USE EVASIVE MANEUVERS. EVEN THOUGH THEY OPERATE AT SUCH EXTREME HEIGHTS, A SAM IN FRONT, AT A PROPER LEAD, AND A B-52 IS JUST SO MUCH JUNK FALLING FROM THE SKY.
FIFTEEN B-52s WERE SHOT DOWN BY THE NORTH VIETNAMESE DURING THE CHRISTMAS CAMPAIGN OF 1972.

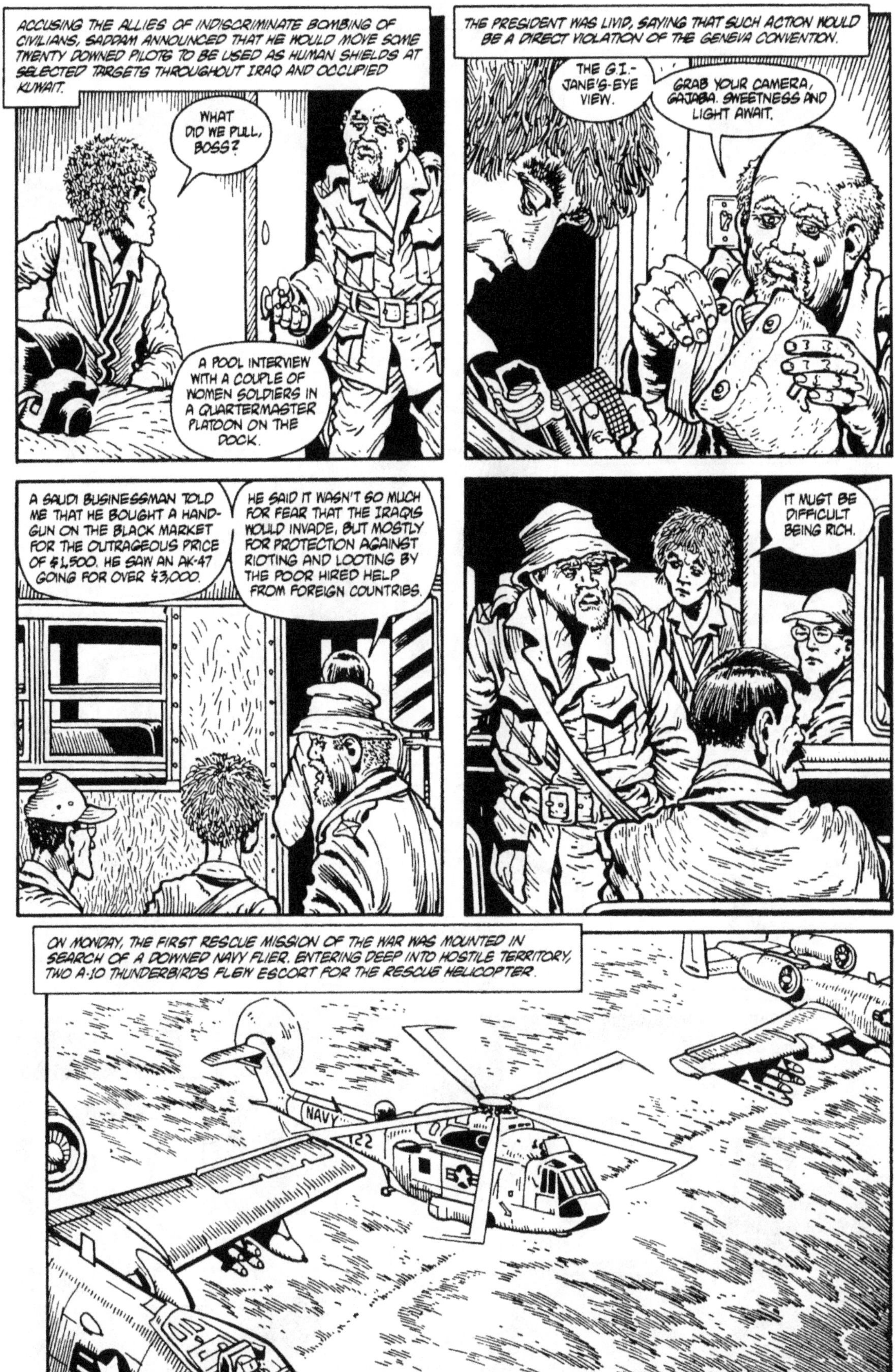
ACCUSING THE ALLIES OF INDISCRIMINATE BOMBING OF CIVILIANS, SADDAM ANNOUNCED THAT HE WOULD MOVE SOME TWENTY DOWNED PILOTS TO BE USED AS HUMAN SHIELDS AT SELECTED TARGETS THROUGHOUT IRAQ AND OCCUPIED KUWAIT.
WHAT DID WE PULL, BOSS?
A POOL INTERVIEW WITH A COUPLE OF WOMEN SOLDIERS IN A QUARTERMASTER PLATOON ON THE DOCK.
THE PRESIDENT WAS LIVID, SAYING THAT SUCH ACTION WOULD BE A DIRECT VIOLATION OF THE GENEVA CONVENTION.
THE G.I.-JANE'S-EYE VIEW.
GRAB YOUR CAMERA, GAJABA. SWEETNESS AND LIGHT AWAIT.
A SAUDI BUSINESSMAN TOLD ME THAT HE BOUGHT A HAND-GUN ON THE BLACK MARKET FOR THE OUTRAGEOUS PRICE OF $1,500. HE SAW AN AK-47 GOING FOR OVER $3,000.
HE SAID IT WASN'T SO MUCH FOR FEAR THAT THE IRAQIS WOULD INVADE, BUT MOSTLY FOR PROTECTION AGAINST RIOTING AND LOOTING BY THE POOR HIRED HELP FROM FOREIGN COUNTRIES.
IT MUST BE DIFFICULT BEING RICH.
ON MONDAY, THE FIRST RESCUE MISSION OF THE WAR WAS MOUNTED IN SEARCH OF A DOWNED NAVY FLIER. ENTERING DEEP INTO HOSTILE TERRITORY, TWO A-10 THUNDERBIRDS FLEW ESCORT FOR THE RESCUE HELICOPTER.
NAVY
122

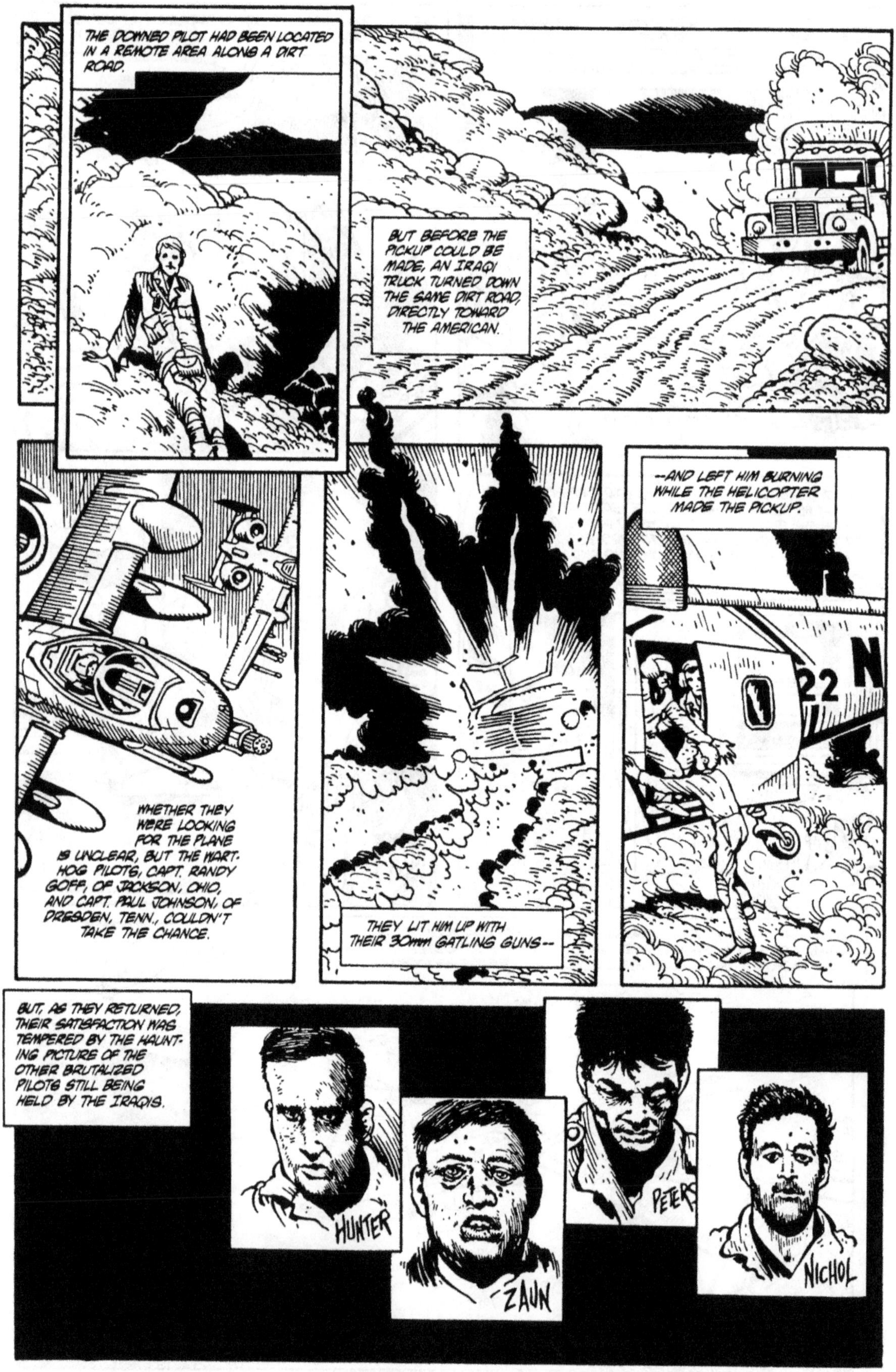
THE DOWNED PILOT HAD BEEN LOCATED IN A REMOTE AREA ALONG A DIRT ROAD.
BUT BEFORE THE PICKUP COULD BE MADE, AN IRAQI TRUCK TURNED DOWN THE SAME DIRT ROAD, DIRECTLY TOWARD THE AMERICAN.
WHETHER THEY WERE LOOKING FOR THE PLANE IS UNCLEAR, BUT THE WART-HOG PILOTS, CAPT. RANDY GOFF, OF JACKSON, OHIO, AND CAPT. PAUL JOHNSON, OF DRESDEN, TENN., COULDN'T TAKE THE CHANCE.
THEY LIT HIM UP WITH THEIR 30mm GATLING GUNS--
--AND LEFT HIM BURNING WHILE THE HELICOPTER MADE THE PICKUP.
22 N
BUT, AS THEY RETURNED, THEIR SATISFACTION WAS TEMPERED BY THE HAUNTING PICTURE OF THE OTHER BRUTALIZED PILOTS STILL BEING HELD BY THE IRAQIS.
HUNTER
ZAUN
PETERS
NICHOL

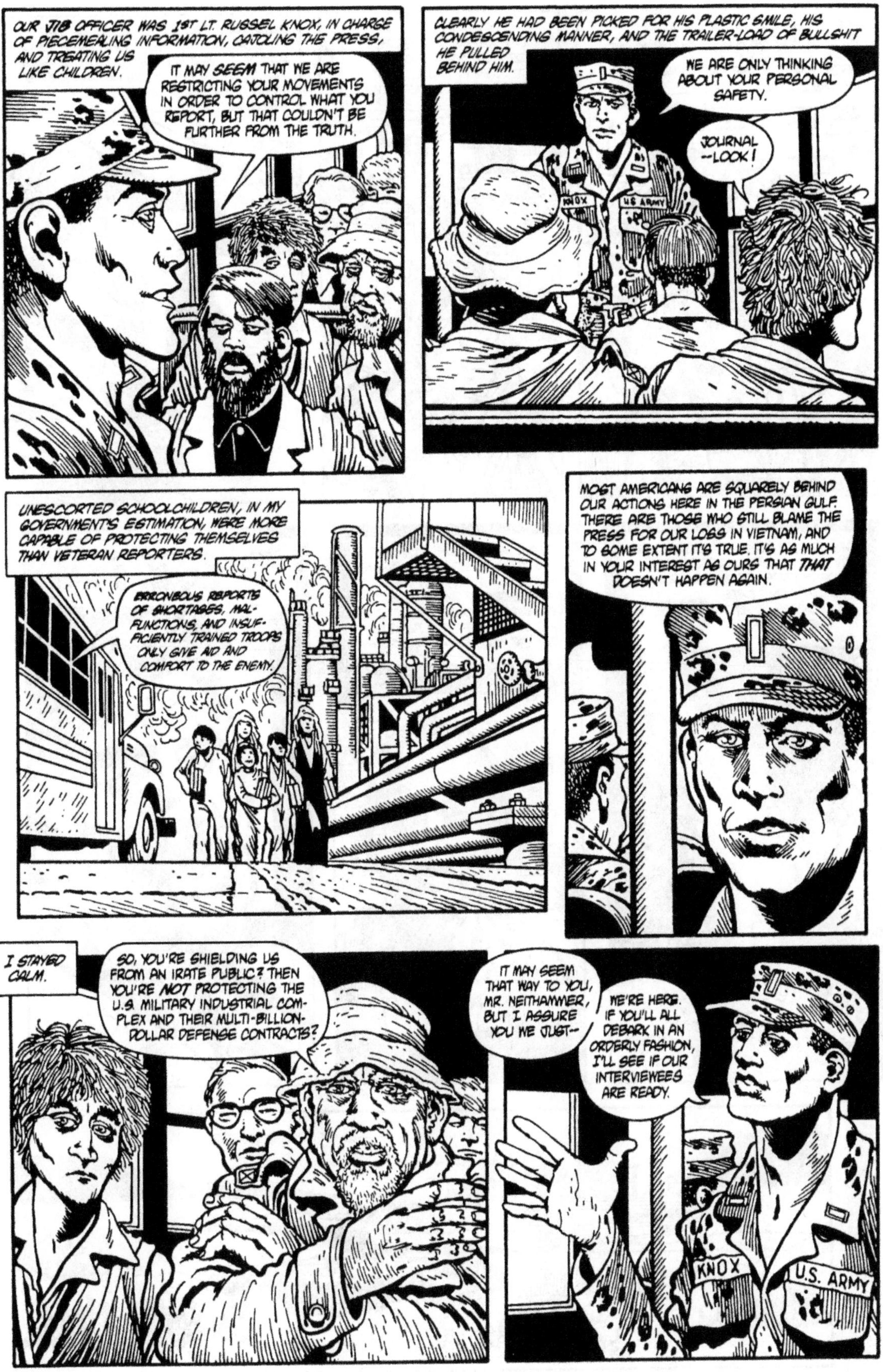

OUR JIB OFFICER WAS 1ST LT. RUSSEL KNOX, IN CHARGE OF PIECEMEALING INFORMATION, CAJOLING THE PRESS, AND TREATING US LIKE CHILDREN.
IT MAY SEEM THAT WE ARE RESTRICTING YOUR MOVEMENTS IN ORDER TO CONTROL WHAT YOU REPORT, BUT THAT COULDN'T BE FURTHER FROM THE TRUTH.
CLEARLY HE HAD BEEN PICKED FOR HIS PLASTIC SMILE, HIS CONDESCENDING MANNER, AND THE TRAILER-LOAD OF BULLSHIT HE PULLED BEHIND HIM.
WE ARE ONLY THINKING ABOUT YOUR PERSONAL SAFETY.
JOURNAL --LOOK!
KNOX
U.S. ARMY
UNESCORTED SCHOOLCHILDREN, IN MY GOVERNMENT'S ESTIMATION, WERE MORE CAPABLE OF PROTECTING THEMSELVES THAN VETERAN REPORTERS.
ERRONEOUS REPORTS OF SHORTAGES, MALFUNCTIONS, AND INSUFFICIENTLY TRAINED TROOPS ONLY GIVE AID AND COMFORT TO THE ENEMY.
MOST AMERICANS ARE SQUARELY BEHIND OUR ACTIONS HERE IN THE PERSIAN GULF. THERE ARE THOSE WHO STILL BLAME THE PRESS FOR OUR LOSS IN VIETNAM, AND TO SOME EXTENT IT'S TRUE. IT'S AS MUCH IN YOUR INTEREST AS OURS THAT THAT DOESN'T HAPPEN AGAIN.
I STAYED CALM.
SO, YOU'RE SHIELDING US FROM AN IRATE PUBLIC? THEN YOU'RE NOT PROTECTING THE U.S. MILITARY INDUSTRIAL COMPLEX AND THEIR MULTI-BILLION-DOLLAR DEFENSE CONTRACTS?
IT MAY SEEM THAT WAY TO YOU, MR. NEITHAMMER, BUT I ASSURE YOU WE JUST--
WE'RE HERE. IF YOU'LL ALL DEBARK IN AN ORDERLY FASHION, I'LL SEE IF OUR INTERVIEWEES ARE READY.
KNOX
U.S. ARMY

KURDISH REBELS REPORTED ALLIED BOMBING AND AIR RAIDS HAD KILLED OR WOUNDED NEARLY 4,000 IRAQI MILITARY PERSONNEL IN THE FIRST THREE DAYS OF THE CONFLICT.

THE KURDISTAN DEMOCRATIC PARTY REPORTED PEOPLE WERE FLEEING THE CITY IN PANIC, DEFYING MILITARY ORDERS AND CHECKPOINTS.

THROUGHOUT BAGHDAD, MOST OF THE POPULATION HAD BEEN REDUCED TO GETTING THEIR HOUSEHOLD WATER FROM THE TIGRIS RIVER. MUCH OF THE CITY'S INFRASTRUCTURE WAS REPORTED DAMAGED.

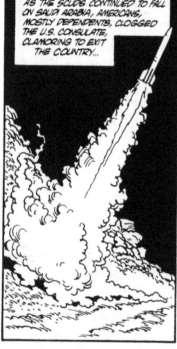

AS THE SCUDS CONTINUED TO FALL ON SAUDI ARABIA, AMERICANS, MOSTLY DEPENDENTS, CLOGGED THE U.S. CONSULATE, CLAMORING TO EXIT THE COUNTRY...

PETER ARNETT OF CNN WAS THE ONLY WESTERN JOURNALIST KNOWN TO STILL BE IN BAGHDAD. HE DESCRIBED THE CITY AS DESERTED—MOST CIVILIANS HAD EITHER LEFT FOR THE COUNTRY, OR WERE STAYING INDOORS.

WHILE THE BUTCHER OF BAGHDAD FOULED THE AIRWAYS WITH HIS POISON, CALLING FOR A HOLY WAR—

—ALLIED TROOPS WAITED.

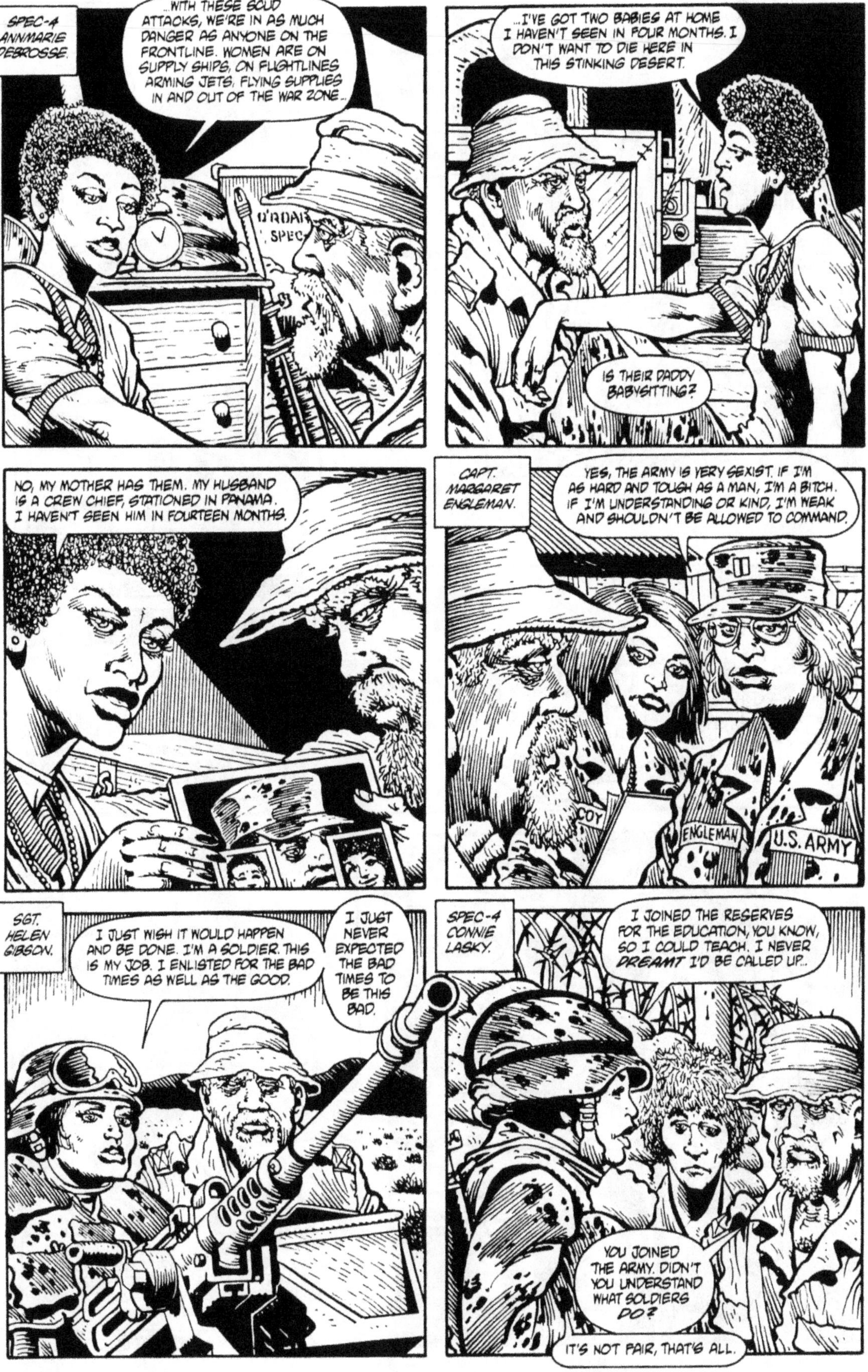
SPEC-4 ANNMARIE DEBROSSE.
...WITH THESE SCUD ATTACKS, WE'RE IN AS MUCH DANGER AS ANYONE ON THE FRONTLINE. WOMEN ARE ON SUPPLY SHIPS, ON FLIGHTLINES ARMING JETS, FLYING SUPPLIES IN AND OUT OF THE WAR ZONE...
...I'VE GOT TWO BABIES AT HOME I HAVEN'T SEEN IN FOUR MONTHS. I DON'T WANT TO DIE HERE IN THIS STINKING DESERT.
IS THEIR DADDY BABYSITTING?
NO, MY MOTHER HAS THEM. MY HUSBAND IS A CREW CHIEF, STATIONED IN PANAMA. I HAVEN'T SEEN HIM IN FOURTEEN MONTHS.
CAPT. MARGARET ENGLEMAN.
YES, THE ARMY IS VERY SEXIST. IF I'M AS HARD AND TOUGH AS A MAN, I'M A BITCH. IF I'M UNDERSTANDING OR KIND, I'M WEAK AND SHOULDN'T BE ALLOWED TO COMMAND.
ENGLEMAN
U.S. ARMY
SGT. HELEN GIBSON.
I JUST WISH IT WOULD HAPPEN AND BE DONE. I'M A SOLDIER. THIS IS MY JOB. I ENLISTED FOR THE BAD TIMES AS WELL AS THE GOOD.
I JUST NEVER EXPECTED THE BAD TIMES TO BE THIS BAD.
SPEC-4 CONNIE LASKY.
I JOINED THE RESERVES FOR THE EDUCATION, YOU KNOW, SO I COULD TEACH. I NEVER DREAMT I'D BE CALLED UP...
YOU JOINED THE ARMY. DIDN'T YOU UNDERSTAND WHAT SOLDIERS DO?
IT'S NOT PAIR, THAT'S ALL.

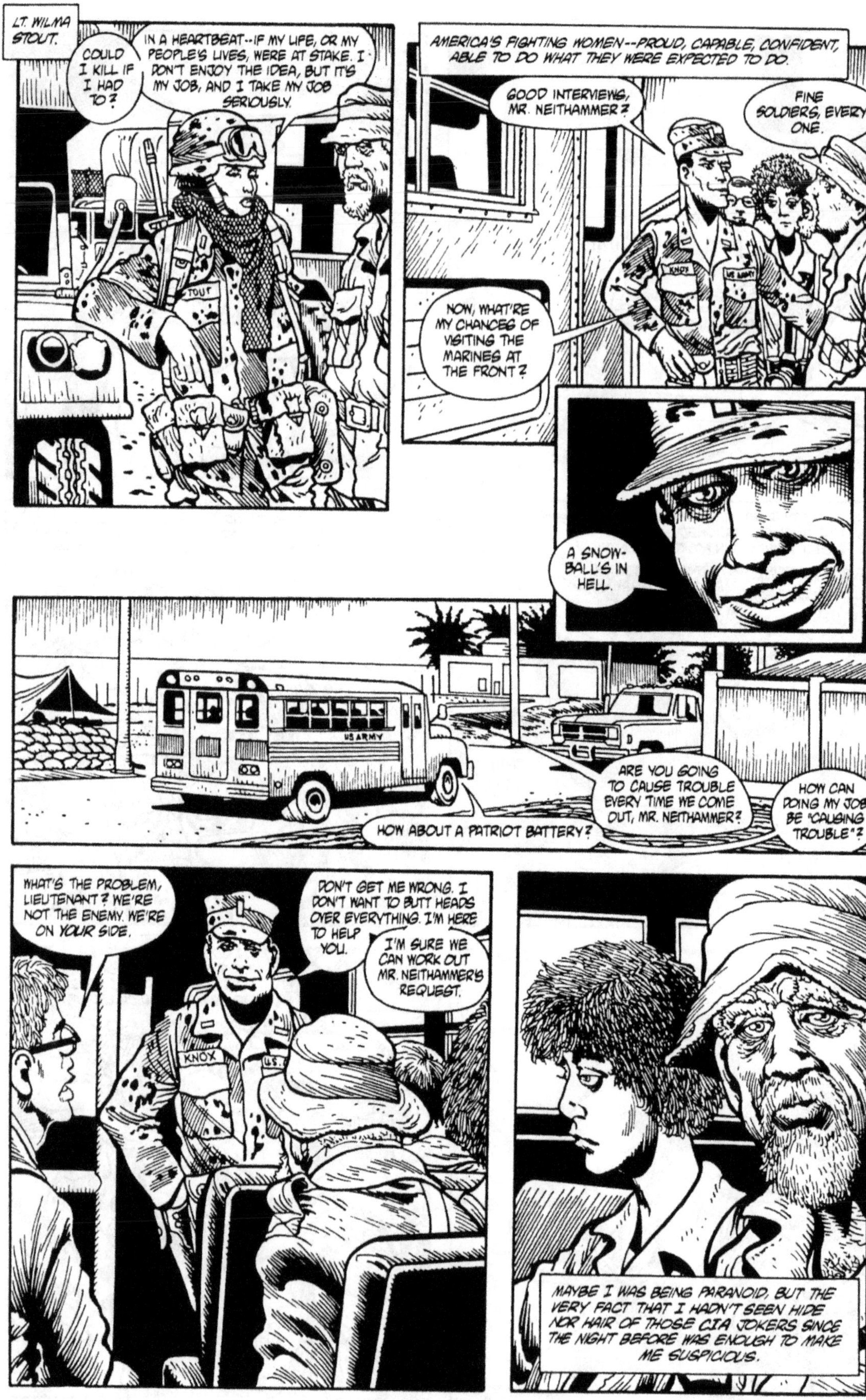

LT. WILMA STOUT.
COULD I KILL IF I HAD TO?
IN A HEARTBEAT--IF MY LIFE, OR MY PEOPLE'S LIVES, WERE AT STAKE. I DON'T ENJOY THE IDEA, BUT IT'S MY JOB, AND I TAKE MY JOB SERIOUSLY.
TOUT
AMERICA'S FIGHTING WOMEN--PROUD, CAPABLE, CONFIDENT, ABLE TO DO WHAT THEY WERE EXPECTED TO DO.
GOOD INTERVIEWS, MR. NEITHAMMER?
FINE SOLDIERS, EVERY ONE.
NOW, WHAT'RE MY CHANCES OF VISITING THE MARINES AT THE FRONT?
A SNOW-BALL'S IN HELL.
US ARMY
HOW ABOUT A PATRIOT BATTERY?
ARE YOU GOING TO CAUSE TROUBLE EVERY TIME WE COME OUT, MR. NEITHAMMER?
HOW CAN DOING MY JOB BE "CAUSING TROUBLE"?
WHAT'S THE PROBLEM, LIEUTENANT? WE'RE NOT THE ENEMY. WE'RE ON YOUR SIDE.
DON'T GET ME WRONG. I DON'T WANT TO BUTT HEADS OVER EVERYTHING. I'M HERE TO HELP YOU.
I'M SURE WE CAN WORK OUT MR. NEITHAMMER'S REQUEST.
KNOX
MAYBE I WAS BEING PARANOID, BUT THE VERY FACT THAT I HADN'T SEEN HIDE NOR HAIR OF THOSE CIA JOKERS SINCE THE NIGHT BEFORE WAS ENOUGH TO MAKE ME SUSPICIOUS.

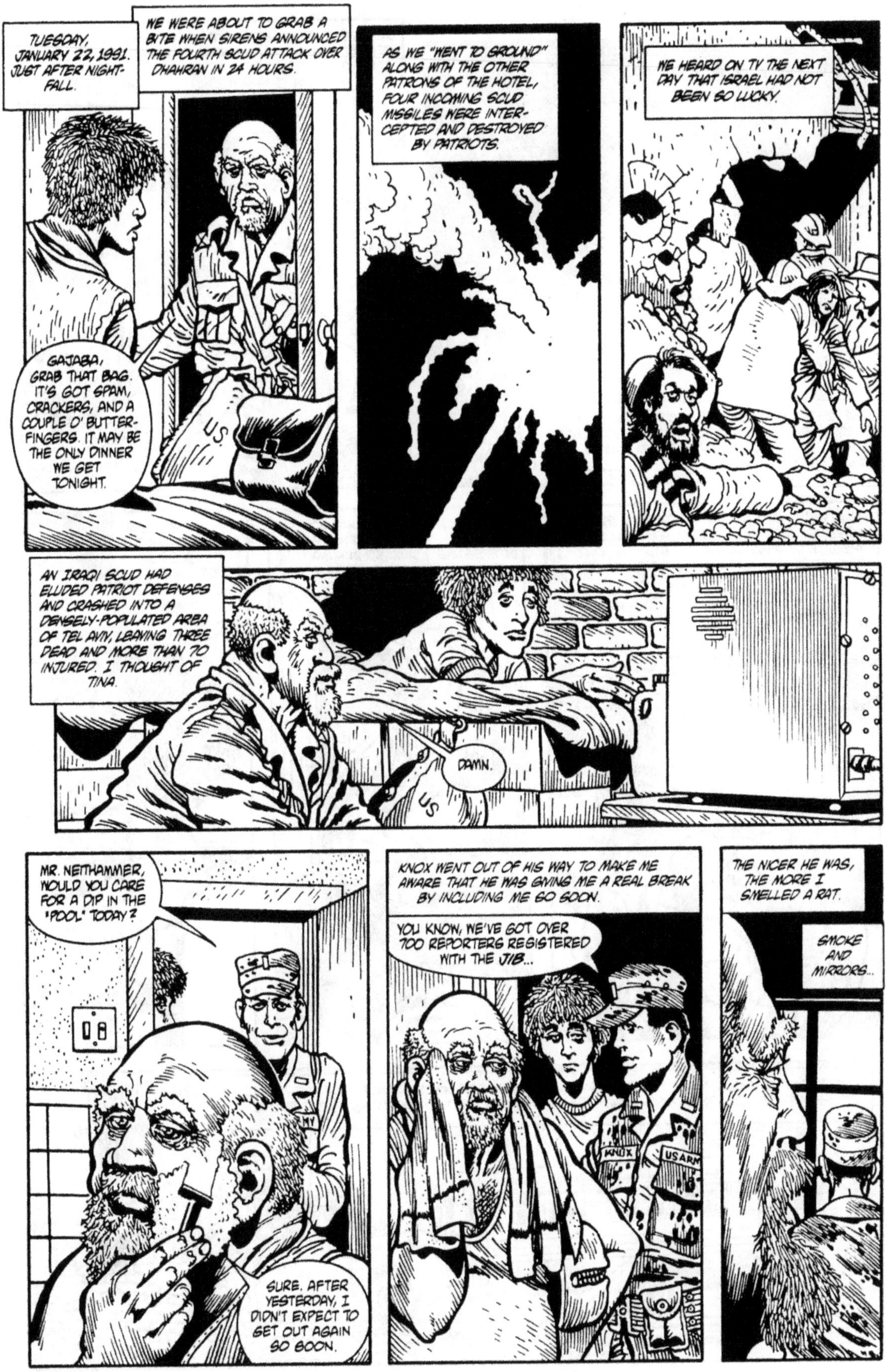
TUESDAY, JANUARY 22, 1991. JUST AFTER NIGHTFALL.
WE WERE ABOUT TO GRAB A BITE WHEN SIRENS ANNOUNCED THE FOURTH SCUD ATTACK OVER DHAHRAN IN 24 HOURS.
GAJABA, GRAB THAT BAG. IT'S GOT SPAM, CRACKERS, AND A COUPLE O' BUTTERFINGERS. IT MAY BE THE ONLY DINNER WE GET TONIGHT.
U.S.
AS WE "WENT TO GROUND" ALONG WITH THE OTHER PATRONS OF THE HOTEL, FOUR INCOMING SCUD MISSILES WERE INTERCEPTED AND DESTROYED BY PATRIOTS.
WE HEARD ON TV THE NEXT DAY THAT ISRAEL HAD NOT BEEN SO LUCKY.
AN IRAQI SCUD HAD ELUDED PATRIOT DEFENSES AND CRASHED INTO A DENSELY-POPULATED AREA OF TEL AVIV, LEAVING THREE DEAD AND MORE THAN 70 INJURED. I THOUGHT OF TINA.
DAMN.
US
MR. NEITHAMMER, WOULD YOU CARE FOR A DIP IN THE "POOL" TODAY?
SURE. AFTER YESTERDAY, I DIDN'T EXPECT TO GET OUT AGAIN SO SOON.
KNOX WENT OUT OF HIS WAY TO MAKE ME AWARE THAT HE WAS GIVING ME A REAL BREAK BY INCLUDING ME SO SOON.
YOU KNOW, WE'VE GOT OVER 700 REPORTERS REGISTERED WITH THE JIB...
KNOX
US ARMY
THE NICER HE WAS, THE MORE I SMELLED A RAT.
SMOKE AND MIRRORS...

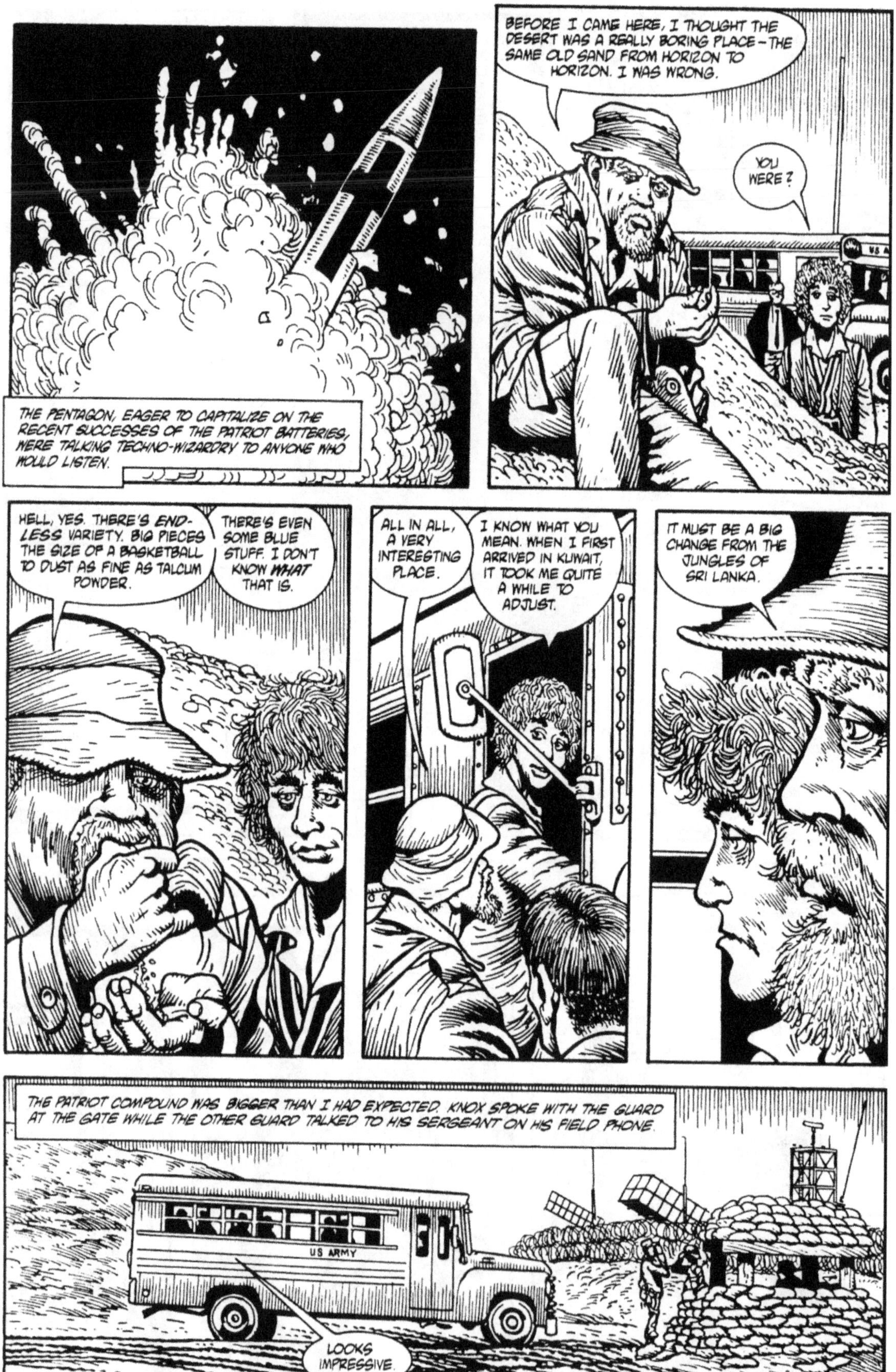
THE PENTAGON, EAGER TO CAPITALIZE ON THE RECENT SUCCESSES OF THE PATRIOT BATTERIES, WERE TALKING TECHNO-WIZARDRY TO ANYONE WHO WOULD LISTEN.
BEFORE I CAME HERE, I THOUGHT THE DESERT WAS A REALLY BORING PLACE—THE SAME OLD SAND FROM HORIZON TO HORIZON. I WAS WRONG.
YOU WERE?
HELL, YES. THERE'S ENDLESS VARIETY. BIG PIECES THE SIZE OF A BASKETBALL TO DUST AS FINE AS TALCUM POWDER.
THERE'S EVEN SOME BLUE STUFF. I DON'T KNOW WHAT THAT IS.
ALL IN ALL, A VERY INTERESTING PLACE.
I KNOW WHAT YOU MEAN. WHEN I FIRST ARRIVED IN KUWAIT, IT TOOK ME QUITE A WHILE TO ADJUST.
IT MUST BE A BIG CHANGE FROM THE JUNGLES OF SRI LANKA.
THE PATRIOT COMPOUND WAS BIGGER THAN I HAD EXPECTED. KNOX SPOKE WITH THE GUARD AT THE GATE WHILE THE OTHER GUARD TALKED TO HIS SERGEANT ON HIS FIELD PHONE.
US ARMY
LOOKS IMPRESSIVE.

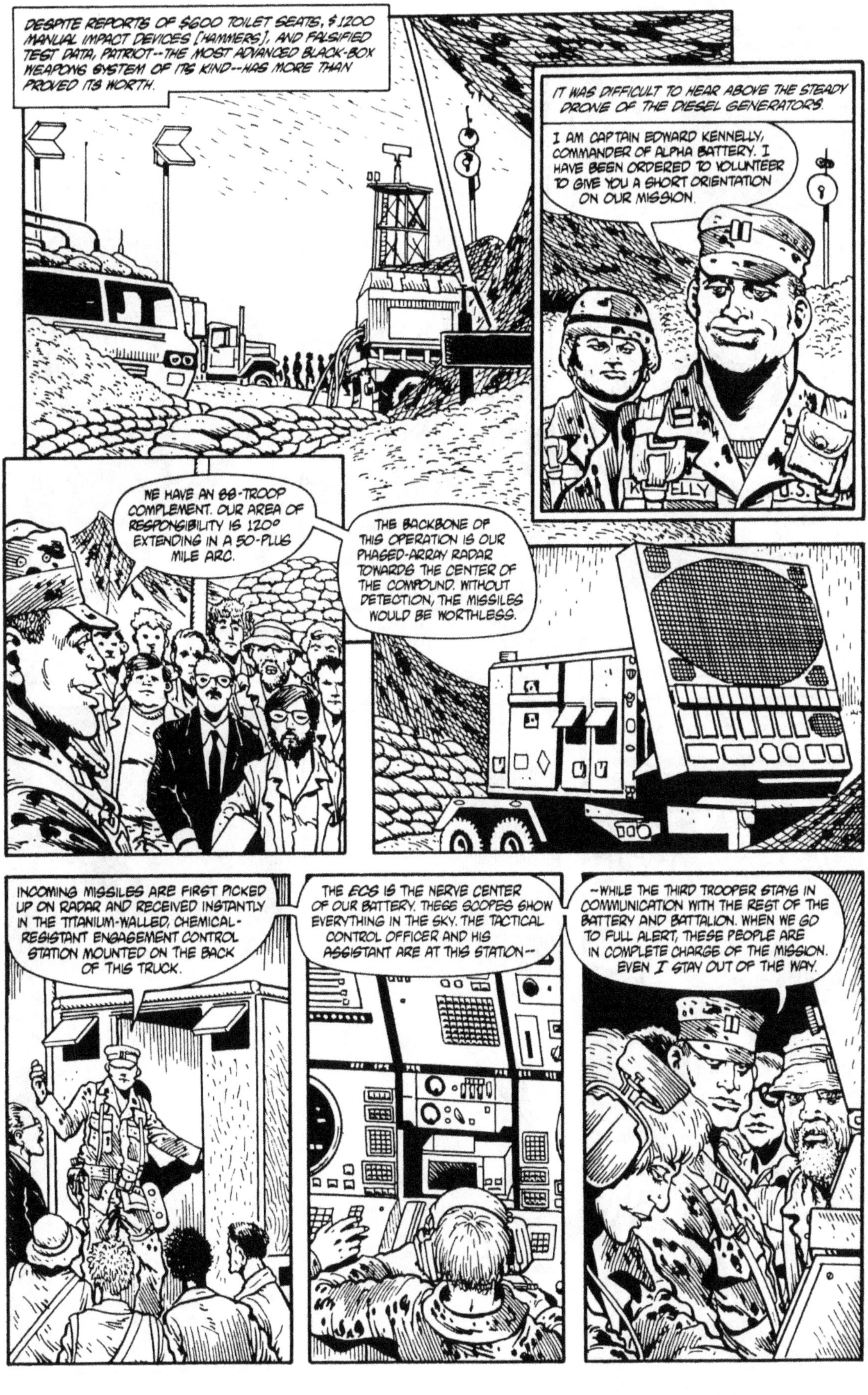
DESPITE REPORTS OF $600 TOILET SEATS, $1200 MANUAL IMPACT DEVICES [HAMMERS], AND FALSIFIED TEST DATA, PATRIOT--THE MOST ADVANCED BLACK-BOX WEAPONS SYSTEM OF ITS KIND--HAS MORE THAN PROVED ITS WORTH.
IT WAS DIFFICULT TO HEAR ABOVE THE STEADY DRONE OF THE DIESEL GENERATORS.
I AM CAPTAIN EDWARD KENNELLY, COMMANDER OF ALPHA BATTERY. I HAVE BEEN ORDERED TO VOLUNTEER TO GIVE YOU A SHORT ORIENTATION ON OUR MISSION.
WE HAVE AN 88-TROOP COMPLEMENT. OUR AREA OF RESPONSIBILITY IS 120° EXTENDING IN A 50-PLUS MILE ARC.
THE BACKBONE OF THIS OPERATION IS OUR PHASED-ARRAY RADAR TOWARDS THE CENTER OF THE COMPOUND. WITHOUT DETECTION, THE MISSILES WOULD BE WORTHLESS.
INCOMING MISSILES ARE FIRST PICKED UP ON RADAR AND RECEIVED INSTANTLY IN THE TITANIUM-WALLED, CHEMICAL-RESISTANT ENGAGEMENT CONTROL STATION MOUNTED ON THE BACK OF THIS TRUCK.
THE ECS IS THE NERVE CENTER OF OUR BATTERY. THESE SCOPES SHOW EVERYTHING IN THE SKY. THE TACTICAL CONTROL OFFICER AND HIS ASSISTANT ARE AT THIS STATION--
--WHILE THE THIRD TROOPER STAYS IN COMMUNICATION WITH THE REST OF THE BATTERY AND BATTALION. WHEN WE GO TO FULL ALERT, THESE PEOPLE ARE IN COMPLETE CHARGE OF THE MISSION. EVEN I STAY OUT OF THE WAY.

HOW DO YOU KEEP FROM KNOCKING DOWN OUR OWN AIRCRAFT, OR WORSE -- A CIVILIAN PASSENGER PLANE?

THAT'S THE PRIMARY FUNCTION OF THE TCO, TO PROTECT THE "FRIENDLIES".

HE DECIDES WHEN IT'S A SCUD AND WHEN IT'S NOT.

WHAT DO THESE GIZMOS DO?

IDENTIFICATION FRIEND OR FOE TRANSMITTERS, ATTACHED TO THE RADAR'S ANTENNA, TRIGGER THE AIRCRAFT'S TRANSPONDERS WHICH REPLY WITH A SECRET CODE, CHANGED DAILY.

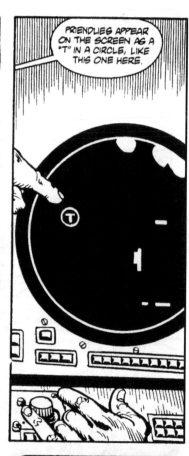

FRIENDLIES APPEAR ON THE SCREEN AS A "T" IN A CIRCLE, LIKE THIS ONE HERE.

CIVILIAN AIRCRAFT APPEAR AS A CIRCLED "S". ALLIED AIRPLANES APPEAR AS EMPTY CIRCLES.

SAFE PASSAGE CORRIDORS ARE PROGRAMMED FOR AIRLINERS. THE SYSTEM IS UPDATED AND CHANGED ALL THE TIME.

HMMM - CAN'T THE SCUDS OUTSMART THE SYSTEM BY FLYING EVASIVELY?

"A SCUD IS EASY TO CLASSIFY. THEY ONLY GO IN TWO DIRECTIONS, UP AND THEN DOWN. THEY APPEAR AS A TRIANGLE ON THE SCREEN. WITH A TERMINAL VELOCITY OF AROUND 5,000 MILES PER HOUR, THEY'RE EASY TO SPOT.

"WHEN THEY IDENTIFY AN INBOUND SCUD, THE TCA MOVES THE CURSOR OVER THE BOGIE, HITS THE HOOK AND LOCKS THE CURSOR ON. HE SETS THE SYSTEM TO RIPPLE FIRE MODE, HITS THE 'ENGAGE' BUTTON, AND THE ANTI-MISSILE IS ON ITS WAY."

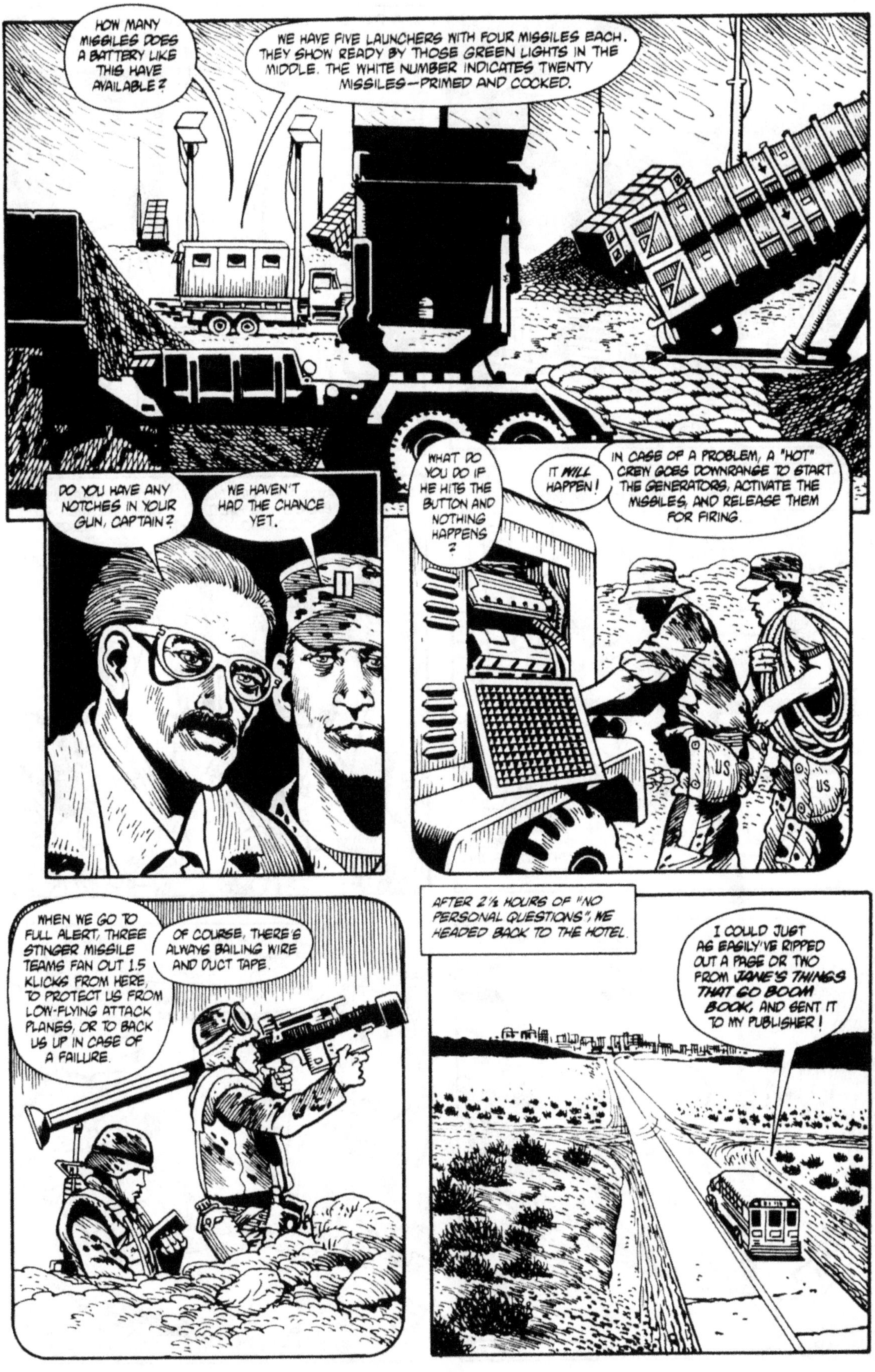
HOW MANY MISSILES DOES A BATTERY LIKE THIS HAVE AVAILABLE?
WE HAVE FIVE LAUNCHERS WITH FOUR MISSILES EACH. THEY SHOW READY BY THOSE GREEN LIGHTS IN THE MIDDLE. THE WHITE NUMBER INDICATES TWENTY MISSILES—PRIMED AND COCKED.
DO YOU HAVE ANY NOTCHES IN YOUR GUN, CAPTAIN?
WE HAVEN'T HAD THE CHANCE YET.
WHAT DO YOU DO IF HE HITS THE BUTTON AND NOTHING HAPPENS?
IT *WILL* HAPPEN!
IN CASE OF A PROBLEM, A "HOT" CREW GOES DOWNRANGE TO START THE GENERATORS, ACTIVATE THE MISSILES, AND RELEASE THEM FOR FIRING.
US
US
WHEN WE GO TO FULL ALERT, THREE STINGER MISSILE TEAMS FAN OUT 1.5 KLICKS FROM HERE, TO PROTECT US FROM LOW-FLYING ATTACK PLANES, OR TO BACK US UP IN CASE OF A FAILURE.
OF COURSE, THERE'S ALWAYS BAILING WIRE AND DUCT TAPE.
AFTER 2½ HOURS OF "NO PERSONAL QUESTIONS", WE HEADED BACK TO THE HOTEL.
I COULD JUST AS EASILY'VE RIPPED OUT A PAGE OR TWO FROM *JANE'S THINGS THAT GO BOOM BOOK*, AND SENT IT TO MY PUBLISHER!

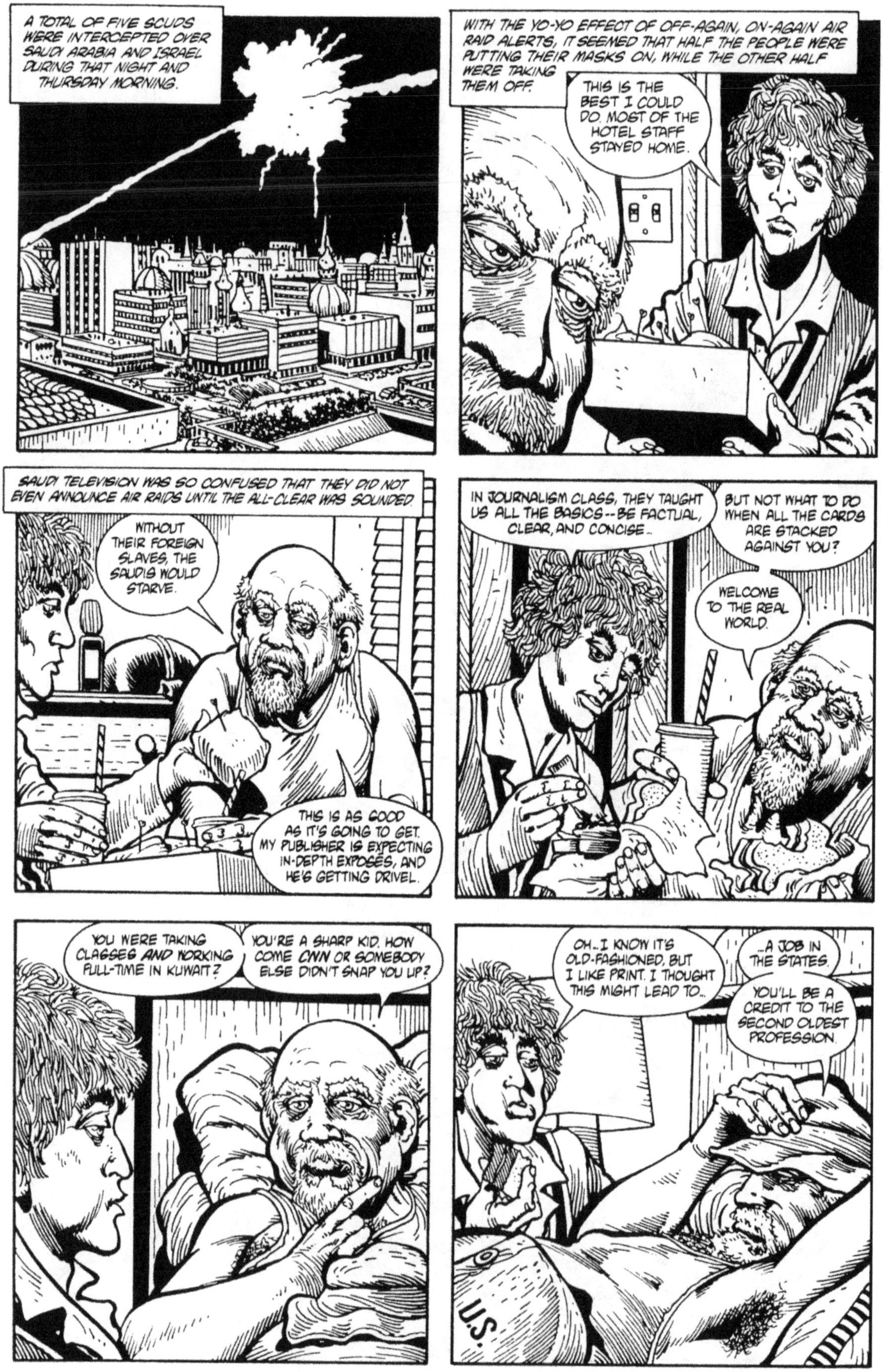
A TOTAL OF FIVE SCUDS WERE INTERCEPTED OVER SAUDI ARABIA AND ISRAEL DURING THAT NIGHT AND THURSDAY MORNING.
WITH THE YO-YO EFFECT OF OFF-AGAIN, ON-AGAIN AIR RAID ALERTS, IT SEEMED THAT HALF THE PEOPLE WERE PUTTING THEIR MASKS ON, WHILE THE OTHER HALF WERE TAKING THEM OFF.
THIS IS THE BEST I COULD DO. MOST OF THE HOTEL STAFF STAYED HOME.
SAUDI TELEVISION WAS SO CONFUSED THAT THEY DID NOT EVEN ANNOUNCE AIR RAIDS UNTIL THE ALL-CLEAR WAS SOUNDED.
WITHOUT THEIR FOREIGN SLAVES, THE SAUDIS WOULD STARVE.
THIS IS AS GOOD AS IT'S GOING TO GET. MY PUBLISHER IS EXPECTING IN-DEPTH EXPOSÉS, AND HE'S GETTING DRIVEL.
IN JOURNALISM CLASS, THEY TAUGHT US ALL THE BASICS--BE FACTUAL, CLEAR, AND CONCISE...
BUT NOT WHAT TO DO WHEN ALL THE CARDS ARE STACKED AGAINST YOU?
WELCOME TO THE REAL WORLD.
YOU WERE TAKING CLASSES AND WORKING FULL-TIME IN KUWAIT?
YOU'RE A SHARP KID. HOW COME CNN OR SOMEBODY ELSE DIDN'T SNAP YOU UP?
OH...I KNOW IT'S OLD-FASHIONED, BUT I LIKE PRINT. I THOUGHT THIS MIGHT LEAD TO...
...A JOB IN THE STATES.
YOU'LL BE A CREDIT TO THE SECOND OLDEST PROFESSION.
U.S.

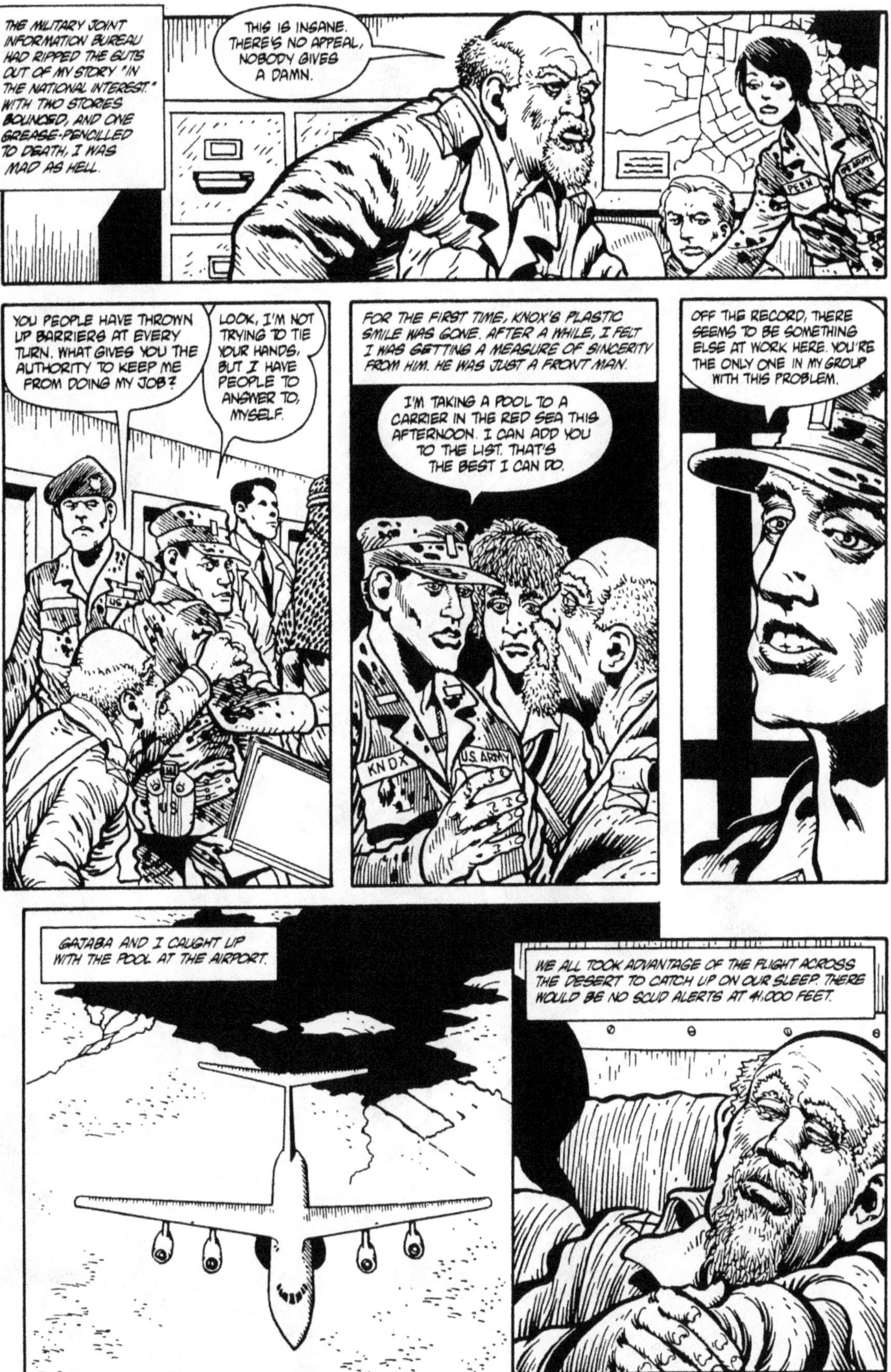
THE MILITARY JOINT INFORMATION BUREAU HAD RIPPED THE GUTS OUT OF MY STORY "IN THE NATIONAL INTEREST." WITH TWO STORIES BOUNCED, AND ONE GREASE-PENCILLED TO DEATH, I WAS MAD AS HELL.
THIS IS INSANE. THERE'S NO APPEAL, NOBODY GIVES A DAMN.
PEEN
US ARMY
YOU PEOPLE HAVE THROWN UP BARRIERS AT EVERY TURN. WHAT GIVES YOU THE AUTHORITY TO KEEP ME FROM DOING MY JOB?
LOOK, I'M NOT TRYING TO TIE YOUR HANDS, BUT I HAVE PEOPLE TO ANSWER TO, MYSELF.
US
US
FOR THE FIRST TIME, KNOX'S PLASTIC SMILE WAS GONE. AFTER A WHILE, I FELT I WAS GETTING A MEASURE OF SINCERITY FROM HIM. HE WAS JUST A FRONT MAN.
I'M TAKING A POOL TO A CARRIER IN THE RED SEA THIS AFTERNOON. I CAN ADD YOU TO THE LIST. THAT'S THE BEST I CAN DO.
KNOX
U.S. ARMY
OFF THE RECORD, THERE SEEMS TO BE SOMETHING ELSE AT WORK HERE. YOU'RE THE ONLY ONE IN MY GROUP WITH THIS PROBLEM.
GAJABA AND I CAUGHT UP WITH THE POOL AT THE AIRPORT.
WE ALL TOOK ADVANTAGE OF THE FLIGHT ACROSS THE DESERT TO CATCH UP ON OUR SLEEP. THERE WOULD BE NO SCUD ALERTS AT 41,000 FEET.

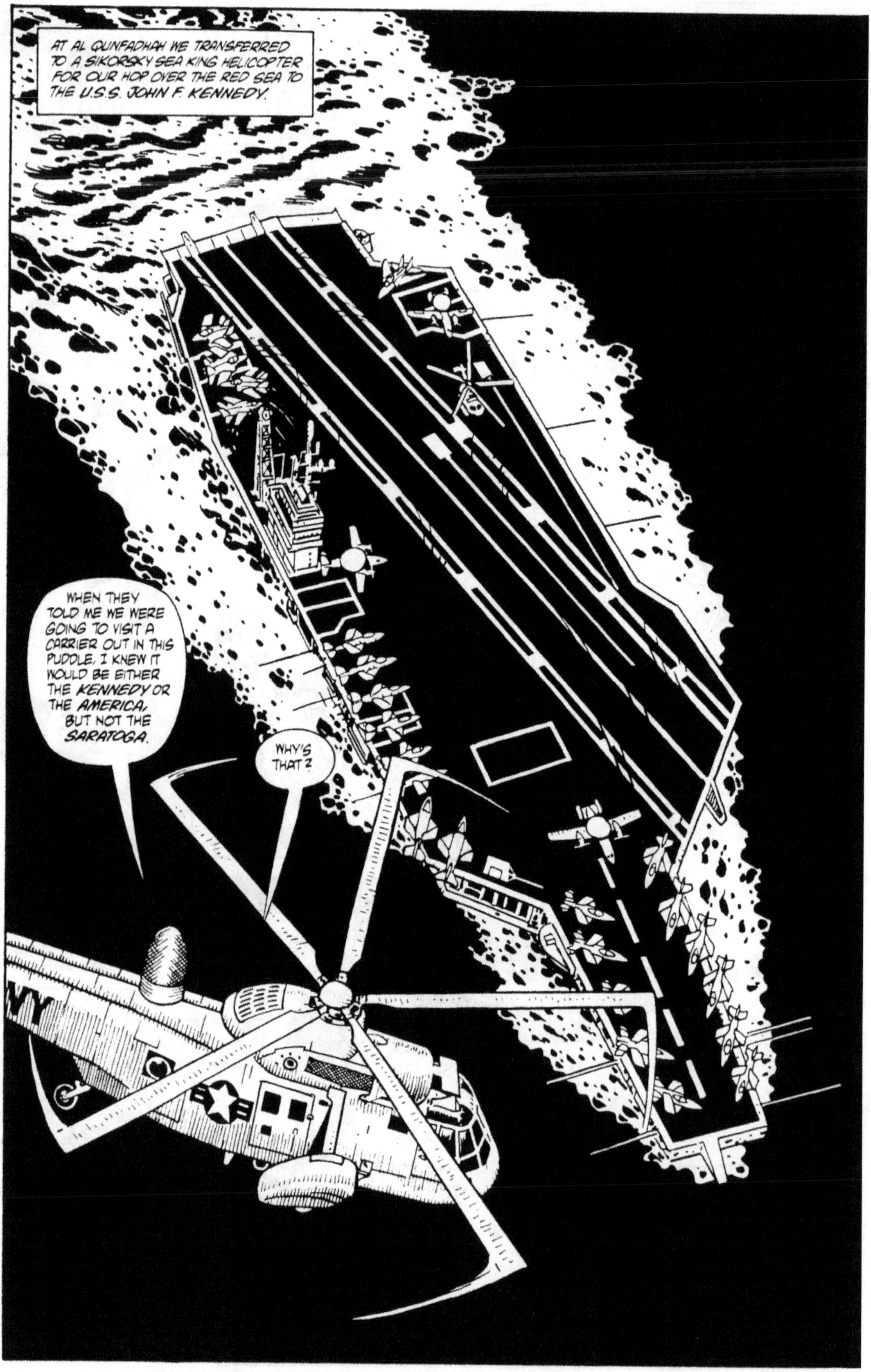
AT AL QUNFADHAH WE TRANSFERRED TO A SIKORSKY SEA KING HELICOPTER FOR OUR HOP OVER THE RED SEA TO THE U.S.S. JOHN F. KENNEDY.
WHEN THEY TOLD ME WE WERE GOING TO VISIT A CARRIER OUT IN THIS PUDDLE, I KNEW IT WOULD BE EITHER THE *KENNEDY* OR THE *AMERICA,* BUT NOT THE *SARATOGA.*
WHY'S THAT?
NAVY

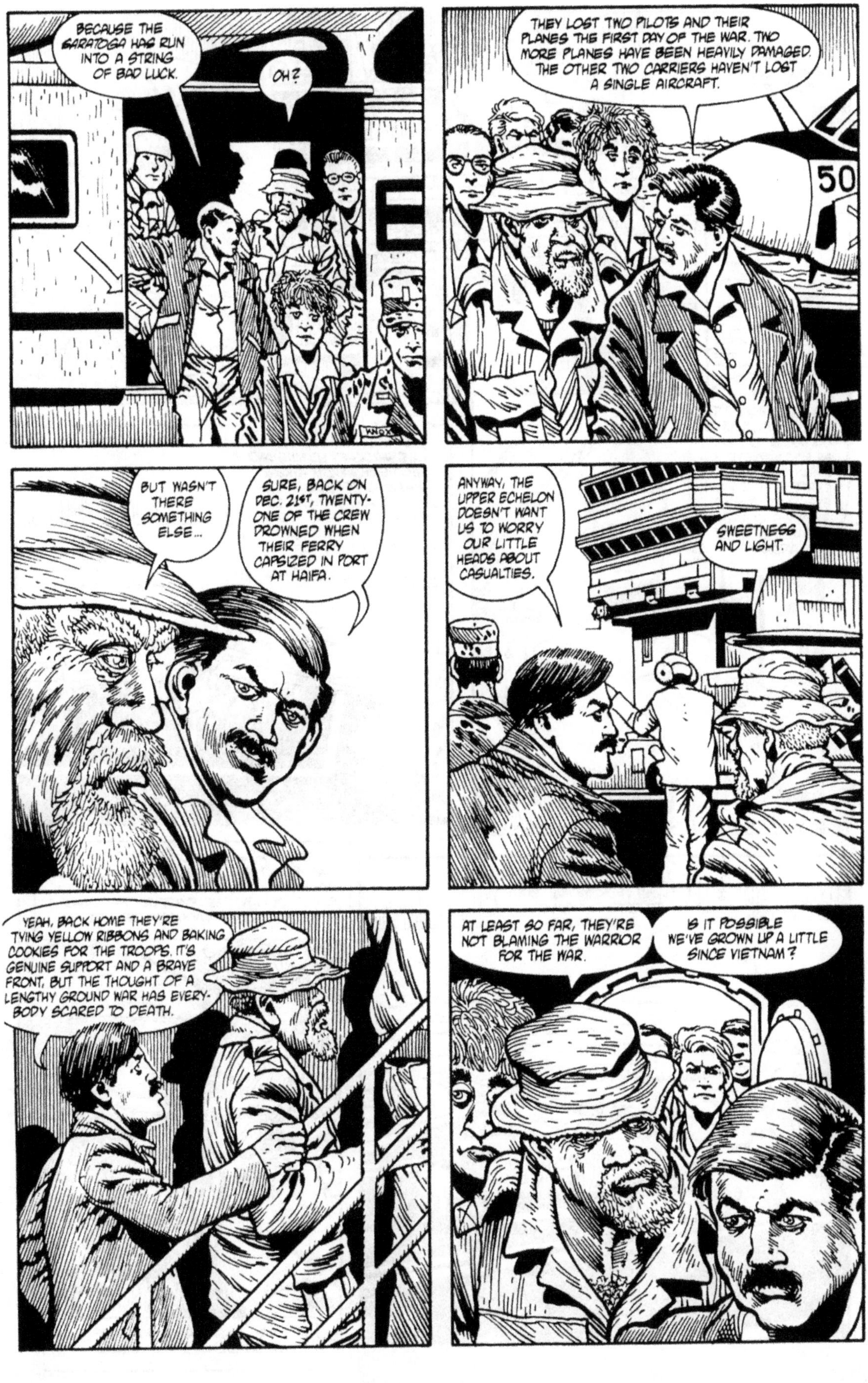
BECAUSE THE SARATOGA HAS RUN INTO A STRING OF BAD LUCK.
OH?
THEY LOST TWO PILOTS AND THEIR PLANES THE FIRST DAY OF THE WAR. TWO MORE PLANES HAVE BEEN HEAVILY DAMAGED. THE OTHER TWO CARRIERS HAVEN'T LOST A SINGLE AIRCRAFT.
50
BUT WASN'T THERE SOMETHING ELSE...
SURE, BACK ON DEC. 21ST, TWENTY-ONE OF THE CREW DROWNED WHEN THEIR FERRY CAPSIZED IN PORT AT HAIFA.
ANYWAY, THE UPPER ECHELON DOESN'T WANT US TO WORRY OUR LITTLE HEADS ABOUT CASUALTIES.
SWEETNESS AND LIGHT.
YEAH, BACK HOME THEY'RE TYING YELLOW RIBBONS AND BAKING COOKIES FOR THE TROOPS. IT'S GENUINE SUPPORT AND A BRAVE FRONT, BUT THE THOUGHT OF A LENGTHY GROUND WAR HAS EVERYBODY SCARED TO DEATH.
AT LEAST SO FAR, THEY'RE NOT BLAMING THE WARRIOR FOR THE WAR.
IS IT POSSIBLE WE'VE GROWN UP A LITTLE SINCE VIETNAM?

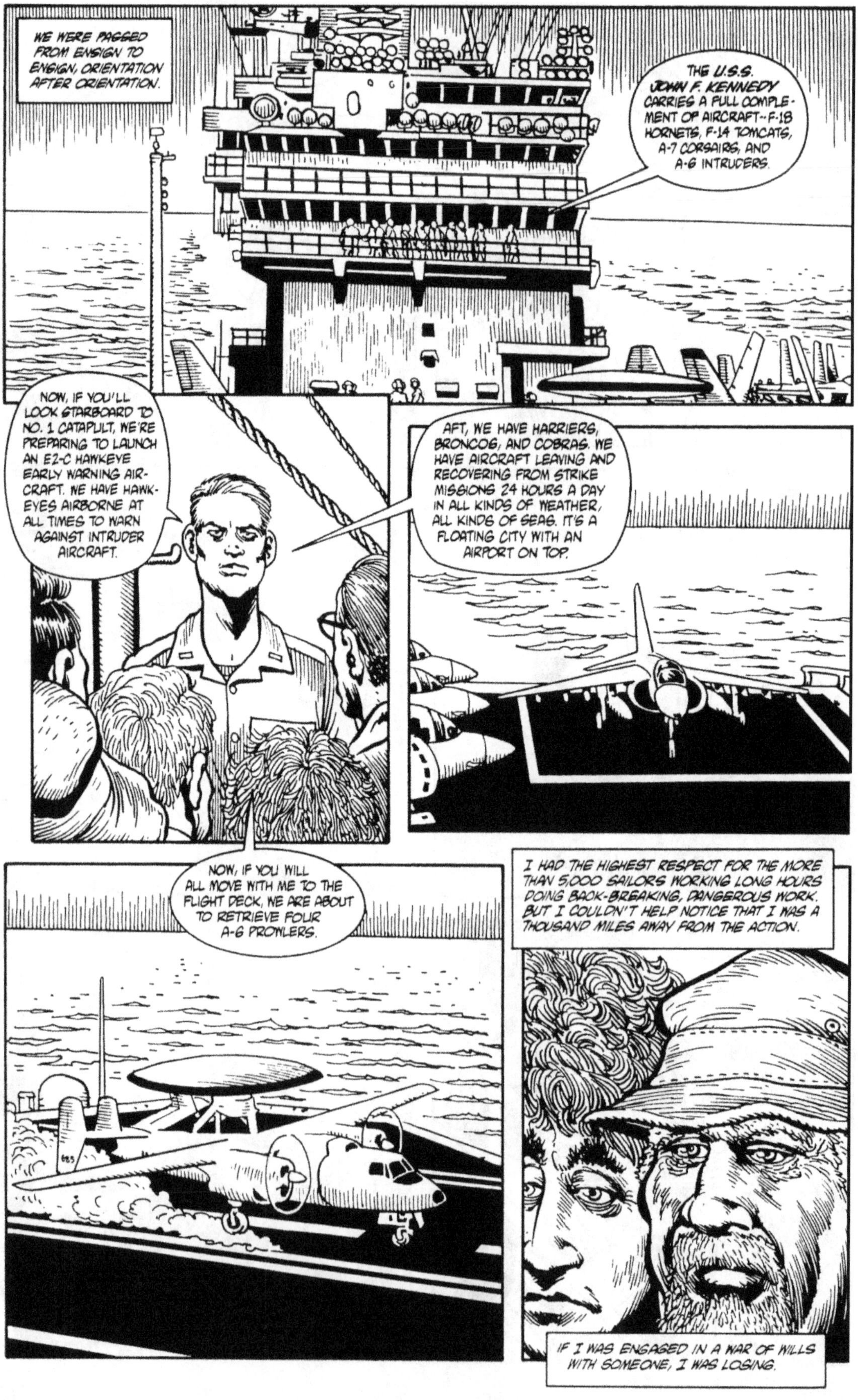
WE WERE PASSED FROM ENSIGN TO ENSIGN, ORIENTATION AFTER ORIENTATION.
THE U.S.S. JOHN F. KENNEDY CARRIES A FULL COMPLEMENT OF AIRCRAFT--F-18 HORNETS, F-14 TOMCATS, A-7 CORSAIRS, AND A-6 INTRUDERS.
NOW, IF YOU'LL LOOK STARBOARD TO NO. 1 CATAPULT, WE'RE PREPARING TO LAUNCH AN E2-C HAWKEYE EARLY WARNING AIRCRAFT. WE HAVE HAWKEYES AIRBORNE AT ALL TIMES TO WARN AGAINST INTRUDER AIRCRAFT.
AFT, WE HAVE HARRIERS, BRONCOS, AND COBRAS. WE HAVE AIRCRAFT LEAVING AND RECOVERING FROM STRIKE MISSIONS 24 HOURS A DAY IN ALL KINDS OF WEATHER, ALL KINDS OF SEAS. IT'S A FLOATING CITY WITH AN AIRPORT ON TOP.
NOW, IF YOU WILL ALL MOVE WITH ME TO THE FLIGHT DECK, WE ARE ABOUT TO RETRIEVE FOUR A-6 PROWLERS.
I HAD THE HIGHEST RESPECT FOR THE MORE THAN 5,000 SAILORS WORKING LONG HOURS DOING BACK-BREAKING, DANGEROUS WORK. BUT I COULDN'T HELP NOTICE THAT I WAS A THOUSAND MILES AWAY FROM THE ACTION.
IF I WAS ENGAGED IN A WAR OF WILLS WITH SOMEONE, I WAS LOSING.

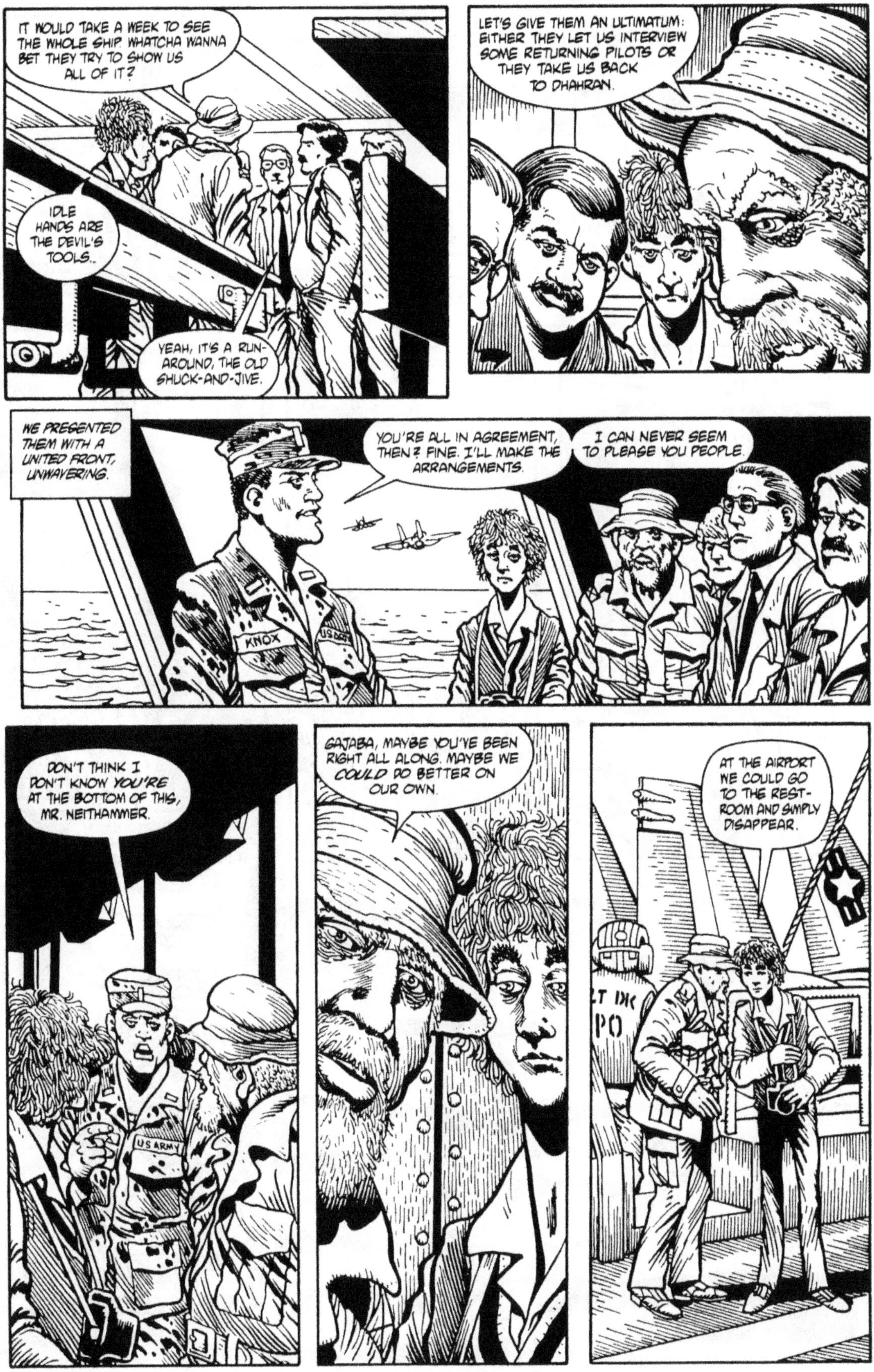
IT WOULD TAKE A WEEK TO SEE THE WHOLE SHIP. WHATCHA WANNA BET THEY TRY TO SHOW US ALL OF IT?
IDLE HANDS ARE THE DEVIL'S TOOLS..
YEAH, IT'S A RUN-AROUND, THE OLD SHUCK-AND-JIVE.
LET'S GIVE THEM AN ULTIMATUM: EITHER THEY LET US INTERVIEW SOME RETURNING PILOTS OR THEY TAKE US BACK TO DHAHRAN.
WE PRESENTED THEM WITH A UNITED FRONT, UNWAVERING.
YOU'RE ALL IN AGREEMENT, THEN? FINE. I'LL MAKE THE ARRANGEMENTS.
I CAN NEVER SEEM TO PLEASE YOU PEOPLE.
KNOX
DON'T THINK I DON'T KNOW YOU'RE AT THE BOTTOM OF THIS, MR. NEITHAMMER.
US ARMY
GAJABA, MAYBE YOU'VE BEEN RIGHT ALL ALONG. MAYBE WE COULD DO BETTER ON OUR OWN.
AT THE AIRPORT WE COULD GO TO THE REST-ROOM AND SIMPLY DISAPPEAR.

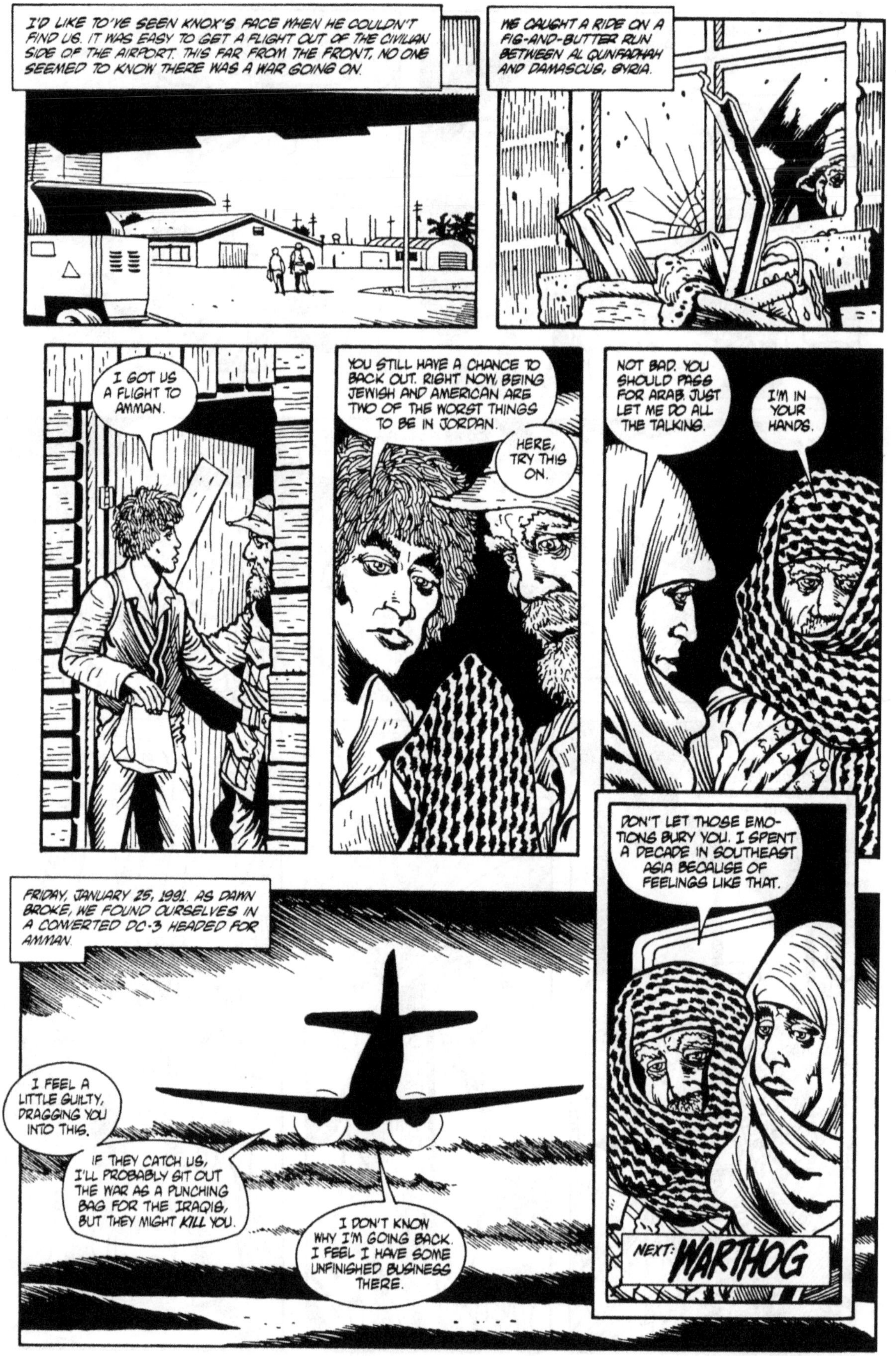
I'D LIKE TO'VE SEEN KNOX'S FACE WHEN HE COULDN'T FIND US. IT WAS EASY TO GET A FLIGHT OUT OF THE CIVILIAN SIDE OF THE AIRPORT. THIS FAR FROM THE FRONT, NO ONE SEEMED TO KNOW THERE WAS A WAR GOING ON.
WE CAUGHT A RIDE ON A FIG-AND-BUTTER RUN BETWEEN AL QUNFADHAH AND DAMASCUS, SYRIA.
I GOT US A FLIGHT TO AMMAN.
YOU STILL HAVE A CHANCE TO BACK OUT. RIGHT NOW, BEING JEWISH AND AMERICAN ARE TWO OF THE WORST THINGS TO BE IN JORDAN.
HERE, TRY THIS ON.
NOT BAD. YOU SHOULD PASS FOR ARAB. JUST LET ME DO ALL THE TALKING.
I'M IN YOUR HANDS.
FRIDAY, JANUARY 25, 1991. AS DAWN BROKE, WE FOUND OURSELVES IN A CONVERTED DC-3 HEADED FOR AMMAN.
I FEEL A LITTLE GUILTY, DRAGGING YOU INTO THIS.
IF THEY CATCH US, I'LL PROBABLY SIT OUT THE WAR AS A PUNCHING BAG FOR THE IRAQIS, BUT THEY MIGHT KILL YOU.
I DON'T KNOW WHY I'M GOING BACK. I FEEL I HAVE SOME UNFINISHED BUSINESS THERE.
DON'T LET THOSE EMOTIONS BURY YOU. I SPENT A DECADE IN SOUTHEAST ASIA BECAUSE OF FEELINGS LIKE THAT.
NEXT: WARTHOG

ABOUT DON LOMAX

DON LOMAX was drafted into the Army in 1965 and, along with most draftees went to Vietnam in the fall of 1966 during President Johnson's targeted build-up to reach his goal of half a million troops in-country by the summer of 1967. Being an orphan company without a particular mission at the time, upon arriving in the Cha Rang Valley on Highway 19 in the near geological center of the country, his unit (the 98th Light Equipment Maintenance Company) was assigned a plethora of duties from convoying supplies, to airport guard duty at Qui Nhon Airport, to repairing Fuel bladders, with a little shit burning thrown in for fun. All the while he took mental notes and sketched the people, the gear, and the countryside thinking, "This would make a great comic." And it did.

VIETNAM JOURNAL, the comic book was first published by Apple Publishing in 1987 and was eventually nominated for a Harvey Award. He has had a long career now approaching 50 years in magazine and comic books including a stint at writing The 'Nam and The Punisher for Marvel in the '90s. Other spin-offs, High Shining Brass, Valley of Death, and Tet '68 are still available in print and download on-line, as well as the Vietnam Journal series from Caliber Comics.

But Don Lomax is by no means a one trick pony. For nearly 50 years he has had comics and cartoons appearing in a score of national magazines on a regular basis including Easyrider, CARtoons, Heavy Metal, Overdrive (Knights of the Road), Police and Security News (Above and Beyond), American Towman, and many others. But he also worked for most of the major comic book imprints including Pacific, Marvel, First, Americomics, Fantagraphics, Transfuzion, Eros and of course Caliber.

Lomax has four great children, two girls and two boys with ten grandchildren, and twelve great grandchildren (at last count). His sons are both veterans, his oldest Bryan served in Panama during operation Just Cause and Torrin with the Special Forces during several tours in Iraq and Afghanistan. Both are retired now. Lomax now lives in Illinois with the light of his life, his wife, Zenaida and is hard at work on Series Two of Vietnam Journal. (well, not THAT hard at work. When you love what you do it can't really be called work, can it?)

ALSO AVAILABLE FROM CALIBER COMICS

QUALITY GRAPHIC NOVELS TO ENTERTAIN

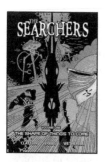

THE SEARCHERS
VOLUME ONE
THE SHAPE OF THINGS TO COME

THE SEARCHERS: VOLUME 1
The Shape of Things to Come

Before *League of Extraordinary Gentlemen* there was *The Searchers*. At the dawn of the 20th Century the greatest literary adventurers from the minds of Wells, Doyle, Burroughs, and Haggard were created. All thought to be the work of pure fiction. However, a century later, the real-life descendents of those famous characters are recuited by the legendary Professor Challenger in order to save mankind's future. Series collected for the first time.

"Searchers is the comic book I have on the wall with a sign reading - 'Love books? Never read a comic? Try this one! ....money back guarantee...'" - Dark Star Books.

WAR OF THE WORLDS: INFESTATION

Based on the H.G. Wells classic! The "Martian Invasion" has begun again and now mankind must fight for its very humanity. It happened slowly at first but by the third year, it seemed that the war was almost over... the war was almost lost.

"Writer Randy Zimmerman has a fine grasp of drama, and spins the various strands of the story into a coherent whole... imaginative and very gritty."
- war-of-the-worlds.co.uk

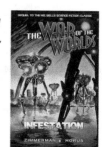

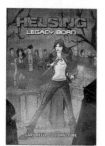

THE WAR OF THE WORLDS
INFESTATION
ZIMMERMAN • HORUS

HELSING
LEGACY BORN
GARY REED
JOHN LOWE

HELSING: LEGACY BORN

From writer Gary Reed (Deadworld) and artists John Lowe (Captain America), Bruce McCorkindale (Godzilla). She was born into a legacy she wanted no part of and pushed into a battle recessed deep in the shadows of the night. Samantha Helsing is torn between two worlds...two allegiances...two families. The legacy of the Van Helsing family and their crusade against the "night creatures" comes to modern day with the most unlikely of all warriors.

"Congratulations on this masterpiece..."
- Paul Dale Roberts, Compuserve Reviews

"All in all, another great package from Caliber."
- Paul Haywood, Comics Forum

DEADWORLD

Before there was The Walking Dead there was Deadworld. Here is an introduction of the long running classic horror series, Deadworld, to a new audience! Considered by many to be the godfather of the original zombie comic with over 100 issues and graphic novels in print and over 1,000,000 copies sold, Deadworld ripped into the undead with intelligent zombies on a mission and a group of poor teens riding in a school bus desperately try to stay one step ahead of the sadistic, Harley-riding King Zombie. Death, mayhem, and a touch of supernatural evil made Deadworld a classic and now here's your chance to get into the story!

DEADWORLD
REQUIEM FOR THE WORLD

DAYS OF WRATH
WAYNE VANSANT

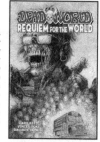

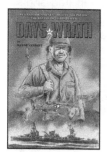

DAYS OF WRATH

Award winning comic writer & artist Wayne Vansant brings his gripping World War II saga of war in the Pacific to Guadalcanal and the Battle of Bloody Ridge. This is the powerful story of the long, vicious battle for Guadalcanal that occurred in 1942-43. When the U.S. Navy orders its outnumbered and outgunned ships to run from the Japanese fleet, they abandon American troops on a bloody, battered island in the South Pacific.

"Heavy on authenticity, compellingly written and beautifully drawn."
- Comics Buyers Guide

THE BOBCAT

Described as the Native American *Black Panther*.
1898. Indian Territory. Will Firemaker is a Cherokee Black-smith who is finding out that the world of ancient lore and myth of his Tribe, that Will had always thought of as tribal fairytales, are actually true, and they're telling him he must replace his best friend from the animal kingdom, The Great Cat, as the guardian of his people. This sends him down a path of shock and disbelief as beings from the ancient past begin to manifest themselves in the world of reality. And as malevolent forces rise up in the wake of the fledgling Industrial Age, the future rushes head on into the Old West. Tahlequah will never be the same...

THE BOBCAT
HOSTLER MENSLING

TIME GRUNTS
VOLUME ONE: THE MONSTERS WITHIN

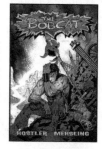

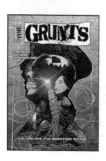

TIME GRUNTS

What if Hitler's last great Super Weapon was – Time itself! A WWII/time travel adventure that can best be described as *Band of Brothers* meets *Time Bandits*.

October, 1944. Nazi fortunes appear bleaker by the day. But in the bowels of the Wenceslas Mines, a terrible threat has emerged . . . The Nazis have discovered the ability to conquer time itself with the help of a new ominous device!

Now a rag tag group of American GIs must stop this threat to the past, present, and future . . . While dealing with their own past, prejudices, and fears in the process.

LEGENDLORE

From Caliber Comics now comes the entire Realm and Legendlore saga as a set of volumes that collects the long running critically acclaimed series. In the vein of The Lord of The Rings and The Hobbit with elements of Game of Thrones and Dungeon and Dragons.

Four normal modern day teenagers are plunged into a world they thought only existed in novels and film. They are whisked away to a magical land where dragons roam the skies, orcs and hobgoblins terrorize travelers, where unicorns prance through the forest, and kingdoms wage war for dominance. It is a world where man is just one race, joining other races such as elves, trolls, dwarves, changelings, and the dreaded night creatures who steal the night.

LEGENDLORE
THE REALM CHRONICLES
TIME SLIP

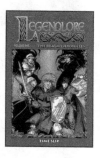

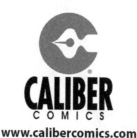

CALIBER®
COMICS
www.calibercomics.com

CPSIA information can be obtained
at www.ICGtesting.com
Printed in the USA
LVHW101615220721
693426LV00005B/254